Frank,

Lies, lies & lies.

Embarassing, I told
the author,

No WARTS!

All the best

Ben

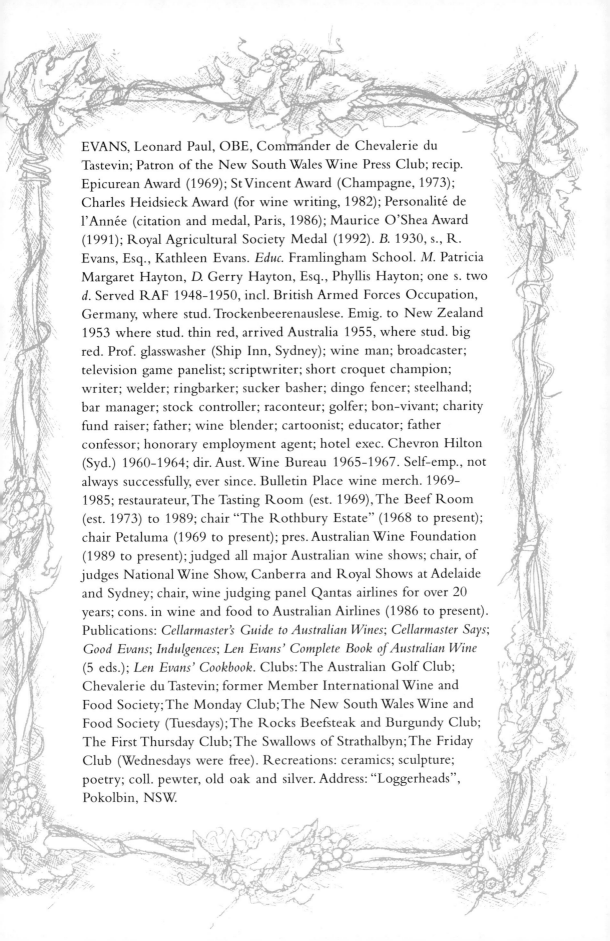

EVANS, Leonard Paul, OBE, Commander de Chevalerie du Tastevin; Patron of the New South Wales Wine Press Club; recip. Epicurean Award (1969); St Vincent Award (Champagne, 1973); Charles Heidsieck Award (for wine writing, 1982); Personalité de l'Année (citation and medal, Paris, 1986); Maurice O'Shea Award (1991); Royal Agricultural Society Medal (1992). *B.* 1930, s., R. Evans, Esq., Kathleen Evans. *Educ.* Framlingham School. *M.* Patricia Margaret Hayton, *D.* Gerry Hayton, Esq., Phyllis Hayton; one s. two *d.* Served RAF 1948-1950, incl. British Armed Forces Occupation, Germany, where stud. Trockenbeerenauslese. Emig. to New Zealand 1953 where stud. thin red, arrived Australia 1955, where stud. big red. Prof. glasswasher (Ship Inn, Sydney); wine man; broadcaster; television game panelist; scriptwriter; short croquet champion; writer; welder; ringbarker; sucker basher; dingo fencer; steelhand; bar manager; stock controller; raconteur; golfer; bon-vivant; charity fund raiser; father; wine blender; cartoonist; educator; father confessor; honorary employment agent; hotel exec. Chevron Hilton (Syd.) 1960-1964; dir. Aust. Wine Bureau 1965-1967. Self-emp., not always successfully, ever since. Bulletin Place wine merch. 1969-1985; restaurateur, The Tasting Room (est. 1969), The Beef Room (est. 1973) to 1989; chair "The Rothbury Estate" (1968 to present); chair Petaluma (1969 to present); pres. Australian Wine Foundation (1989 to present); judged all major Australian wine shows; chair, of judges National Wine Show, Canberra and Royal Shows at Adelaide and Sydney; chair, wine judging panel Qantas airlines for over 20 years; cons. in wine and food to Australian Airlines (1986 to present). Publications: *Cellarmaster's Guide to Australian Wines*; *Cellarmaster Says*; *Good Evans*; *Indulgences*; *Len Evans' Complete Book of Australian Wine* (5 eds.); *Len Evans' Cookbook*. Clubs: The Australian Golf Club; Chevalerie du Tastevin; former Member International Wine and Food Society; The Monday Club; The New South Wales Wine and Food Society (Tuesdays); The Rocks Beefsteak and Burgundy Club; The First Thursday Club; The Swallows of Strathalbyn; The Friday Club (Wednesdays were free). Recreations: ceramics; sculpture; poetry; coll. pewter, old oak and silver. Address: "Loggerheads", Pokolbin, NSW.

EVANS on EARTH

The Story of Len Evans' Affair with Wine

Jeremy Oliver

A Lothian Book

Acknowledgements

This book would have never materialised without the time and help of many people including: Tony Albert, Lorraine Bambrough-Kelly, Nick Bulleid, Frank Christie, Deeta Colvin,Doug Crittenden, Brian Croser, Dennis de Muth, Frank Doherty, Peter Doyle, David Dunstan, Keith Dunstan, Annie Ellis, Trish Evans, Diana Fisher, Sarah Gough, James Halliday, Sigmund Jorgensen, Max Lake, Dan Murphy, Anders Ousback, Bob Oxenbould, John Parkinson, Colin Richardson, and Hermann Schneider, to you and to many others, I am indeed indebted. And to you, Len Evans, without whom, as they say at the Oscars, this book would never have been possible, my gratitude.

A Lothian Book
Lothian Publishing Company Pty Ltd
A division of Thomas C. Lothian Pty Ltd
11 Munro Street, Port Melbourne, Victoria 3207

Project commissioned and managed by Lorraine Bambrough-Kelly, The Writer's Style

First published 1992
Copyright © Jeremy Oliver 1992

Cover design by Jennifer Peta Richardson
Cover photograph by Sandy Edwards, Sandy Edwards Photography
Designed by Jennifer Peta Richardson

National Library of Australia
Cataloguing-in-Publication data:
Oliver, Jeremy, 1961—
Evans on earth.

ISBN 0 85091 512 0.

1. Evans, Len, 1930- . 2. Vintners - Australia - Biography. 3. Wine industry - Australia - History. 4. Authors, Australian - 20th century - Biography. 5. Businessmen - Australia - Biography. I. Title.

663.20092

Disclaimer

Foreword

Occasionally, in the course of conversation I ask, "Have you met Len Evans?" If my wine-loving acquaintance hesitates for a moment, I know he hasn't – for once met, never forgotten.

Len is larger than life. Outrageous, loveable, occasionally most offensively rude; generous to a fault; I have never met anyone so genuinely kind and extravagantly hospitable. The only trouble is that it is virtually impossible to reciprocate. He also happens to be a brilliantly good taster, as a raconteur few are his equal.

I must confess, rather like the author of this book, that I am biased. For some unaccountable reason – for Len and I are rather akin to chalk and cheese – we have long been the closest of friends. We write to each other regularly confiding in escapades and exchanging the lastest stories. We even share one private joke: we address each other as "S.A.". The initials are not those of an honour bestowed, or the outward manifestation of some higher educational attainment, nor anything to do with South Australia. When I drew his attention to his name, followed by S.A. (meaning in this case Société Anonyme) below the name of a Bordeaux Château of which at the time he was proprietor, he nearly died laughing. "It's official," he said. No, S.A. in our case means something *far* ruder, though it is always used as a term of endearment, and indicates great affection.

I first met Len in the early to mid 1970s when he was showing his wines at a tasting in London. To be truthful I was more impressed by his embullient presentation than his wines. He was our principal host when my wife and I paid our first visit to Australia. Our plane was 24 hours late owing to a false fire alarm over the Indian Ocean, but Len was there to meet us at Sydney airport on an unexpectedly cold and wet, dismal, crack-of-dawn, whisking us away in his vintage Bentley to the club where we rested before the first marathon "single bottle" dinner. Ostensibly held in my honour, I found myself in the company of the Prime Minister and a room full of Australia's best tasters. This was merely the prelude to a fabulous tour of all the major Australian wine districts – with Len as companion and guide. If at times I found his kindness overpowering, his warmth, generosity, enthusiasm and great sense of humour were irresistible.

Fortunately many of those connected with wine, whether as producers, middlemen or consumers are pretty pleasant, civilised people. But in my forty years in the trade I have never met anyone like Len. He is irrepressible, incorrigible, incorruptible, incandescent: *Bacchus incarnate*.

What we pommies would simply call "the best of fellows".

Michael Broadbent, M.W.
Christie's, London

Contents

*I*ntroduction

*L*ong before I decided to make my career in wine I knew about Len Evans. Or to put it correctly, I thought I did. The first wine book I ever bought was the third edition of his *Complete Book of Australian Wine* which I used as a bible. Like many who had never met him, I was in awe of his profile and achievements, jealous of his abilities, and desperately longed to drink even a fraction of the great wines of which he appeared to consume unspeakable quantities.

For an Australian, and a migrant Australian at that, to have fostered and maintained such an international profile in wine had an air of unreality about it. To a young agricultural student overwhelmed by Len Evans' publicity, reputation and incredible stature, his ego and popularity led to suggest a lofty remoteness and aloofness.

My research into this book reveals that many others have made the same mistake about Len Evans. As a youthful entrant to the field of wine writing and education (I studied winemaking in 1984 at Roseworthy College to augment my agricultural science degree), I was fortunate enough to meet him on several occasions, once or twice to ask for his guidance. He had little reason to talk to me apart from friendliness and perhaps curiosity, and I always found him generous with his time and advice. I was amazed at the interest he showed in my career while it was still searching for direction.

Today, now that I have established myself as a wine writer and educator of sorts, I haven't had that much regular contact with the man, but have never forgotten his words to me, or how accurate they turned out to be.

Like all who know him well and understand what his contribution has meant to the growth of Australian wine, I am still astonished at what Len Evans has achieved in a little over thirty years since he first revealed himself to those at the Chevron Hilton in Sydney. I would only ever have written this book with his authorisation, for by presenting the story of his affair with wine, my intention is to acknowledge Len Evans' achievements in a way that has yet to be done.

His is a story that deserves to be told. Despite the fact that Len Evans, unceremoniously referred to as "Evans" by those who know him, has received an OBE for services to the wine industry and to the community, and has collected a number of other wine industry awards, he has still to receive appropriate recognition for what his endeavours have given to countless people; some known to him, most not.

More than anyone else, Evans has carried high the standard for wine in Australia. With the "Cellarmaster" column in the *Bulletin,* he became the country's first regular wine columnist and he has been, without question, our most influential wine writer; an innovative wine retailer and restaurateur at Bulletin Place in Sydney; and as an educator of wine he knows no peer. He has overturned the Australian wine show system, and has brought Australian wine to the attention of the international community. Through sheer force of character, he has cajoled and bludgeoned the world's wine opinion leaders into taking it seriously.

One could be forgiven for imagining Evans' life to be a continual joyride, but his business career has more in common with a rollercoaster ride of giddy heights and desperate lows. He has owned châteaux in France and has been forced to sell wine from his own cellar to stay in business. His grand vision for a global wine company of the highest quality was almost within grasp when suddenly snatched away.

Evans has been both an individual and a tall poppy in Australia and has suffered the consequences. The wine industry, for which he has done more than any other individual, has sometimes encouraged him and occasionally spurned him. Today, it rightly recognises Len Evans as its elder statesman, albeit one cast in his own iconoclastic mould.

Evans has never been motivated by profit, but rather by what he can achieve for himself and for others. As James Halliday says, the fact that Evans has made what wealth he has is only because those projects which motivated him were of such quality and vision that a return was more or less inevitable. Evans has always spent money faster than he has earned it, often in a spirit of awesome selflessness and generosity.

The keys to his success are the scope and breadth of his vision and his dogged determination to see through to completion any project he commences. To this day his greatest disappointment remains the wine venture he had planned in California with his friend, partner and financier, Peter Fox, whose untimely death abruptly halted the scheme and also forced the sale of his two French châteaux.

Most of his projects, such as Rothbury Estate, Bulletin Place and the Evans Wine Company, were many years ahead of their time. Those that remain - the Hunter Valley and Adelaide Hills wineries of Rothbury and Petaluma - are still waiting for the rest of us to catch up.

The Evans' flair is known to stretch reality. It is instantaneous, spontaneous, Elizabethan, grandiose, frequently bordering on wild and uncouth, expensive, explosive and usually very noisy. Nevertheless it is always generous, selfless and sharing. The creative side to his character is most recently expressed in the shape, form and character of "Loggerheads", the home he designed overlooking Rothbury Estate in the Hunter Valley.

Evans on Earth is not a conventional biography. It is a chronicle of stories, told by Evans and others, of Evans' lifelong affair with wine - how he fell into it and where it has taken him. Although my story is deliberately, unquestionably and unapologetically angled in his favour, it neither pretends he was close to perfection or an angel. Anyone as passionate, opinionated and as active as Evans will inevitably create rivalry, jealousy and criticism. Where there is a case to put against Evans it is discussed and evaluated positively – the results further underline his individuality and greatness.

You can't plan in advance what sort of person you want to lead your country, your religion or your wine industry. If we could, our leaders would probably all resemble the same person – squeaky clean, crisply presented and probably utterly straightforward and predictable. Australian wine has Len Evans, a rough diamond and an individual and, as a close friend observes, as despotic, narcissistic and pig-headed a person as ever there was.

That doesn't alter the reality that Evans does display the essential qualities of leadership – vision, an ability to get the job done, to teach and to delegate, and to work with others in a true style of consensus and mutual benefit.

Evans on Earth provides the reader with an opportunity to get to know Len Evans, his views, his past, present and future. Writer, wine man, golfer, gambler, raconteur, satirist, schemer, entrepreneur, artist and architect; he takes some knowing.

The **A**scent

*Len Evans — an illustrious and diverse career — from deer culling
and timber cutting in New Zealand to the uncrowned king of the
Australian wine drinking revolution.*

All achieved, he claims, without direction or ambition.

The
*W*elsh Nomad

One of the marvellous things about wine
is the trouble it gets you into.
L. P. E.

The first wine ever to pass Len Evans' lips was tipped from a bottle of Château d'Yquem, the world's best and most famous sweet wine. Having pinched it from his father's cellar, the young Evans had secreted it in his bedroom. If you are going to immerse your life in wine, you may as well start at the top! "I would sip thimble-sized portions from this bottle until it actually developed a flor-like covering of yeast," he confesses. By the time he finished it the wine must have tasted terrible. "I hate to think how long I kept it for," he wonders. "It was the only sweet and sour wine I've ever had!"

Today Len Evans would love to know what that "darned" vintage actually was, but guesses it must have been about 1937. "At the same time," he continues, "I sent away to the newly emergent Australian wine promotion for information about the Australian Empire ports and sherries. Talk about from the sublime to the ridiculous!" But the taste of wine had triggered something deep inside Len Evans. Where it will ultimately lead is anyone's guess.

Conceived in the classic wine year of 1929, Leonard Paul Evans came into the world only weeks after Don Bradman had left a blazing trail across the lush green outfields of England. Ask anyone in Australia who personifies cricket and the answer is Bradman. Ask the same question about wine and the answer is Len Evans.

Evans was born to Welsh parents, Kathleen and Robert "Chick" Evans on 31 August 1930 in the English harbour town of Felixstowe, Suffolk, close to the city of Ipswich. With some regret, I suspect, he concedes that 1930 was an awful year for wine. The Evans family then returned immediately to Wales for three years before emigrating to England in what Len describes as a depressed condition.

Evans' only sibling is his younger brother Martin, born sixteen years his junior. Martin Evans became a behavioural scientist and, at one stage, was the United Kingdom's director for teacher education on drug and alcohol abuse. Today Len and Martin are close, though they still argue at times.

Throughout his youth Len Evans idolised his father, Chick Evans, who began his lifelong association with the military in 1919, immediately after the First World War. He started as a flying rigger with the Royal Flying Corps, the forerunner to the Royal Air Force. Flying riggers were those daredevils of questionable mind who would alter and tighten the rigging of biplanes by strolling onto the wings during flight. "He was very much the serviceman in uniform," says Evans, "who if distant at times, was a good father. He represented authority, even if it was expressed to others and not necessarily directly to me."

Surviving the rigours of aviation, Evans senior sought sanctuary in a desk job and so moved into administration, although during the Second World War he was commissioned as a Provost Marshall to the airforce's military police in India. Meanwhile, the young Len Evans and family were bombed out three times, which today he states as the reason he turned to alcohol.

Once peace had broken out, as described in *Beyond the Fringe*, and after unsuccessfully tilting at a business career, Evans senior rejoined the airforce as a civilian consultant, eventually retiring after a relationship with military service of over fifty years.

Before his father's travels and his own nomadic wanderings, Len did not see much of his parents, although in 1955 he was their guest in Singapore. He didn't really rekindle his relationship with them until his return to England in 1967, another twelve years later, and spent more time with his family from the 1970s onwards. "By then my father was more retiring and had become very proud of both his sons," Len

For a time at least Evans did retain a air of innocence and harmlessness.

Evans recalls. Chick Evans died in 1987, aged 85. "Dad was loads of fun and had a great sense of humour. He was a gregarious man, a real old charmer."

According to Len Evans, he inherited his personality in equal parts from each of his parents. "My mother, who still lives hale and hearty in Felixstowe at the age of 81, is utterly honest, straightforward and direct. I get that from her. No-one would ever be in any doubt about exactly what she's thinking."

For a brief period after the war Chick Evans became moderately prosperous as a businessman, and although he was basically a beer drinker, managed to stockpile a small collection of wine. Although this ultimately became a temptation to the young Len, he still says he doesn't know exactly where he got this "wine thing" from.

Chick Evans could afford to send his eldest son to Suffolk's leading public school, Framlingham, where Evans progressed happily, taking keenly to his studies and even becoming a school prefect. His ultimate reward was a scholarship to Cambridge and entrance to an architectural degree. At Framlingham Evans also initiated a custom of serving contraband sherry and madeira to a small band of select guests after chapel on Sundays. The hospitality bug was already biting, even if illicitly so. "We didn't do it to break the law by drinking at school, but we all thought we were frightfully smart about it," he confesses.

In 1948 Evans declined his offer to Cambridge, abandoning formal education in favour of professional golf, although he still refers to architecture as his true love. He has since created evidence for this aplenty: witness the buildings of Rothbury Estate, Bulletin Place and his present home, "Loggerheads", where his instinctive flair for shape and design has created extraordinary results.

After a time as a trainee at Ipswich's Purdis Heath Golf Club, Evans was called up for his national service, then still mandatory in the U.K., as a physical training instructor with the airforce. He was posted all over England and even sent to Germany where, although he found the wine plentiful if not memorable, he admits today he hadn't the faintest idea what he was drinking.

Demobbed from the services in 1950, Evans swung back to golf in earnest, spending time at several clubs as a trainee professional, before becoming assistant professional at Potters Bar Golf Club from 1951 to 1952. Golf was highly enjoyable on the course and offered the glittering prospect of fame and fortune. Teaching others to play it on a full-time basis must, however, have numbed Evans' creative mind. When it finally dawned that he was cut out for more than cleaning clubs for the rest of his life, Evans made a characteristically venturesome decision and in March 1953 emigrated to the far-flung Commonwealth outpost of New Zealand. Within a mere twelve hours of his arrival in this strange habitat, Evans had found employment with the New Zealand Forestry Service as a timber cutter and deer culler.

He relished felling trees and hunting game, although found female company on the rare side of scarce. This detail was swiftly overcome.

It must have been a charmed, if basic and physical existence. If weekends were too hot for hunting, Evans and his company would simply desert to the nearest beach, sleep in caves and wash down the fish they cooked by the sea with flagons of rough New Zealand red. He loved the Daniel Boone existence. Already a rather broad and tough nut, with a low centre of gravity, Evans and his English comrades were happy to make their own entertainment. Each week they would provoke a similar number of Yugoslavs into a fight. On one occasion, the Slavs didn't show up at the pub at the appropriate time, so Evans and his pugnacious team compensated by turning on each other!

Descending from the mountains in 1954, Evans found more conventional employment in a small factory which made golf buggies and car mufflers. Its owner was a golf fanatic and allowed Evans to play and teach the game two days a week, working four days in the factory. He ran a disorganised and inefficient factory, and despite there being no sequence between the machines, still managed to produce eighty mufflers a day.

He left Evans, who by now had become foreman of the car muffler plant, in charge while away on a fortnight's holiday. There was another foreman responsible for the electrical side of the business, and it was nothing for Evans to persuade him to devote a day to reorganising the factory into a logical sequence. Production immediately trebled and the owner returned to find his factory churning out a prodigious 240 mufflers a day. It wasn't long, however, before Evans' mandatory two years' service as government "factory fodder" after his immigration ticked over.

He was now a completely free man, twenty-four years of age and able to take any job he wanted. So he immediately gave his employer notice. Too proud to meet Evans personally, the owner arranged for a book-keeper friend to offer Evans a junior partnership in the firm.

"I wasn't a bit interested," Evans recalls, "but asked 'Why me?' It was because of what I had done with the factory."

Evans at Mount Isa in 1956.

"We wish you great success, because you are going to be a very successful man," the book-keeper told a rather startled Len Evans. "You do more than you have to."

"It was my first great lesson in life," Evans reflects, "and one I've never forgotten. Having employed people since 1960, I've always seen that those who get on are always the ones who do more than they have to."

Evans' new-found liberty took him to Sydney, where he arrived in May 1955, quite unready for the worst and most depressing period of his life. The only work he could find was a job as a welder on a General Motors production line, eight monotonous cars an hour, eight dreary hours a day. Then came the wet Sydney winter, the final straw. It must have been a bad season, but it was enough to encourage Evans to move northwards to the bush, up to the heat of Goondiwindi, Queensland. He was working outdoors again, clearing trees, ring-barking, sucker-bashing (clouting the shoots off ring-barked trees) and scrub clearing. He loved the work, but when he watched an Aborigine being hit with a shovel by the camp boss, he gave the boss one back and packed his swag for Brisbane.

Again opportunities were scarce, so Evans replied to an advertisement in the *Courier Mail* for inexperienced fencers to erect a rabbit-proof fence at Boulia. Exasperated by so-called "gun fencers" telling him how to do his job, the contractor had made a point of demanding fresh talent. No applicant, says Evans, was less experienced in fencing than he.

Fence constructed, in 1956 Evans returned to civilisation and the practice fairway. Making it his priority, he gave his golf the biggest chance he ever would, played the best golf of his life, and then threw it all away. "I discovered the world of difference between being a professional golfer and a golf professional," he says. Playing the tour in the Far East, he won The Selectar Cup, a tournament in Singapore. "Later on I gave the trophy away," he shrugs. Many people, some who know Evans better than others, have since wondered at the wisdom of his quitting golf, but Evans was in no doubt at the time. Now aged sixty-one and after a heart bypass, he still hits a monstrously long, straight one-wood without even appearing to try. Like many others, I find this absolutely infuriating and grossly unfair.

So, unable to return to New Zealand because of lack of funds, Evans made it as far as Mount Darwin and Mount Isa, far north-west Queensland, where he stayed, holding down several jobs at once. He was simultaneously a labourer and steel-hand, a foreman and stores manager. He ran a chicken and duck farm which was put out of action by a solitary dingo in a single night, and gave golf lessons at the weekends, setting the pace he has lived at ever since. In the free time he sometimes found in the evenings, Evans immersed himself by writing and performing revues for charity.

By now, Evans says, he had already become a "considerable" drinker of wine, thanks to his extensive exposure to it in the United Kingdom, New Zealand and Germany. He would inevitably arrive at Mount Isa parties laden with wine, and still recalls the disbelief on the bottleshop manager's face when once he asked for an entire crateful. Evans didn't think they considered him a poofter for his wine drinking, but rather saw it as a charming aberration. In any case, doubts would quickly have evaporated once he started courting his future bride, Patricia Hayton, who just happened to be the local beauty queen.

In 1957 Evans first became acquainted with the well-known Hill-Smith family of Yalumba fame when, on a camping trip around Australia, his route from Alice Springs to Adelaide took in the Barossa Valley. Clutching an introduction from a mutual friend, he met Margie and Mark Hill-Smith, with whose family he remains very close, and saw at first-hand that life in the wine industry had its compensations.

Wine was not foremost in Evans' mind as far as his career was concerned, but writing certainly was. He had begun, and rather successfully at that, to submit scripts to several radio and television shows, and kept an eye peeled for a chance to move to Sydney to further his scripting opportunities. Additional part-time income would be the ticket. Scanning through advertisements in the "Casual Work Available" section of a Sydney paper, he saw a vacancy for a "Casual young man, glass washer, Ship Inn, Circular Quay". "Being about the most casual man I knew," he says, "I applied for the job." It was the last job Len Evans says he ever applied for. And so his toe was dipped into the hospitality industry, working under a manager named Jack Moody, with whom he still keeps in contact.

Most days Evans would work from 6 a.m. to 10 a.m., which gave him time to attend script rehearsals and to write, but on Saturdays he worked from 6 a.m. to 6 p.m., the statutory closing time in those days. He was contributing a number of television scripts in several States and also began writing as a humorist for the *Observer* magazine, which later amalgamated with the *Bulletin*.

"I used to wander around Sydney," says Evans, "and found my way to Bulletin Place, only two hundred yards from the Ship Inn, where I saw this very old building, which turned out to have been built in 1816. I would stop and wonder what could be done with it and the other great old buildings in the area." Time would tell.

Working his way up through the ranks at the Ship Inn, Evans graduated to first barman, then to bar manager. One particular day he was assisting a stock controller whose rounds included his hotel. Evans thought it logical to name the item he was counting first, and then to name the number of stock counted, allowing the controller time to find the item on his lists before its quantity was read out – a simple and typical piece of Evans thinking which had its ramifications. Shortly afterwards, Evans was offered full-time employment as a hotel stock controller and systems analyst, a position he gladly accepted, recognising the additional financial security it would bring. Evans had now arrived full-time in the liquor industry; he was in it up to his knees.

Most importantly, by accepting the stock-controlling offer, Trish Hayton, patently an intelligent woman who had not until then been willing to agree to wed a freelance humour columnist who augmented his income by washing glasses, regardless of his skills at either, accepted him. Trish and Len Evans were married at St Mathias in Oxford Street, Paddington, on 18 July 1959. It was a small wedding party of around thirty friends. In the *Len Evans Cookbook*, it is recorded that the red wine at the wedding breakfast was Fiorelli, the white, Bianchini.

Evans' job involved analysing the gross percentages and potential profits of hotels. He was quick and accurate, and instead of taking the usual two weeks gave his clients their results by the following day. In 1959 he was already earning £60 per week, healthy pay in those days. It was while working in stock control that he met Mark Cotter, a former mayor of Scone and a very superior type of publican who owned the Lennox Hotel in Parramatta; a very dignified man who knew how to get the best from people, as Evans recalls. Cotter introduced Evans to the Chevron Hilton, where the young systems analyst first came across its manager, Frank Christie.

Now financially secure, Len and Trish Evans rented a small flat in Paddington for £4 10s a week. They renovated their loungeroom themselves, and began the endless collection of antiquities that has come to typify any Evans building project. Evans unleashed healthy doses of his unique and spontaneous creativity on a table-top, painting it "with Dali-like surrealism".

By 1959 Len Evans was beginning to convert his enthusiasm for wine into genuine knowledge. His cause was furthered greatly the day he ambled into the new gallery of the Hungarian-born Sydney art dealer and bon vivant, Rudy Komon. Komon had recently taken over the old McWilliams wine salon on the corner of Jersey Road and Paddington Street, Woollahra, just a stroll down the road from the Evans residence. Seconds later, as Evans recalls, a glass of wine was in his hand and its contents had become the topic of conversation. He soon learned that Komon was President of the Wine and Food Society of New South Wales, a judge at the Sydney Wine Show, and spent much of his time consummating his love for wine.

A few weeks later, Evans found himself enrolled as a student at an introductory wine appreciation course conducted by Rudy Komon at the Sydney Showgrounds. Evans enjoyed it, and after the last session confronted his teacher to tell him so.

"And which wine do you most like drinking?" asked Komon.

"I rather like gewürztraminer," Evans replied, keenly.

"Don't worry," consoled Komon. "You will grow out of that." Of course neither Evans nor Komon could then have guessed that on this occasion the sorcerer had commenced training his apprentice.

Thirstily, Evans accumulated more and more wine, finding much to his and his bride's concern that their marital bed was rising instead of sagging in the middle. Fortunately, much was able to be relocated in the cellar of a particularly trustworthy friend, whose honesty over a long period of time Evans still finds admirable. The Evans' next move was into a house with a cellar, or as Trish Evans used to call it, a cellar with a house.

By that time the incessant flow of trade samples of liquor had begun. Among the first to arrive at the Evans' home was a set of fifty Baitz Liqueurs from Louise of the popular Melbourne-based cocktail king.

Trish Evans was then employed by a personnel consultancy, where she became firm friends with a colleague, Jan Oxenbould. They decided that their husbands might just get on together, so Trish invited the Oxenboulds round to dinner. After the meal, which had included a respectable quantity of decent wine, Evans asked Bob Oxenbould if he wanted to try a liqueur. He presented the entire set of Baitz bottles, which Bob Oxenbould estimates they nearly finished that night, draining at least something, or rather a lot from every bottle. Evans regrets that he doesn't know how or when the Oxenboulds left the flat.

Nevertheless, Bob Oxenbould says they quickly established themselves as kindred spirits who liked a spot of drink with a bit of food. They also shared an obsession for fishing, even though Oxenbould is totally allergic to fish and becomes violently ill on eating it by mistake. It's that kind of eccentric that Len Evans likes to collect as his friends.

The
*C*hevron Hilton:
the Alternative University

*He arrived as a pushy young fellow, and it was clear
that nothing was going to stop him from getting where he
wanted to go.*
Frank Christie, General Manager, The Chevron Hilton,
Sydney.

*I*n 1960 Sydney witnessed the building of the Chevron Hilton, the most ambitious
hotel project it had ever seen. In all likelihood, today it would still be the harbour
city's largest hotel complex had funding not run dry after only 220 of the intended
1 100 rooms been completed.

Amazingly, the building's full complement of food and beverage facilities had
been constructed, leaving a fully operational hotel able to wine, dine and entertain
many times more people than it could recline. The Chevron Hilton could seat 3 000
people in different rooms in a single night if there were double seatings for some
shows. The jewels in its crown were the 650-seat Silver Spade Theatre Restaurant and
its 800-seat ballroom. The Oasis Lounge could seat another 600, the Chevron's Grill
Room 200, while function rooms of varying sizes catered for another 200. In
addition, there was a variety of public and cocktail bars.

Aware that the project was excessively burdened with its wealth of embellishments,
the Hilton chain opted to sever its ties with the hotel, although it did allow the
Chevron to retain the "Hilton" suffix until its sale, provided it was managed
according to the Hilton chain's international standards. Heavily over-capitalised, the
Chevron was never able to shake off its phenomenal interest burden and eventually
collapsed into receivership, but not before it had radically altered Sydney's perception
of wine and food, due largely to the inspiration of a young and energetic Len Evans.

The Chevron's inaugural General Manager was Frank Christie who, before
taking up the appointment, had represented the interests of its owners, Chevron
Sydney Ltd, one of the Korman companies, as an adviser in the project's preparatory
stages.

Early in 1960 Christie received a call from a young man saying he had arrived
in the hotel's personnel department with a scheme for a perpetual inventory system,
designed to afford the hotel better control over its stocks of beverages. Up fronted
Evans, cocksure that he had devised the system to suit the Chevron and that he was

just the very person to implement it. "He was a very persuasive young man," Christie remembers, "and it sounded like he had a lot to offer." Impressed by both Evans' plan and persona, he agreed that Len Evans should begin work full-time at the Chevron.

This was unquestionably Evans' great opportunity and he was in his element. It wasn't long before he became the hotel's Assistant Beverage Manager, then its Beverage Manager, before a time as its Food and Beverage Manager. When Evans left the hotel for the Australian Wine Board, and only four years after first meeting Frank Christie, Evans had become his right-hand man, the Chevron's Executive Assistant Manager. He and Christie had developed a firm friendship that they still maintain. Both now meet monthly as board members of Ridge's Hotels, which owns properties at Kosciusko and Thredbo in the Australian Alps.

As far as Len Evans is concerned, those years at the Chevron, from 1960 to 1964, were his five great years of university, a more practical training than the Cambridge University education he had knocked back. Notorious Evans' characteristics began to emerge: an insuperable desire to learn everything about wine and to teach it to others, an ability to be innovatory, an inevitable Elizabethan touch, the Options Game to guess a wine's identity, consummate hospitality, an ability to mix easily with the biggest names and the now legendary Evans' capacity for surprise.

By playing out a length of rope that would leave the average hotel manager speechless, Frank Christie candidly concedes his role in creating the phenomenon that Len Evans has become. At the end of the day he's obviously proud of it. "He arrived as a pushy young fellow, and it was clear that nothing was going to stop him from getting where he wanted to go," he says. "After about a year he always made it known that he was going to have his own vineyard. We gave him the opportunity to develop his feelings for wine and for himself," he says.

From day one Frank Christie saw something unique in Evans and presented him with the opportunity to taste the very greatest of wines. Even then Christie

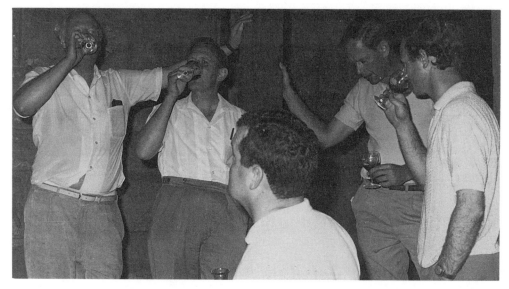

Early wine guessing-games in the cellar at the Evans' home. From left:
Douglas Lamb, Bruce Tyson (McWilliams), Evans, Graham Gregory and Dr Ray Healey.

remembers Evans bemoaning that everyone drank far too much beer and whisky, and didn't enjoy wine enough.

When Evans joined the Chevron, he expected to have the chance to learn about wine from others more qualified. Imagine his surprise to find himself the palate in residence, the local source of wine knowledge, in spite of how little he says he knew. Perhaps Evans underestimated his own ability for, as Christie recalls, even in those days it was obvious he had a natural palate, and his recognition and discussion of wine was unusually precise. "He would use a lot of other people to help him develop his skills and knowledge. He kept in close contact with the wine companies, talking and arguing with them, learning about what they were doing, and matching their ideas and opinions against his own."

Evans did stray on occasions, but Christie left him in little doubt that expensive mistakes were to be made but once. With the Chevron's Catering Manager, Ken Kendrick, Evans once threw a private party for the opening of a new floor show at the Silver Spade. Together, Kendrick and Evans had devised a spectacular banquet tossing together sundry food items destined to be thrown away, since they no longer appeared on a menu. Evans cribbed a few odd bins of wines and samples and, predictably enough, the dinner unfolded as a sensational event.

Never one to fraternise willingly with those whose company he plainly didn't enjoy, Evans' big mistake was not to invite the hotel's Food Controller, not considered a popular man. Retaliating, the spurned controller costed all the wine and food devoured by the Evans party at full margin. Next morning, when the staff accounts went through as usual to Frank Christie, he baulked instantly at a preposterous bill "with wine expenditure quite out of this world". Minutes later he confronted Evans with the biggest dressing-down of his life, even though his head was hurting long before his ears began to burn. Evans squeezed in about four "Yes, sirs" during Christie's lecture, but recognised the value of the lesson.

Today, Christie is amused that Evans remembers the occasion so vividly. "He took a liberty I hadn't given him. I was prepared to go along on the understanding that his ideas were helpful and good for all of us." In the *Len Evans Cookbook*, Evans records that he never repeated the offence, and that "temperance in all things has dominated my life ever since".

It's easy to forget how primitive was the Australia of the early 1960s. Wine for sale was closeted behind counters, out of the public's reach. To examine a bottle required an attendant to hand it over. Infected with the wine bug, Evans put the bottles where the public were, out from behind the counters and onto the shop floor. He was the first to put wine in displays, in aisles, on open shelves, in bins, split barrels and stacked cartons, setting the standard which all modern wine shops have since followed. People loved to come to handle the wine and buy, says Evans. Thirty years ago, Roy Mayer, a Lindemans salesman, told him "You're bloody mad, Len. They'll knock it off by the case." But they didn't.

Shortly afterwards Evans found himself at the Kings Cross Rex Hotel. Underneath an enormous Lindemans sign was a replica of his own display. He telephoned Mayer immediately. "You bastard, you've pinched my bloody idea!" Mayer replied: "It's the sincerest form of flattery, mate."

Evans also introduced the concepts of "Private Bin" wines and "Cellarmasters' Suggestions" to help promote individual wines. We now take these ideas for granted, but someone had to think of them first. Nevertheless, wine companies bucked strongly at the time, telling Evans they didn't want to give away or display the vintages or bin numbers of their wines. He replied that those details meant a lot to him. Once Cellarmasters' Suggestions became a huge success he was proven right.

Now appointed Beverage Manager at the Chevron, Evans set about stocking the cellar, for it to become the greatest retail cellar then seen in Australia. Only small amounts of top Australian wine was then available in bottles, which he stacked against all the top French wines, all the Premier Grands Crus, all the great vineyard Burgundies and all the great Champagnes.

With three of his friends, Department of Agriculture officer Graham Gregory, Max Lake and Rudy Komon, Evans helped persuade Murray Tyrrell to begin bottling his own wine in 1962. Before then, all Tyrrell's wine had been sold in bulk, much of it to other wine companies. Murray Tyrrell was then new to the game and had not long been in charge of the family winery, having taken over from Dan Tyrrell, who had died in the late 1950s after working an incredible seventy-six consecutive vintages. Evans ordered sixty cases of his second bottlings, twenty cases of each Vat wine.

"Don't you mean six cases?" queried an incredulous Tyrrell. Evans confirmed he meant sixty. "Christ, that will cover the wages for a few months!" barked Tyrrell, now infamous as the "Mouth of the Hunter".

Although Evans supported the Hunter Valley from the outset, winegrowing there was then a mere fraction of its present scale. "Tullochs which, thanks to people like Johnnie Walker, were well known in Sydney, were open to sell bottled wine," he says. "At McWilliams and Lindemans you could taste but not buy because everything was shipped to Sydney for bottling. At Elliotts you could buy wine, at Tyrrells you could buy it in bulk, while at Draytons both bulk and bottled wine were for sale."

Evans lined the Chevron walls with the great Lindemans whites of the 1950s and early 1960s, alongside the classic Maurice O'Shea reds from Mount Pleasant for all of six and seven shillings a bottle. Years later, Dick Heath, former Hardys chief winemaker, showed him a letter written in 1960 to the Hardys Board, showing concern at the build-up of old red wine stocks.

"The Chevron fixed that alone," Evans declares. "It was an exciting time. We would hold incredible tastings of Australian wines. On one occasion we had five or six vintages of Thomas Hardy wines back to 1945, plus an entire line of Lindemans wines from the so-called great years in the Hunter, including four or five Granges when Grange Hermitage was tantamount to a dirty word. I can remember making a great success of the '55 Grange, but I didn't like the '56, so I sent it back. Penfolds agreed with me that it wasn't good enough. What's it worth a bottle now? Many thousands!"

In 1962 Evans found himself summoned one day by Ernie Gower, who managed Seppelt's office in Sydney. Great Western was releasing a range of great old wines made by the legendary Colin Preece. "One was the J34, the 1953 cabernet that won all sorts of prizes, another the K81, either 1949 or 1951, all up for a song," Evans remembers. "So I bought the lot."

Two years later, another lot was released, but by this time he found himself competing against ten or twelve other buyers, from the Menzies Hotel, the

Wentworth Hotel, the Sebel Townhouse, and other hotels and restaurants. Australia was rapidly waking up to the quality of its wine.

Evans would select and purchase large amounts of wine, including some entire stocks, to then be given the Chevron's own label. One wine, as Frank Christie warmly recalls, was the entire vintage of a St Patrice Claret, which became the hotel's star performer. It was a 1957 Reynella Shiraz vintage, bottled in 1959, and bought from Douglas Lamb. Whether Christie's fondness for the wine stemmed from its vinous character and qualities, or that it must have made him a small fortune, costing only 6s 7d a bottle and selling for a heavily marked-up £2, I can't tell.

Evans and a team from Thomas Hardy, including Dick Heath, Guf Pfafflin and, once he had started with his family's company, the young Jim Hardy, would venture northwards on wine-buying expeditions to the Hunter Valley. There being no freeway at this time, it took the group an entire day to travel to the Hunter, although their precise route was hardly chosen for speed. They would rendezvous by 8.30 a.m. at Hardys' Sydney office for a couple of brandies before embarking for Brooklyn, on the Hawkesbury River. There they would pick up fresh oysters to accompany what Evans remembers as a marvellous Hardy wine in a white bottle. "It was a 1945 white with a green colour," he says. "Lovely wine; I'll never forget it." "We'd have a couple of bottles of that and then turn towards the Hunter, although first we'd stop at the Wattagan State Forest for an enormous T-bone steak and tomatoes, washed down with '54 Cabernets or a '45 Thomas Hardy Claret."

Next they would set a course for Cessnock, the only town of any size in the Lower Hunter Valley wine region. Cessnock only offered one place to stay, the Wentworth Hotel in the middle of town. By now it would be 6.30 p.m., all of three hours since the steak so the hunger pangs would be returning. Having checked in, the group would head directly to the dining room for a full English dinner, come rain, cold, sleet, frost or 105-degree heat. "We would religiously have roast beef and Yorkshire pudding or roast pork and apple sauce and whatever," says Evans, "and then we'd go for a walk up and down the totally deserted streets of Cessnock."

Before the end of the six o'clock closing in the late 1960s, Australian pubs were forced to sell their last drinks at this ridiculously early hour. The licensing laws of the time were a little more than a reprehensible legacy of austere and archaic traditions, and created far more problems than they prevented, including the infamous "six o'clock swill", when every member of a drinking "school" would line up at the bar at five minutes to six to buy the largest glass of beer possible for each person in the group. They had until twenty minutes past six, at which time the doors of the hotel were legally forced to close, to down the lot, frequently eight or more glasses. It was little wonder that few Australians were then to be seen walking the streets at night. Few were able to.

Being the sensitive and moderate wine drinkers they were, Evans and his group would return unhindered and unaided from their walk just in time to drop into the Residents' Bar at the hotel where, at 9 p.m., they would enjoy a simple and delicate supper of meat balls.

A modern visitor would scarcely recognise the Hunter Valley of the 1960s. On a crowded weekend, twenty or thirty people might visit from Sydney to call on the seven wineries in existence at the time.

Evans credits Max Lake for starting the 1960s wine boom in the Hunter, which began with fever for red wine, then very quickly switched to white. "Lakey got everyone enthusiastic about wine and his contribution as a writer was very considerable. He was writing very well and had published three important books, *Hunter Wine, Hunter Winemakers* and *Classic Wines of Australia*, all excellent works and extremely important in their day. He spoke tremendous truths in them and they helped a whole generation of wine lovers.

"I loved helping Max plant the vineyard at Lake's Folly (in 1963 and 1964), being part of those days, and I enjoyed drinking many great wines from his cellar with him. As I evolved, I was able to reciprocate at Bulletin Place."

The Hunter Valley's wine industry grew out of all proportion from the late 1960s to the mid 1970s. In his book *The Hunter Valley*, James Halliday recounts that in 1956 only 467 hectares were planted to vines in the Hunter, which by 1977 had stretched to 4 127 hectares, as the rate of wine consumption increased more rapidly than that of any other alcoholic beverage in Australia.

Well-known leading Melbourne wine retailer, Doug Crittenden, accompanied Evans on another of his Hunter Valley wine buying trips in the early 1970s. Evans was, by then, buying wine for his cellar and restaurant at Bulletin Place, Sydney.

Both were tasting straight from Murray Tyrrell's casks. There were two special, separate samples, as Crittenden recalls, each from a 250-gallon cask. Evans shoved a glass of one of them at Crittenden demanding, "What do you think of that?". Crittenden replied that it had fantastic body and palate. "Well, what do you think of this?" Evans enquired, handing over a glass from the second barrel. Crittenden said he liked the second for its bouquet, the first for its body. "I like them for much the same reasons," agreed Evans. "Let's put the two together and we'll call them our mutual idea of a great Hunter red."

Murray Tyrrell later blended the two and the result was a certain Bin D2404, labelled "Tyrrells Hunter River Dry Red 1970", with the annotation "Exclusive to Crittendens and the Bulletin Wine Club". A note on the label said it was chosen by Evans and Crittenden "as their concept of what a top Hunter wine from a good year should be". Enthusiasts should note the straightforward use of the word "good" by Tyrrell in his formative days, before every season came to be declared the "Vintage of the Century". Crittenden agrees it was a "bloody good wine". Still in top condition today, it drinks softly and subtly, showing the sort of richness and development that only low-cropped Hunter vineyards can deliver with shiraz.

In 1974 Evans took another major Melbourne retailer, Dan Murphy, to visit Tyrrell and to taste his wines. Murphy, tongue firmly wedged in Irish cheek, said: "I hope he won't produce any of his reds."

"Why not?" cried Evans defensively.

"Murray can't make a good red wine," continued Murphy. "He's hopeless with reds, but his whites are all right."

Into the cellar they strode. "I've brought Dan with me, Murray," said Evans, blunt as ever. "He tells me you can't make a decent red!"

In 1962, Frank Christie promoted Evans to the position of Food and Beverage Manager at the Chevron, with responsibility for 350 staff, including eighty cooks and apprentices. In the *Len Evans Cookbook* Evans records that it was the last time in

Australia that two full brigades of chefs operated in traditional fashion, with separate teams of sauciers, grillardins, rôtisseurs, garde-mangers, pâtissiers and poissoniers.

Evans' placement instantly made him senior to a highly skilled operator by the name of Tony Bohdan, who was simultaneously appointed the hotel's Catering Manager. "Until then I had found Bohdan abrupt and determined," he says, "and he thought I was very much the Assistant Clown Prince."

Evans chose to visit Bohdan to break the ice. "I realise you know a lot more about food than I do," he said, "but I have some advice. If you expose me, or bring me down in any way, shape or form, I will take you down with me." Bohdan quickly nodded his agreement. Evans then said: "Now my chief worry is whether or not the cooks will accept me."

Bohdan smiled and asked why, saying "Surely after what you've just told me, the cooks' chief worry is whether you will accept them."

Evans says that was the best lesson he ever received as an executive. "If you are put in charge of something, be in charge. The responsibility is all yours. The decision-making process, right or wrong, has never been difficult for me," he states. "But I'm not suggesting I make the right decisions all the time."

The Evans-Bohdan partnership became both happy and profitable; they led a successful and innovative team with a flair for the grand scale. The ex-officio third part of the Chevron culinary triumvirate was a hotel guest, in Sydney to present television stations with an idea for a cooking programme. It was Graham Kerr, described by Evans as a tall, self-confident English Scot from New Zealand. They quickly became friends.

Tony Bohdan and Graham Kerr helped Evans to acquire a huge knowledge about food. Frank Christie remembers watching as Evans, Bohdan and Kerr would all huddle over a table discussing recipes, several of which would later appear on the menu.

Their Chevron innovations included the Baron of Beef presentation, grand flambés in front of 600 people, and the Chevron's Hawaiian presentations, for which decapitated coconuts were filled with something described as "Polynesian stew". It may not sound that exciting today, but remember that in 1960s Australia it was a brave man who would choose to eat anything other than steak and potato.

Food has always been part of Len Evans' picture. In the *Bulletin* magazine, he wrote that it was Tony Bohdan who taught him more about food than anyone else. At the Chevron, Evans might throw in a promotional food-related thought, then sit back fascinated as Bohdan then translated his concept into practical ideas. A terse "No, that's no good" might spell the end of a particular train of thought, but Evans refused to question Bohdan's judgement.

Evans' good friend Bob Oxenbould illuminates with the memories of the grand Chevron occasions, some of them perceptibly clearer than others. He believes the Silver Spade was one of the great restaurants and rates its functions as years ahead of their time.

Perhaps the most incredible of all was the Elizabethan Dinner, reviving a popular Evans theme. It is still firmly lodged in the minds of those who attended, although they could easily be forgiven for thinking they had stepped straight into a passing time warp.

Forever seeking any excuse to pull out a costume, Evans had distributed explicit instructions to each patron to dress in authentic Elizabethan garb. At the tables, guests were equipped with ancient daggers instead of cutlery, intended to slice chunks of meat from the huge cuts presented by teams of appropriately attired and buxom serving wenches. Great Danes, starved no doubt for days beforehand, roamed the sawdusted and straw-covered floors, scavenging for bones tossed over the diners' shoulders. Etiquette and decorum became more mediaeval by the minute.

How did Evans manage to persuade Frank Christie, a patently sensible man, to condone, and then to participate in bizarre events of that nature? "It just seemed like a good idea at the time," shrugs Christie, sounding less like the traditional accountant-styled hotel manager all the time. "It was a huge success. Len thought he could revive some of the great themes of the past. Rather than have an elegant event, like a standard banquet with immaculate linen and waiter service, here we were, supposedly feasting as they did in the seventeenth century."

Evans created a name for himself in Sydney with his spectacular events, which were usually centred on simple but very good food, great wine and riotous fun with his own magic touch. Thirty years on, little has changed. "They were enormous gimmicks, but we got away with it," he laughs.

At the Chevron he was surrounded by stars, Governors-General and Prime Ministers, including Sir Robert Menzies who came to know Evans well. "Look at the people I got to meet there – Vivien Leigh, Frank Sinatra, Judy Garland, Henry Ford II, Ethel Merman, Nelson Eddy, Louis Armstrong, Nat King Cole, Rudolf Nureyev and Dame Margot Fonteyn. Candice Bergen was there when only nineteen years old – she was a great beauty. At one time I had Sammy Davis Jnr, Shelley Berman and Eartha Kitt on a single floor together, all appearing at different venues in Sydney."

Evans would invite Bob and Jan Oxenbould to the General Manager's table on opening nights, where the top comedians and most popular acts of the day, like Katherine Grayson, Jane Powell, and Rowan and Martin would entertain them just a few metres away.

During his last two years at the Chevron as Frank Christie's assistant, Evans' biggest challenge was the Nat King Cole season at the Silver Spade which lasted just a single week. It was the first time ever that two floor shows were staged at the Chevron on a single night. Antediluvian licensing laws prohibited public admission until 6 p.m. although special dispensation was granted to enable the Chevron to serve the last drinks by 12 midnight, provided they cleared the bar by 12.10 p.m. An additional half-hour was permitted to facilitate the removal of patrons by 12.30 a.m.

Since Nat King Cole's show lasted just over an hour, Evans' dilemma was how to seat 650 people in the Silver Spade at 6 p.m., have their orders taken and two-thirds of their meal served by 7 p.m., when Cole came on to perform from then until just after 8.15 p.m. The final course would then be served, bills presented, monies collected and the room emptied by 8.45 p.m., leaving an entire half-hour for the room to be completely stripped and re-set by 9.15 p.m. when another throng of 650 poured in.

Once he realised how tight was his schedule, Evans approached Nat King Cole, saying what an impossible job he had given his staff, who of course would have little choice but to clear the plates during the floor show. As Evans tells the story, "He then gave me a great big grin and a wide smile with all those huge marvellous white teeth and said, 'Len, I've been a star for seventeen years. And do you know what makes a star?' I said, 'No, Mr Cole.' 'He is a star when no-one clears a plate during his show'. Consequently, not a soul moved in that room during the show. "And it was fun," says Evans, "enormous fun." It was the Chevron's biggest week ever.

It was nearly the Chevron's second biggest week ever. While Frank Christie was overseas on holiday, Evans had accepted a booking from the Beatles to stay there during their memorable Australian tour. On his return, Christie immediately cancelled the booking, assuming it would excessively disrupt the hotel's routine. So John, Paul, George and Ringo camped immediately across the road at the Sydney Sheraton.

While the Sheraton scored all the attention, the publicity and the Beatles, the Chevron got the crowds, the riots and the police, as thousands of hysterical people backed into its frontage, while police kept the front of the Sheraton clear.

"It was a mistake," Christie concedes. "But it was great for our kids who could look out and wave from the balcony."

It wasn't long before Christie restored face with Evans. In 1964, while overseas for three months with his wife Joan, Christie was woken by an early morning call. It was Evans, explaining in the dead of the Parisian night that he had been unable to secure an act for the Silver Spade for a period after Christie's expected return. "You go ahead, Len, and make all the arrangements. There's not much I can do from here," Christie advised, unable to be any more constructive from that distance.

By his return there was still no act. Knowing that almost anything was preferable to his own particular variety of soft shoe shuffle, Christie met with an agent to hear a demonstration tape. Time was running out, so he felt he had little choice but to book the act, which sounded acceptable. His name was Wayne Newton.

"Who the hell is Wayne Newton?" flared Evans, instantly cancelling the booking. Rising to the occasion, Christie bravely countermanded Evans' rejection.

As fate would have it, Wayne Newton became a gigantic success at the Silver Spade, the second biggest attraction ever to Nat King Cole, and his manager, Carlos Gastell, never forgot Len Evans. Every time he visited Sydney thereafter he made sure to send him Wayne's love.

Once you understand Len Evans, it's of little surprise that the most important thing he did at the Chevron involved lunch. With Christie, he formed the Friday Table, a luncheon club which came to play a pivotal role in Australia's evolving sophistication about wine. The club was the chrysalis from which Bulletin Place ultimately unfolded as the most important centre of wine consciousness this country has known.

Together, they invited the elite of Sydney's wine and food community to a weekly lunch provided by the hotel, for which the members were each to bring a wine. The Chevron kitchen was given an exacting proving-ground for its culinary talent and Christie and Evans guaranteed a fine luncheon in excellent company once a week.

The original members of the Friday Table were Frank Christie; Rudy Komon; Max Lake, surgeon and future vigneron at Lake's Folly; Joe Franks, then the President of the Australian Catering Institute; Ron Tarrant, celebrated journalist and then editor of *Pix*; Lawrence Rodriguez, a doctor in King's Cross; David Manuel; Ken Kendricks, the Chevron's Catering Manager, later replaced by Tony Bohdan; and Evans. David Manuel developed a form of ulcer (due to his work, says Evans) and, sadly, dropped out.

At the time, Rudy Komon and Max Lake shared the wine spotlight in Sydney, both recognised as then having the most knowledge and best palates at the table. Lake was then acknowledged as Australia's leading wine academic and author. Dan Murphy, Victoria's leading wine man of the day, who ranked with Komon and Lake as equals in wine knowledge, had yet to venture into journalism in Melbourne. By the time he left the Chevron, Evans was already rivalling each of them.

The table paid equal attention to wine and food. The Friday Table provided a perfect environment for the likes of Komon, Lake and Evans to perform in their element. To Tony Bohdan it was a personal challenge to create and re-create dishes from all over the world with locally sourced materials, before then laying down the gauntlet to the members to identify the food, the sauce and other various accompaniments. The cuisine brought to the table was enough to stretch the imagination. Joan Christie used to wait keenly on Friday afternoons to hear from Frank of Bohdan's latest culinary breakthrough. Her interest was justified. Of course, the members were also expected to comment on the wines, which were always served masked.

On one occasion, a huge steaming bowl arrived at the table, accompanied by thin slices of pink meat. Each member was presented with a set of wooden skewers and listened while Tony Bohdan told them to treat the dish as a fondue. The meat was a tremendous hit and enjoyed by everyone, while Bohdan sat back, basking in the flattering remarks. What was it then – aged beef, prime fillet, young vealer? Silence fell momentarily when it was revealed to be horse. Bohdan had christened the dish "Mongolian Hotpot"!

Perhaps the most memorable dish ever served at the Friday Table was a fat pie which Tony Bohdan produced with a featherweight crust so tanned it was almost red. Each person was served a portion which included a large white sausage of chopped chicken, white almonds, ravioli and dates amid a plethora of forcemeats and delectables. The table was again silenced, albeit briefly.

It turned out that Bohdan had been studying Irving Stone's book about Michelangelo, which included a description of a Venetian pre-renaissance dish which was, as Evans recounts, the master's main sustenance while in the throes of creation. Max Lake says the table felt privileged to be transported back six centuries. They ate well, considering each serve measured twelve inches by eight. Evans says that, "In this case it was the Ecstasy first and the Agony after."

It's easy to give compliments, especially when the food is free, so Bohdan took measures to guard against complacency amid the sensitive palates of his guests. One day he presented them with a marine dish, a fillet of fish served with a sauce whose colour Max Lake remembers as "lavender moving into regal purple". Knowing something about these things, Lake was also aware that in the animal kingdom purple is the colour for danger.

Neither sauce nor fish had any taste to speak of, yet everyone was expected to comment. They all, fortunately, since they weren't aware they were on trial, agreed the sauce was tasteless, the fish also, although none had the faintest idea what it was. Bohdan admitted that the fish was indeed ordinary and that the sauce was flour and water coloured purple with grape juice. "They put out this garbage to see if they could trust us," cries an anguished Max Lake. But once the trial was passed, out came a dish that really stunned them.

On another occasion, an incredible broth appeared. The guesses of those at the table were speculative in the extreme, no-one even coming close to figuring out how the kitchen had achieved its result. Bohdan explained. Two days before the luncheon the Chevron had played host to a convention of Australian Ford dealers. "I think we served them four hundred roast chickens," he said. "These are the pan drippings of all four hundred, washed, put into a stock and cleared." Outfoxed, but by a master. The table came to expect that, once in a while.

Pushing foodmanship to the absolute limit, Bohdan once presented bull's testicles, sautéed in oil, then braised with olives in a rich tomato paste with stock and various herbs. He had to repeat the announcement to his startled audience, through which, to their eternal credit, they continued munching resolutely onward.

Months later, Max Lake recalls, there appeared on his plate a brown, rather glandular-looking object. Having studied it, tasted it and enjoyed it, he arrived at the conclusion that bull's balls had reappeared for an encore. He settled back in his chair, expectantly waiting for the testosterone to raise its effect, but nothing happened. To his eternal disappointment, the mystery dish turned out to be udder of cow!

Members were briefed to bring a wine worth talking about. The less likely anyone was to recognise what the wine was, the more merit was acquired by the person who brought it. Best bottles from cellars were saved for the single and devious purpose of tricking each other. What ensued was a fledgling options game.

Early on at the Friday Table, members would stop at little or nothing to gain an advantage in the identification of the wines presented. Although concealed with paper, bottles were dextrously handled to detect physical clues. Fingers would be run up necks to feel for wax, as used for the old Great Western bottles. Searching hands would also explore underneath, for French bottles come with a punt in their posteriors. Sometimes a punt would be covered with cardboard to conceal the bottle's gallic origins. At other times, a piece of cardboard might be put over the flat bottom of an Australian bottle to suggest it too had a punt and was really French. One day, a punt covered with tin was duly fingered by Frank Christie. He picked up the bottle, caught the edge of the tin and cut his hand quite badly. The Friday Table then moved into decanters.

Discussion around the Friday Table was animated on most, if not all occasions, so it generated sufficient decibels to warrant its removal from the Grill Room to a private space in a corner of the Silver Spade. Evans took all in his stride, learning furiously about wine from the finest assembly of tutors in the country. "He was much the same character then as today," says Frank Christie. "If you disagreed with him you got the shaft!" Evans claims the Friday Table "was undoubtedly the rudest bunch of egoists extraordinary to be found, who continually attempted to score off the others and delighted in the ensuing verbal ping-pong."

Frank Christie, who was present throughout the life of the Friday Table, says that, although the luncheon meetings were generally quite friendly, there was the odd occasion when Rudy Komon would react to the commentary, erupt and cry: "You barbarians, you don't know what is going on!" He was especially direct to his emerging protégé. "You talk like that, Evans, but you are a simple barbarian!"

An extremely volatile man, Rudy Komon would get his point across through sheer strength of personality. There's a good deal of that in Evans as well. When you put the two together, comments Frank Christie, sparks would sometimes fly.

"Often at a lunch Rudy would disagree with Len, but Len would prove to be right. On other occasions it might be Len who was wrong. But underneath there was a genuine appreciation of each other, and after a time Rudy recognised that Len had the palate and the knowledge. It was mostly a friendly clash of two people with very similar personalities and egos."

Doug Crittenden knew both well and agrees that they have much the same type of personality. "Both wanted to run everything, but they never underestimated each other."

In later years, once Evans had established himself as Australia's wine authority without peer, their mutual territories were more firmly pegged out, allowing their friendship, always based on mutual respect and affection, to further blossom. Brian Croser, winemaker and wine industry politician, frequently saw both of them towards the end of Rudy Komon's life. He never once witnessed any friction between the pair, even when judging alongside them at the Sydney Wine Show from 1975 to Komon's last year in 1979.

There's no doubt that, together, Evans and Komon formed a formidable intellectual partnership based on similar interests, attitudes and abilities, each finding a kindred soul in the other. "Both individuals were migrants to Australia, both extremely capable and intelligent, and each capable of making an impression on we bovine Australians," observes Max Lake.

Komon used to encourage, cajole, support and even ridicule Evans when he thought it necessary. "He always egged me on and made me try harder," Evans recalls. "He could be a terrible bastard and at times a real old sod." Evans was once moved to record that Rudy Komon could be both "rude and common".

Komon was always prepared to give freely of his time to talk to his pupil, but hardly ever to anyone else. "But you see, Len," he might say, "this wine is much better than that, because this one has true Hunter character. It will last, it will last just like Bin 1590." Evans would stand next to him, carefully and quietly taking in everything he said.

Dan Murphy doesn't think he ever saw Evans pay as much respect to anyone as he did to Komon. "To Len, whatever Rudy said was absolutely right, especially when it came to wine," he says. Some people who knew them both thought Evans paid Komon's knowledge of wine more deference than was due, but there is no doubt that from the 1950s to the 1970s, Rudy Komon was at the forefront of wine appreciation and understanding in Australia.

"Komon had an incredible knowledge of every great Lindemans wine of that era," says Murphy, "and could easily nominate any one of them to the four-figure number they carried. He would be absolutely correct every time, over a very large range. He used to revere those great Hunter reds and spoke about them with enormous respect."

Not far below Komon's gruff exterior was a genuine, if extremely wicked, sense of humour. He was once commissioned by Evans to act as Cellarmaster for a special wine dinner at the Chevron, for which Evans was taking extreme care to ensure a smooth passage. During the dinner, Komon was approached by a young waiter reverently cradling a bottle of 1947 Maurice O'Shea Hunter Valley red. "Have you shaken the bottle?" boomed Komon at him, in his best and most threatening Czechoslovakian accent.

The terrified waiter quickly answered, "No, sir, but I will!" going on, as Evans describes, performing like a cocktail barman.

Frank Thorpe, then the President of the New Zealand Wine and Food Society, was once a guest at the Friday Table. Being a sporting winemaster, Evans refrained from asking him to comment on the Australian wines, but felt free to set him loose on a German white. Thorpe decided to capture his impressive audience by starting big. "This wine reminds me of one I tasted last year with Prince Metternich," he began, before waxing lyrical how, while standing together on the slopes of the Rhine, they had both realised that they had fought on different sides during the war. Not only that, but the Prince had served with the Panzer Corps and Thorpe in the New Zealand Antitank Brigade. Sipping that wine, they delved further to find that, not only had they fought in the same theatre of war – North Africa – but in the same battle. "Comparing notes," Thorpe concluded, "here we were, in the brotherhood of wine, and we found that we had fired and fought against each other twenty years before."

Evans records that Ron Tarrant could contain himself no longer. "It's a good thing you were both bloody incompetent!"

Sir James Hardy, then simply "Gentleman Jim", was another guest. As was customary, everyone took a turn to initiate discussion on a wine. It being his turn, Hardy tasted one, swirled it around his mouth for a while, and sat there, while his audience sat captive, expectantly awaiting the inevitable pearl of knowledge. He didn't begin well: "I can't say where it comes from, I can't tell you the grape and I'm not sure of the year," he said. "But I can tell you one thing – it's very easy on the gums!"

The Friday Table's ideas began to filter through to Sydney's fast-growing population of wine and food devotees. In its time, the Friday Table was unquestionably the highest level meeting place of its kind in Australia. Its most important product, of course, was Len Evans.

"I was schooled by people like Rudy Komon to realise how good Australian wine was and to realise its enormous potential," he says. It was also Komon who introduced Evans to another of his great friends, Peter Doyle.

Doyle remembers Rudy Komon as a great character and great person, who would accompany his guest to Doyle's restaurant and then take a quick peek into the kitchen. If he had successfully sold a painting, Komon would buy the best food on offer for his guest, says Doyle. If, however, the deal had not gone as planned, he would still ask "What is the best?" Perhaps it might be whiting, john dory or lobster. He would then declare: "I will have the lobster, my guest will have fish and chips. You will tell him there is only one lobster left." If the deal had gone through, says Doyle, he would order two or three lobsters!

One particular day, Evans was Komon's guest and Komon had told him, "I will take you into the kitchen to see my great friend Peter Doyle. I don't think he has any lobsters. But we will look anyway."

"He was about to pull his old trick and say there was only one lobster and that he would have it," laughs Doyle. Only moments earlier, at 1 p.m., when the restaurant's kitchen was working at breakneck speed for the lunch-time rush, a delivery of lobsters had arrived. The crate had split wide open and between eighty to one hundred lobsters had begun to explore the entire kitchen floor. "So Rudy couldn't get out of it," says Doyle.

"This is my very good friend Len Evans," Komon introduced, before conceding, "I suppose I will have to buy him a lobster." Then, without batting an eyelid, Komon strode around the room, finally singling out a plump specimen. "That one will do," he pronounced, as if lobster underfoot was an everyday occurrence at Doyle's kitchen.

One Evans-inspired idea was to invite to the Chevron in 1962 the First Thursday Club, an industry-based meeting of top wine professionals he joined in 1960, usually attended by rivals from the various large wine companies. They would meet monthly with prominent amateurs, wine merchants and retailers to taste wine, discuss public trends, exchange knowledge, technical advances and different viewpoints.

Evans vividly remembers that Rudy Komon almost ruined the inaugural First Thursday Club dinner at the Chevron. The trouble began when Komon was not served the correct portion of duck he wanted. "After all," concedes Evans, "why should the waiter not give him the breast or the leg or whatever it was he wanted?"

Komon became upset and as soon as the dinner was half over, an obviously distraught Evans left for his terrace in Paddington. Shortly after his arrival home there

At lunch in Ye Olde Crusty Cellar with a gathering of wine industry people.
Opposite Evans is the late Ted Maloney, an early food author and advertising executive,
while two from Evans' left is the late Ted Mead of Leo Buring's.

was a knock on the door. Graham Gregory had left the dinner, saying Evans shouldn't worry about Rudy Komon, who, everyone agreed, could be a pig at times, so they dragged out a consolatory bottle of wine.

Next moment, there was another knock on the door. This time it was Max Lake, who had also left the dinner bemoaning Komon's impossible behaviour. Another bottle was opened. "We were just getting stuck into that," says Evans, "and there was another knock on the door. It was Rudy, saying "Why get upset with me? It isn't necessary."

He came in, so they shared yet another bottle, but by 2 a.m. the argument had started all over again. The commotion became too much for Trish Evans who, having bravely attempted to sleep, appeared at the top of the stairs Boadicea-fashion, threatening to kick the lot of them out of the house.

Evans didn't seem to need sleep. He lived instead on his astonishing reserves of energy, drive and love of his job. The time to leave the Chevron drew near when he found he was growing tired of the routine it demanded.

He had been working five days a week to anywhere between 8 p.m. and any time at night, usually past midnight. He also had a Saturday shift, a morning or evening, and then worked every other Sunday, which added up to a relentless eighty-two-hour week.

Evans says that two poignant memories depict his Chevron life. One Monday he received a mayday call. Thugs in a public bar had activated the fire sprinkler heads by holding burning paper under them. Water was everywhere and by the time he had rushed down, it had risen to a foot deep. Not only that, but an elderly man had informed security that someone was in danger of drowning in the lavatories.

A huge male, obviously very drunk, had toppled forward in the lavatory, jamming his head under the door in about six inches of water. Leaping into action, Evans tried moving his head away, but without luck. Jumping over the lavatory door, he managed to pull the giant out, stand him upright and clean him a little, but to no avail, for the man immediately vomited. At least, Evans deduced, he was still alive.

Until this occurred, Evans had been patiently awaiting the arrival of a bridal party. Now he found himself in the pitch dark, the power having been switched off, with a sixteen-stone mastodon over his shoulder who at anytime was likely to vomit again.

Having struggled outside, Evans was again vomited on, just as word arrived that the bridal party had arrived. Bolting to the front of the hotel, Evans strode down the steps to greet the limousine. He bowed and showed the party into the waiting lift. Only then did he realise that, not only was he saturated to the skin, but his shirt and jacket had been fouled as well. He still wonders what the guests must have thought.

In 1964, the Chevron conducted a massive Bake-off competition with forty contestants. Each had specified the particular electric or gas stove of their preference, so the ballroom was fitted with enormous gas and electricity installations.

"The starting time was 8.30 a.m.," Evans explains. "I walked into the preparation areas with Frank Christie and saw the contestants, all the ranges and stoves. On each preparation area were precisely the ingredients the contestants required. The entire room was in readiness. The General Manager said, "Very well done, Len, etc., etc.""

"What he didn't know, which I did, was that there had been a ball in that room until 1 a.m. that morning, at which time we managed to shoo the last person away.

From that moment an army of people descended, cleaning up the place totally in about twenty minutes, before about seventy people – carpenters, electricians and display people – moved in forty stoves and set up that room in seven-and-a-half hours for the 8.30 a.m. start.

"I left around 5.30 a.m. when I could see all was going well, went home, had a shower, put on another suit, had some eggs and bacon, and came back straight away. For me that encapsulated hotel life. Unbelievably exciting. I just loved it."

Eventually becoming restless at the Chevron, Evans was keen to find a position as General Manager at a major hotel, having enjoyed the taste of higher authority while Frank Christie took three months leave. Harry Sebel offered him a job at the Sebel Town House, but Frank Christie persuaded him not to take it. "I don't think I was then quite ready to be a General Manager," says Evans, "but that wasn't the point. In fact I was certainly not ready, but I thought I was."

Evans wonders if he could ever have delegated responsibility the way Frank Christie did. "While maintaining complete control over them, Frank gave his staff full licence to try new things and create new themes and concepts." It's hardly surprising that Len Evans admires Frank Christie so. He is a doyen of the Australian hotel industry and Evans recognises the doors he opened for him.

Christie left the Chevron in 1966 to go to the Hotel Australia, in Sydney. He is also remembered for managing the Melbourne Hilton from its construction in 1973 until his retirement in 1987.

In 1989, Evans bumped into Harry Sebel. "I've watched your career and I've always regretted you not taking the job," said Sebel. "Either you'd have lasted three months with me, or you and I would now own the greatest chain of hotels in Australia."

Spreading the Word

*My house is mortgaged, my car bloody and battered from the
scuffles in traffic, my children walk barefoot, and my wife has
needed a new hairdo for the past six weeks. But I am sitting
on 2 000 bottles of good red wine.*
L.P.E.

*E*vans left the Chevron Hilton to work for the Australian Wine Board, which he
persuaded to establish an entity known as the Wine Information Bureau. The
Bureau's brief was to promote Australian wine by encouraging writers to publicise
it in all available forms of media, and also arranging and conducting wine classes and
tastings Australia-wide. The Wine Information Bureau gave Evans the opportunity
to stamp himself as a national wine personality and authority.

Before Len Evans joined the Australian Wine Board on 1 January 1965 as its first
National Promotions Executive, the promotion of Australian wine was primitive at
best, as indeed was its consumption. Six bottles of fortified wine were sold each year
for one bottle of table wine, with an average national wine consumption of around
5.5 litres per head per year. Wine public relations activity was largely a reactive affair
and any promotional monies then available were squandered on institutional advertising.

The Australian wine industry was finding the going tough in the 1960s. Most
wineries were making no money and were only just able to survive. Hardly helped
by influences divine, they were greatly set back by a run of extremely difficult seasons
of unfavourable weather.

Doug Crittenden remembers that in the early 1960s it was almost impossible to
sell white wine. Recognising this, Murray Tyrrell would sell his red only on the
condition that buyers also bought white. Red was itself in short supply.

Acclaimed Melbourne journalist and long-time friend of Len Evans, Keith
Dunstan says that Evans arrived at a time when the wine industry was totally dead.
People like John Brown (Brown Brothers) and Eric Purbrick (Château Tahbilk) were
not even bottling their own wine, selling it instead to merchants like Rhine Castle.
The public would then bottle their own wine for around 10c a bottle.

Evans recalls that to make an entire vat or 500 dozen of a single red wine was then
a pretty big effort. "If ten vats were made, say 5 000 dozen, which was in those days
an immense quantity, people like me or Ray Kidd from Lindemans would pick out

the two to four best casks for bottling, while the rest would be sold in bulk to whoever would buy it."

John Addison and Ken Reid (both now deceased), the New South Wales heads of Hamiltons and McWilliams, were good friends of Evans and served on the Australian Wine Board's Promotions Committee, whose responsibility it was to spend the wine industry's advertising and promotional budget. Most of the money was allocated to the cities of Sydney and Melbourne, the largest domestic markets, which leaned towards fortified wine and table wine respectively. Each year the Board spent around £85 000 on television advertising to let Australians know "they could have more fun with wine".

"When they hired me to become the National Promotions Executive they had no idea what to do with me," says Evans. "They simply said 'Here is your pay. Your job is to change the promotion of Australian wine in Australia'."

Whatever they may have been doing wrong at the time, at least the Australian Wine Board found the right person to change their direction. In 1962, Evans had begun to write as "Cellarmaster" in the *Bulletin*, and he was the logical choice. His former employer, Frank Christie, was also very encouraging and supportive.

Undoubtedly, Evans went into the job with two very solid things going for him. He had been an outstanding retailer of wine at the Chevron and since he was Australia's first regular wine writer, he "knew the media". He had dealt himself a decent hand and knew how to play it strongly. And since the views of his masters were frequently contrary, if not diametrically opposed to his own, that was just as well.

Evans did have a predecessor at the Wine Board, although his role has been entirely different, to keep any unsavoury reference to wine out of the newspapers. A former fighter pilot, Blue Greatorix was the wine industry's PR man. He had fostered close ties with the editors and persuaded them to delete any reference to wine if, for example, someone had been hit over the head with a wine bottle. Greatorix would see that an entirely anonymous "bottle" would go to print.

"He would take them to golf at Royal Sydney, to the racing and be charming to everybody and did a wonderful job," says Evans, who took the job on the understanding that his promotions would be of the positive, rather than the negative variety.

As Evans recalls, a lady by the name of Sarah Parkinson was also "paid a disgracefully small wage" to operate a recipe service, whereby she matched recipes from all over the world with Australian wines, which then she distributed for publication to glossy magazines like *House and Garden*, *Vogue*, and the *Women's Weekly*.

So Evans moved in. Scanning through the Board's totally inadequate public relations files, he found that of the seventeen or so wine articles published in the previous year, 1964, he was responsible for fourteen of them. Yet he had never received any encouragement from the Board. But things were about to change.

He remembers an early Wine Board meeting at which he was briefed that his main job was to promote sherry and port, then almost the staples of Australian wine. They told him that "Market research shows that that's what people want".

"You don't understand," Evans retorted. "Market research doesn't show what people want, it only reflects their consumption; what they're having at the time."

"Surely Australians will continue to drink more sherry than they will table wine," argued the Board.

"But I understood that I was hired as a table wine promoter," reminded Evans, "although of course I'll look after sherry. The point is that most people have little or no experience with table wine. It's quite obvious to me what they're going to drink in future."

But where to begin? "I know what they thought I was, but I don't think anyone really knew what I was. I don't think I knew what I was! So I wrote a report."

After about two months of fairly haphazard operation, Evans went to meet the Sydney heads of the Wine Board. Recognising that the £85 000 advertising budget was far too small to achieve any good, his proposal was to develop further the wine tasting programme already initiated in New South Wales and Victoria, involving wine appreciation tastings at clubs, and then to expand it into the other States.

Evans was, by now, writing as a journalist under his fifth pseudonym and had begun to wonder how far he could take it without becoming a very public case of schizophrenia. Reinforcements were required, so he suggested the formation of the Australian Wine Bureau, of which he was to become the first Director.

The Bureau would incorporate and expand Evans' promotional role by employing managers in each State to implement new promotions and would encourage top journalists with a feeling for wine to to write about it. Funding was to be taken from the National Advertising Committee's £85 000.

In late 1965, Evans went off in quest of disciples. By the end of the year, he had started to build his team of writers and educators, hiring Frank Margan in New South Wales, Jack Ludbrook in South Australia and Frank Doherty in Victoria, to write about wine and to syndicate their columns across the papers. "In those days newspapers, magazines, radio and television were screaming for material on wine," recalls Doherty, recently lamented by the wine industry, "and our Wine Bureau tastings for clubs and charities had a two-year waiting list."

Evans initiated a dedicated wine promotional team around Fred McKeever, Arthur Moore and John Stanford. Then, as he says, "We got off our arses and started promoting." It was an incredibly busy and fruitful time, coinciding as it did exactly with the Australian public's wish to learn more about wine and also to drink more of it.

Frank Doherty enjoyed his work with Evans, who would visit Melbourne every couple of months or so. "He left me alone, but taught me a lot, especially about the basics of writing about wine."

In late 1965, Evans arrived in Melbourne to manage "Wine Week", a major public wine promotion conducted yearly by the wine industry in Melbourne, Sydney and Adelaide on a rotating basis. "More often than not," says Doherty, "it had become an occasion for the wine industry to entertain itself on a grandiose scale."

Coming across Evans for the first time, Keith Dunstan decided he was more worth writing about than Wine Week itself. "Len came down to Melbourne and was his usual quiet, retiring self," he laughs. "I thought what a wonderful character he was, full of jokes, and did a number of stories about him in my column," the highly popular "A Place In The Sun", for the *Sun News-Pictorial*. "He was the most wonderful breath of life, which the wine industry desperately needed."

By this time Evans had made some very good friends in Victoria. Among them were Frank Doherty, Eric Purbrick, John Brown and Doug Crittenden, but according to Keith Dunstan, he had an extraordinary capacity to rub others up the wrong way. "He was looked upon by some as a rather cheap little nasty from the Hunter River who was good at getting publicity for himself, but not at doing the job for the industry. I probably didn't do much to alter that impression," he admits.

Frank Doherty concurs, observing that the established older core of Victorian wine people thought that Evans only went to Melbourne to promote himself. "From then on," he says, "as far as I could tell, Len still feels uncomfortable in Melbourne, which is a great pity." Since that time, despite efforts by Evans and his Melburnian friends, Len Evans and Melbourne remain to an extent like imiscible fluids.

However, to the key Melbourne retailers, who at the time amounted to only a handful – Rhine Castle, Doug Seabrook, Doug Crittenden and Dan Murphy – Evans was a livewire. "We loved him," says Murphy, "because even though he was not really that well known in Melbourne in those days, he really promoted wine."

In Melbourne, Evans had much to do with Dan Murphy, of Dan Murphy's Cellar and The Vintage Club, against whom the Melbourne wine fraternity were fond of pitting him in tasting duels. He recalls one occasion when tasting McLaren Vale reds with Murphy. Murphy claimed he detected a gooseberry taste in a 1965 Cud Kay wine from Amery. Evans described the second wine, a 1965 d'Arenberg, as big, fruity, soft and round, having good balance and being without coarseness; a wine ready to drink now or to repay those who kept it for ten years. Asking Murphy for his opinion, he was informed: "Well, it has a highly spiced or smoky nose, which is almost candyish at times, perhaps more like the smell of oleander or that of those spicy perfumed bushes you get in Spain." What's more, Murphy was able to deliver all of that keeping a perfectly straight face!

The Australian Billy Graham. Representing a Wine and Wool Board
promotion to a visiting Russian delegation, 1965.

From time to time Evans was himself guilty of verbal largesse. Years later, he and Tony Albert, one of the founders of Brokenwood, were drinking '45 Mouton together. Evans was in rhapsodising mood: "Isn't it a superb exquisite wine? Everything you expect Mouton to be – tremendous elegance and that wonderful opulent cabernet flavour, the complexity of the nose, violets and cigar boxes, one's perfect idea of a classic Bordeaux from a great year that's absolutely at its peak! And that extraordinary depth of flavour! Even so, you can just see in it that classic hardness at the back of the middle palate that's the mark of the '45s."

Tony Albert turned to him and said simply: "Stuff the hardness!"

Evans greatly admired the style and character of Eric Purbrick, himself a great autocrat, whose family had bought Château Tahbilk in Victoria and still operate it today, two generations later. Purbrick's recent death, in 1991 and at a mature age, has left a vacuum in the tradition of Victorian wine that will be impossible to fill.

Requiring copy for one of his wine columns in the early 1960s, Evans dropped into Château Tahbilk at the very height of vintage. A carload of visitors had arrived simultaneously, but since all the winemaking team were slavishly working in the cellar, there was no-one available to show the other visitors around. Evans clearly remembers one of them, a red-nosed hotelier, gruffly complaining "I buy their bloody wine all the time, and now no bastard will look after us."

There was only one thing to do. Evans decided to fill the breach himself. "I knew about Tahbilk's old cellar and the New Cellar which dated back to 1875," he says. "So I spoke about the old oak casks, the new wines, and then we arrived at the de-stalking machine, at which Eric Purbrick was standing, looking swarthy and leathery, shovelling out stalks into a trailer."

Looking directly at Purbrick, Evans eloquently described that the winery was staffed by migrant people of Italian descent who had originally arrived to look after the mulberry trees. "You don't pay them," he claimed. "You just fill them up with spaghetti and off they go like threshing machines."

"Careful, they might hear you," said the publican, showing signs of concern.

"Don't worry," said Evans, "they don't speak a word of English. We'd never let that happen. Then they'd want Saturdays off as well as Sundays." The group walked by, as a huge forkload of stalks whistled directly past Evans' ear. "Are you certain he doesn't speak English?" queried the publican.

Tradition was always a strong point at Château Tahbilk. The first time Evans was invited there for dinner, a butler served it. Eric Purbrick consistently maintained that black tie was mandatory for special dinners, even if just for family occasions.

Years later, Evans arranged to take James Halliday there, since he had never visited Tahbilk. He rang in, and Alister Purbrick, Eric's grandson, collected the pair in the family's old Rolls-Royce.

Evans queried: "Black tie as usual for dinner?"

"Of course."

"James laughed," says Evans, thinking we'd really put on the con. We were sharing a twin bedroom and after mandatory gins and tonics at 6 p.m., we went for a bath and to dress for dinner. James changed into a sportscoat, crew-neck pullover and corduroys, while I got out the dinner suit.

"I explained to James that I was going to dress formally for dinner, just to send up the old boy. He said, 'You wouldn't!', And I said 'Just for fun'. James said, 'On your head, then.' So I put on my black tie and with James shaking his head at my impudence, we both went down the stairs. There, waiting for us, were Eric, Mary and the whole family, all dressed formally for dinner. Halliday looked round at me and said 'You complete bastard.' It was one of the great cons."

Evans was the first to take wine to Australian country people and make them taste it. His "bivouacs" of tastings and lectures into country areas would take weeks on end, supported by new and Evans-trained additions to his staff like Peter Drayton.

On one occasion, Evans was touring around wineries in an old Holden with Frank Margan and a photographer, Val Sowada, to collect information and data, aimed at building up a photographic library of the wine industry. Their trip took them all over the countryside, covering nearly 6 500 kilometres.

Word was out that the cellar of the Renmark Hotel, at the South Australian riverside town on the Murray, was something special, so Evans and his crew called in to investigate. They were astounded to unearth a treasure-filled vault of old vintages of Australia's greatest wines, made by Maurice O'Shea, Colin Preece and Roger Warren and dating back to the late 1940s. Asking if any were available for sale, they were informed that since the labels were old and dirty, the diners upstairs didn't like buying them. They would, in fact, be "doing the locals a favour" by shifting the stock.

"We bought the entire lot at cost," says Evans. "Decimal currency had just been implemented, and I will never forget the thrill of learning that the 1952 Mildara was 31¢ a bottle, whereas the '53 was a little bit more. We would have to pay 34¢." Into the Holden they went.

The local Wine and Food Society members were naturally distraught at what became known in lore as the "Rape of Renmark".

Len Evans' wine courses in Sydney attracted a great number of potential wine enthusiasts and wine professionals, one of whom was James Halliday. "I would have been just another face in the crowd," says Halliday, "but Evans was the same incredibly fluent speaker that he is now, with just as much enthusiasm. His attitude was very infectious and fired up most of the people who attended his courses. Even then Evans was a great communicator, both of ideas and feelings. We were all singularly impressed with what we heard."

The evangelistic Evans would take wine anywhere. He was a keen fisherman and would raid his cellar to take wine with him onto the fishing boat, although his enthusiasm waned noticeably when he realised the advanced state of thirst shown by his companions hardly did service to the quality of his contributions. Being aware that the skipper on a particular trip was a lifetime beer drinker, and also in genuine fear of keel-hauling, Evans infiltrated on board a few cans of beer in support of his major staple of Penfolds Dry Red, taken from the flagon.

Once they had beached for lunch, the awful truth dawned that the beer had been left on the boat, which was some way off shore. The skipper's disgust was immediate, but since he lacked the energy to row out to get it, he consented to sample the demon plonk. His satisfaction was as immediate as it was unexpected. Declaring instantly that it was the best stuff he'd had for years, the skipper wondered aloud what he had been missing all this while" … and didn't it make the steak taste!"

Evans recalls that he "lay back contentedly in the sand, lulled by the music of the waves, the snoring of his companions and the recurrent shouts of the skipper for more red biddy!"

The Wine Bureau was the catalyst that paved the way for the abundance of wine writing in Australia today, there now being more written about wine per capita in Australia than in any other country. Through the Bureau, Evans was responsible for picking up a number of wine writers and putting them into the papers, as journalists were eager to clutch onto the wine-stained nib, taking to it like ducks to water.

Evans made sure their enthusiasm was brimful with tasting adventures, exercises, parties and tours to wineries. Individuals like the ABC's David Patterson and Peter Young began to discuss wine on the radio, which was quickly recognised by Evans as being equally important as the print media. More writers grasped any excuse to cover wine, although Keith Dunstan says he was sometimes criticised by his editor for excessively turning his back on the rest of human endeavour.

On one educational wine tour, Dunstan was escorted by Evans around the Hunter Vineyards. The first stop was Tulloch's, where Hector Tulloch paraded some ancient wines, dating right back to the early 1950s. "He got some bottles down for us, right down from underneath the winery's hot, uninsulated galvanised iron roof," Dunstan remembers. Evans asked: "Doesn't that do any harm to the wine, to have it up there?" Tulloch replied: "Look, Len, if it doesn't boil, it's all right."

Next stop was Tyrrell's, where Dunstan learned about fermentation. He asked Murray how he knew the fermentation was finished, and Murray replied, "Well, Keith, you just put your arm in up to here [indicating his armpit] and if your arm is not prickling, it's OK."

By 1966, Neville Baker was, according to Evans, already a very good food man who knew wine. Evans approached him saying he had just persuaded Walter Kramer, the *Australian's* first editor, to start a wine and food column, and that he had nominated Baker as its writer. "Then I had to train Neville how to write," says Evans. "But that's the way we got wine going."

James Halliday remembers buying the *Sunday Telegraph* in the mid 1960s for no other reason than to read "Frank Margan's Choice", a tiny little box of forty to fifty words. "I had no idea at the time that Evans was the man behind Margan getting that slot," he says. In this sort of fashion, the activities of the Wine Bureau impacted indirectly on Halliday and on everyone else interested in wine.

But the path the Wine Board Committee would have Evans tread was littered with mines. To begin with, it was the Committee's original intention that no particular brand of wine be mentioned in its publicity – that while it was all right to promote wine as Hunter Valley white or Barossa Valley red, to mention any wine or winery by name was simply not on!

"What would happen if the Hunter got more publicity than Coonawarra?" they asked Evans. In the *Len Evans Cookbook*, he writes that "sheer persistence finally won that day, and we were able to give editors the copy they wanted, instead of the copy the industry thought would be the most suitable".

One Evans plan for a nationwide rosé promotion was knocked back on the irrational basis that not every wine company in Australia made one.

Despite the antediluvian approach of his masters, Evans' approach was succeeding. Red wine stocks around the country quickly became depleted. Instead of seizing the hour and the initiative, the Wine Board then refused to support more promotions for red wine, wrongly convinced that since Australia was selling all it could make, any further effort would only aid the cause of imported wine.

Evans' problems were not confined to the Wine Board Committee's particular brand of marketing vision, or lack of such. He also had to counter the parochial interests of the individual States, especially South Australia, and the industry's bureaucrats who serviced wine exports, then at a meagre level of less than two million litres.

"Some people obviously didn't favour my appointment unless they could control it," Evans believes. Early on, export chief Harry Palmer kept Evans waiting for well over an hour for an appointment. Evans left before Palmer consented to see him, but they happened to cross paths shortly afterwards at a wine tasting and dinner.

When Palmer offered his apology, Evans bluntly rejected it. "You weren't busy today," he said. "To keep somebody waiting to put them in their place is the oldest ploy in the world." What then followed reveals much about Evans' directness towards all people, regardless of who they may be.

"I'm in this business to promote wine internally in Australia and you're into promotion outside Australia," he said. "There's no reason why we should get in each other's hair and I have no intention of getting into yours. But tell me now, sincerely, whether you want to be a foe or a friend."

"What do you mean by that?"

"Tell me whether you want to be a foe or a friend. I really am not interested in worrying about you. If you really want to stuff me up, tell me now so we understand each other. That would be fine. Otherwise I shall treat you as a friend and I expect to be treated as a friend in turn."

For the next two and a half years while Evans was with the Wine Board, Palmer and he worked well together and Palmer was instrumental in Evans' promotional trip on behalf of the Board in 1967.

"Sometimes I think the wine industry has got there in spite of itself. A journalist from the *Financial Review* came to me once, wanting to write a series of profiles on the wine industry and its financial aspects. I arranged a complete itinerary for him, including all the people he should meet – the cream of the industry.

"He came back saying he couldn't believe it. He said he had just been among some of the greatest dills, people who just don't understand, but who also happened to be some of the nicest people he had ever met in his life."

Sometimes Evans would turn a doubter around. Mildara's chief winemaker, Ron Haselgrove used to question many of his ideas, forthrightly saying some were a ridiculous waste of money. "I finally won him over," Evans says, "and he became a strong supporter of mine, my strongest bloody advocate." Haselgrove was a prickly character, says Evans, who did a tremendous amount for the industry, for which he was awarded an OBE. But I liked him.

"Haselgrove was a fanatic for trying to evolve a style of red wine which was like a Bordeaux. He tried it by blending all the regions together, blends between Reynella, Coonawarra and the Hunter. That fabulous '58 Mildara Yellow Label was a fifty-fifty Hunter Coonawarra blend."

Evans describes how Haselgrove once argued with Bill Redman, the grand old man of Coonawarra's famous Redman family, over the price of Redman's wine. In the late 1950s, Redman was charging 3s 6d a gallon for his red and he asked Haselgrove if the price was too high, saying he would knock it down to 3s if he had to.

"No," countered Haselgrove. "I want to make it 10s, because I believe you should have the support you deserve for making the great wines that you are. I want to be part of those red wines for some time and will encourage you to continue."

One could almost excuse the bewilderment displayed by the members of the Wine Board's Promotions Committee, since some of Evans' concepts were light years ahead of their time. In 1965, he suggested they focus their energies towards the under-eighteen age group, convinced the more they read about how older people came to enjoy the good things of life, the more they would aspire to be part of it.

Evans' intentions to teach younger people about the moderate joys of wine with food and how to handle alcohol properly are today finally being addressed, a quarter of a century later. But then he was told it was far-fetched to talk to under-age people about wine.

"It was all part of the arguments of those days. I was just a boy, just an enthusiast," he says. "It was a fascinating time."

Fascinating maybe, but hardly lucrative. After a six-month campaign for improved salaries for his staff, Evans made a stand at a Wine Board Promotions Committee meeting in Hobart. In 1966, John Stanford, then a State Manager, was paid just £42 per week. Evans only received £60 per week.

"They got their £50 after a day of argument, but not a soul spoke of giving me a raise," Evans recalls. "Ian Seppelt, then the Chairman of the Australian Wine Board, stood up and said 'Well, I hope you're satisfied, Len. You've got all you want. I hope we won't hear from you for another year or two.' It was as if they had done me some kind of favour," Evans says, still exasperated today, "which I found extraordinary."

On the flight to Sydney, Evans sat next to Ken Reid, the NSW manager of McWilliams Wines and, coincidentally, the same person who had first suggested that he work for the Wine Board. "Those bastards won't give me a rise and don't understand what I'm doing," muttered Evans. Reid replied that they did understand what Evans was doing and were very grateful for it, but the problem was that the more that he wanted, the more they then had to pay other managers of equivalent status. "I don't blame you in the least for being upset," he said.

So Evans resigned, giving the Board six months notice. "I only left for that reason. They literally said they were going to be mean to me. I couldn't stand the thought of not being appreciated. I had no intention of leaving the Wine Board and had the wine industry paid me properly, I would probably still be there today."

Wine had started its roll in Australia and Len Evans had much to do with it. Without taking any credit from him, some have said his timing was fortunate. Dan Murphy says that, to a degree, it was inevitable that wine would hit the crest in Australia because it was simultaneously happening in England, Europe and America. Individuals like Rudy Komon migrated here, bringing with them their knowledge and love of wine, as indeed did Australians returning from business or holidays in countries where wine was an accepted part of daily culture.

Evans recognises all of these influences. "I don't claim for a second that I made the table wine industry, as some indeed claim I did. No one realised what was in front of them, although people like Rudy Komon did."

Evans recalls a visit Komon made to Adelaide in 1955. When served a glass of Coonawarra red he asked: "And where is this 'Coonavarra'?" Hiring a car immediately, he drove southward to see Coonawarra for himself. "As the Winemaster of the New South Wales Wine and Food Society, this was an unbelievable thing at the time," recognises Evans. He made Coonawarra known in Sydney. No one there had ever heard of Coonawarra.

David Wynn made Coonawarra in Victoria. Tony Nelson, the Austrian-born winemaker at Château Comaum in Coonawarra (which became the Wynns' winery) and a great friend of mine, used to distil his Coonawarra wines into bloody brandy!

"It was a big boom time," Evans reflects. "From the mid 1960s to the early 1970s, sherry was the biggest seller in Australia. Then the Wine Bureau promoted table wines and they sold out. When red wine consumption overtook sherry a memo was sent out to our staff asking them to promote white wine, and then look at what happened."

The broad impact made by the Wine Bureau under Len Evans was incredible. Wine had begun to take its place as part of the Australian psyche, rather than remaining the sole domain of 'plonkos'. In Evans' final six months as the Bureau chief, they collected 307 articles about wine through their media clippings service.

It is a measure of Evans' broad contribution to Australian wine that, once he left the Bureau, his impact became even greater.

This man would do almost anything to promote wine.

Champagne
Days

Evan's self-described lack of ambition saw him open Bulletin Place, a wine centre of two restaurants and Australia's most desirable retail cellar. By the time of its closure Evans was recognised as the country's most important arbiter of wine quality and its most prolific wine critic. His credentials — twenty years of exposure to unsurpassable wine and the fun that went with it.

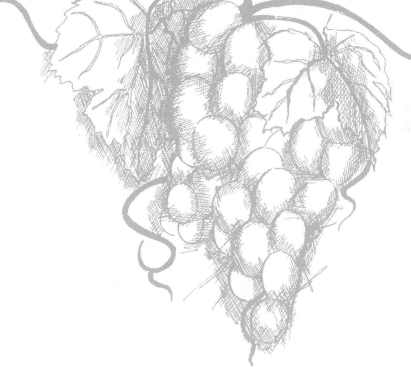

The
*F*iefdom of Bulletin Place

*Len Evans Wines, Bulletin Place, regrets to announce that it
has sold out of 1928 Pichon Longueville.*
Advertisement posted by L.P.E. in Sydney's
Daily Telegraph.

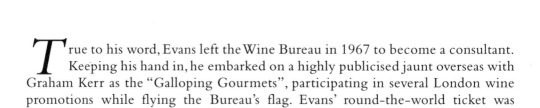

True to his word, Evans left the Wine Bureau in 1967 to become a consultant. Keeping his hand in, he embarked on a highly publicised jaunt overseas with Graham Kerr as the "Galloping Gourmets", participating in several London wine promotions while flying the Bureau's flag. Evans' round-the-world ticket was courtesy of Pan American Airlines, for which he would deliver a verdict on the wines they served in-flight.

On his return, Evans visited Harry Alce, responsible for Millers Hotels and Brewery and the future head of Tooth & Co., who hired him to train his hotel managers about wine which he recognised to be the "coming thing" in Australia. He also asked Evans to advise his company, which also operated the Stockpot chain of restaurants, on the presentation of their food.

Evans' fee was $3 000, and since his salary at the Wine Bureau was just $7 000, he considered himself nearly half way there. In no time at all, he added The Summit Restaurant, The Coachman Restaurant, Travelodge and Qantas to his growing list of consultancies, grossing $19 000 in his first year self-employed.

Throughout his career Evans has been an important source of opinion and knowledge for organisations with interests in Australian wine. He helped to engineer the Tooths Breweries' takeover of Penfolds and, in the early 1970s, was instrumental in selling the Stanley Wine Company to the American food processing company of Heinz. He was rewarded for his efforts with a Rolls-Royce Silver Cloud from Christopher Penfold Hyland, chairman of Tooth and Co., and a cheque for $10 000 respectively which was, at the time, the largest fee he had ever earned. "It should have been over $30 000, but I was too naive to know," he shrugs.

Throughout his on-again-off-again relationship with Penfolds he helped to resuscitate Bin 707 Cabernet Sauvignon in 1976, a label the company had discontinued in 1969. Today it could possibly lay a fair claim to be Australia's leading red wine; certainly its pre-eminent claret style.

Since his first arrival in Sydney, Evans had often appreciated the architecture of an old warehouse in Bulletin Place, a very beautiful building originally built in 1816 for Mary Reiby. In future years, he would enjoy informing visiting Victorians that it was open for business long before Melbourne was even established.

In the late 1950s, he had come to know Ken Berger, who had run a wine merchant's business at a certain old warehouse in the same street, bottling and selling bits and pieces and paying a pound a week as rent for the cellar. Writing in the *Len Evans Cookbook*, he says he was generally too embarrassed to venture into Berger's cellar, but he eventually looked down inside, too shy, he says, of taking up anyone's time! It must have been an off day.

It was a friend of Evans, real-estate dealer Richard de Salis, who persuaded him to move into Bulletin Place. He had heard of someone who had been about to take over a property there, who had previously been a successful operator of the Old San Francisco restaurant. However, he had gone broke while trying to expand and had absconded with the company's funds. It turned out to be the same property Evans had viewed nine years before, now a fairly derelict old warehouse.

"It was harum-scare-em," says Evans, "because now my so-called vaulted ambition comes into it. You see, I really had no ambition to become a wine merchant, but thought it seemed a good idea. Anyway, I took over the cellar with virtually no money and checked with the landlord, Bill Rubenson, if I got all the floors. He affirmed that I did and wanted to know what I was going to do with them, for half were burned out. We had to rebuild a lot and replace the floor of what was to become the Tasting Room, for instance."

Evans, who had saved $5 000 by that time, borrowed another $10 000, and a friend, Dr Ray Healy, whom Evans bought out later, came in for $5 000. He acquired his licence from Buring's Ye Olde Crusty Cellar, a wine and spirit merchant owned by Lindemans, but on settling the matter, and having already transferred the licence to him, Lindemans asked Evans how he was intending to pay the $10 000 licence fee. The company ultimately lent it to him in return for the third mortgage of his house, and the loan was fully paid off a couple of years later.

The property was in a terrible mess and Evans watched closely as over fifty tonnes of rubbish were carted away from its lower floors. One of the few pleasant surprises was the discovery that under about twenty layers of paint stood a wall of ancient Scottish sandstone bricks, which, despite sincere warnings from the builder who wanted to cover them, became the Tasting Room's major feature.

"I saw the place while he was building there," says Doug Crittenden, "and just couldn't see how he was going to do it." Years later you would have thought it had been that way forever. Cluttered with memorabilia, photographs of old dinners, menus and wine lists, the character and atmosphere of Bulletin Place was unique in the Australian wine industry, totally reflective of their creator.

The Bulletin Place cellars were opened with Evans' friends, Graham and Treena Kerr, on 20 July 1969, on the very day that man first stood on the moon.

Evans' first secretary was Mary McDiarmid, and the twenty-one-year-old Annie Tyrrell (now Ellis) was poached from Douglas Lamb, with the brief, as its manager, to open and stock the bottle shop.

Evans began by stocking the cellars with his own wine, of which he had accumulated a serious quantity. "We started with twenty dozen of this, twenty dozen of that, like Bin 27 of Mildara, ten dozen Grange of that vintage, twenty dozen '61 Pinot Hermitage from McWilliams, five dozen '54 Richard and all that sort of stuff," he recalls.

Fitting out the place, Evans first discovered he had to build lavatories, then an office and a room for tasting. "Then I decided to have a small kitchen to give food to my friends," he says, "and of course the kitchen was minute. It was literally no bigger than 10 feet by 8 feet, the tiniest kitchen in the world, a hell-hole of a kitchen."

"Only then did I realise, here I have this tasting room, this complementary dining room, and here I have this little kitchen. It was ridiculous not to make a business of it! So I decided to open the Tasting Room as a commercial enterprise right away."

An atmospheric room, the Tasting Room's marvellous cedar panels came from Milson's great house at Milson's Point, pulled down in 1928 to make way for the Sydney Harbour Bridge. The father of Evans' landlord, also in real estate, had retained some of the house's more appealing features and fittings, keeping them in the loft at Bulletin Place. Two of those windows now form part of "Loggerheads", the Evans homestead in the Hunter Valley.

"At the end of the day, Evans is a frustrated architect come builder and collector," James Halliday explains. "The very top storey of Bulletin Place was crammed with the most incredible pieces and things, large things, like the doors from a Spanish castle, which finally ended up as the doorway between the kitchen and living room at "Loggerheads". He was the great collector, the great creator with a very strong sense of design."

It wasn't long before the Tasting Room was running at full swing, its membership in huge demand. The meal of the day was brought to the table as if each patron was Evans' own personal guest. It comprised a soup or other starter course, then a single main course shared by all. The wines of the day were selected by Evans from those he currently had for sale. With cheese and bread, the all-inclusive charge was just $5.

Evans greeted his patrons with champagne, with perhaps two or three wines to taste at the bar. Then, at 1 p.m. precisely, he, with a characteristic thump of a gavel, would demand that the assembled company take their seats. Next he would address them all concerning the wine, the food and the prices. He presented three or four wines with the first course, another three or four with the main, itself followed by cheese and port. All told, Evans' patrons would taste up to fourteen wines with their lunch. No wonder it was popular.

"In 1970 I remember making a big thing of the '68 white from Lindemans at $1.35 per bottle," says Evans. "It has since become that famous multi-show award-winner which now sells for $85."

His food was very simple, bold and robust, old English in style and invariably excellent in quality. According to Halliday, Evans was almost the first bistro operator in Australia, although Bulletin Place was never called a bistro. "He was far ahead of his time in terms of the style and concept he created, so classic in its simplicity," Halliday acknowledges.

Some guests were unable immediately to comprehend the idea of a single, set main course. A member once brought two Tasmanian guests to lunch one day. One immediately sought out Evans, who was leaning on the bar. "What's going on? Our host tells us we've got to have whatever you are!"

So Evans explained to the "truculent Taswegian" that if they were at his home, they would indeed have the food and wines he put on his table.

"Well, I thought I was in Sydney! What's on today?"

"Steak and kidney pie."

"That's okay, I like steak and kidney pie."

Evans had placed them at the end of a table with two rather prim young ladies. It came 3.30 p.m. and their host spoke to Evans, requesting that while he had to leave, since his two guests were getting on so famously with the ladies, would he mind if they stayed on? "Not at all," Evans replied.

"They stayed and stayed and stayed," he remembers. "Quite often lunch would go through until 6 or 6.30 p.m. and the record for paying guests was 7.30 p.m." But by around 6 p.m., the two Tasmanians departed, hand-in-hand with their two companions.

The next morning, the more vocal of the two Tasmanians rang in. "You know, I wasn't too impressed at the start, but it turned out marvellously. We went for a few rums and a few beers afterwards, then the girls said, 'Let's go and see the sights'. We finished up having dinner, went out dancing and then back to their place. They serve a terrific breakfast. It was the greatest day of my life. What's on for lunch today?"

Throughout its first six years, the Tasting Room was very college-like in format, furnished with just three long refectory tables, church pews and end seats, seating fourteen people to a table. The room had a maximum capacity of forty-two. Groups were shuffled together to make up tables as the arithmetic permitted, so patrons were never entirely certain with whom they would be seated.

One table, known as the Evans Table, was generally occupied by Len's own visitors, guests and friends, so the Tasting Room evolved into a sort of club, there being several informal levels of member, host and guest. Evans handed out his attentions accordingly.

"I never went around kissing arses," he says. "I didn't know half the customers and I wasn't a good customer man. That was never my job. I gave people a place to enjoy themselves. I was considered by many to be a rather arrogant little shit, and I'm quite sure I was. But my attitude was that they were spending a very fair price to have great food and great wine. The wine and food spoke for themselves."

Sally Cleaver, who took over from Bobby Patterson (now McNee) as manager in 1980, altered the room to a more conventional restaurant layout, with smaller tables of four and two. She also hired an excellent chef, Carolyn Divjak, with whose efforts the cuisine improved to a genuinely excellent level.

According to Brian Croser, "Bulletin Place was fantastic, one of the best places to eat. It was always abuzz, managed by good people and full of Sydney business people and internationals.

"It was a social event to go there. There could be twenty masked wines at lunch on a serious day. It sounds indulgent and it was, but it was never vulgar. It was stimulating, civilised, and facilitated the consumption of fine wine with good conversation and food. There was not a mean thing about Bulletin Place."

Evans was the leader of the pack, the grand host and the fount of lunchtime entertainment. He would introduce special guests to the crowd and was never afraid to pick on anyone there for a character weakness, not just at his own table. But he always maintained complete control.

Frank Christie remembers it as "a fun place", full of Len Evans devotees. He was uplifted by their adoration. He'd belt the table with his gavel, tell them to shut up, and everyone would listen to the master speak on his wines and anything else that came to mind. He is able to talk at length on any subject.

"If you went to one of Len's lunches you knew you were going to have a fantastic time. You could end up next to Lord Snowdon, film producers, or world-famous writers and artists," says Sydney publicist Deeta Colvin. "There's never been anything like it in Sydney since. Anyone who came into town who was anybody would visit Len at Bulletin Place."

Lunch could linger on, even winding up around 11 p.m. or midnight, usually with diners standing on chairs and singing songs. Derek Nimmo, in the book *Memorable Meals*, mentions that lunch with Len Evans would usually turn into the most charming of dinners. On those occasions, Evans might burst into his signature tunes of "All Pommies are Bastards" and "Bread From Evans" or perhaps his famous ditty of "Port makes me fart", composed for one of the floor shows held at his home. He never dared print it in "Indulgence", his column in the *Weekend Australian*, even when the subject became the topic of much detailed correspondence and interest. Courage, however, eventually prevailed. Here it is, delivered, according to Evans, in Lion's Day Accent:

I'm a bit of a wine dot
I'm fond of good red.
And I like to drink muscat
Whilst lying in bed.
I love a fine sherry
I'll have a good snort,
But there's one thing I do love,
A good glass of port.
But **FART**, **FART**, port makes me fart.

I've tried it with brandy,
I've tried it with rum,
I've tried it with biscuits to seal up my bum.
I tried to obscure it,
By loving me mum,
But **FART**, **FART**, port makes me fart.

I went down to Dijon
To have a good time.
Three bottles of champers
And four more of wine.
I'd duck, grouse and pheasant,

Far more than I ought.
And then with me custard
Just one glass of port.
FART, **FART**, port makes me fart.

I tried to ignore it,
To pretend it weren't there.
I tried to contain it
And got full of air.
And then I released it,
It went everywhere.
FART, **FART**, port makes me fart.

The moral to this tale is
An ill wind blows no good.
Some get the wind from cabernet
And some from treacle pud.
Some get the wind from radishes
And cabbages and Kings
But I say that true flatulence
It comes from simple things.
Port makes me **FART**.

If not intuitive, Evans' timing when he opened Bulletin Place was in the least fortunate. The mining boom was in full swing and front-page ventures like Poseidon generated heaven-sent volumes of optimism and cash. For the solicitors, accountants, stockbrokers, sharetraders and other businessmen who rode the boom, work was the place you went to before lunch, which would itself generally extend until 4 or 6 p.m.

Opening Bulletin Place as a restaurant in October 1969, Evans quickly captured a loyal following of precisely the right sort of people, like John Beeston, James Halliday and Tony Albert, who developed a long association around the now-famous Monday Table.

Halliday says it was easy to get to know Evans. "Beeston, Albert and I were pretty close to the ideal clients as far as Bulletin Place was concerned. We were up-and-coming lawyers, with money to spend and an acute interest in wine. But it quickly went beyond business to a personal friendship, which we keep up these days through the Single Bottle Club, birthdays and fishing trips."

As a group, those who played the Options Game at the Monday Table were then very keen on French wine, along with the occasional German; Australian wine being yet to develop to anything near its present extent. No merlot or pinot noir was grown in Australia to speak of, and if they decided to drink chardonnay the choice was straightforward – French white burgundy.

Awed by their sheer quality, Evans began his famous Bordeaux dinners, featuring vertical tastings of Latour, Lafite, Montrose, Mouton and several other great growths. In the late 1960s, the wine known today as Australia's most prestigious was still gaining its reputation. Grange Hermitage was hardly world famous, just a "comparatively good Australian table wine known by comparatively few Australians". Yet recognising its class and potential, Evans conducted a Grange dinner in the early 1970s.

"It was an innovative and developmental time," says John Beeston, "and on some occasions at the Monday Table we would have been drinking at the best table in the world. How many people drink first-growth Bordeaux for lunch? We did it regularly."

I am left in no doubt that the Monday Table considerably raised the sights of Australian wine. It fostered an appreciation and developing understanding of the great wines of the world at an unprecedented level in Australia. Evans, Halliday and Beeston (just to name the writers and wine judges among the regular players) then spread the quality message across the breadth of Australian wine through the media, the show system and other wine educational processes.

John Beeston modestly admits that as a critical group, they played a role in guiding the development of styles in Australian wine. Although its contribution would be impossible to measure, all who now enjoy Australian wine owe something to the Monday Table.

"John Beeston was our single greatest customer," says Evans. "So great that when he wasn't lunching with me or a friend he would lunch quite cheerfully by himself. I can't imagine what he would have spent per month."

Once Beeston took a week's holiday, only to be cornered by Sally Cleaver on his return: "Mr Beeston, I didn't know you were going off for a holiday last week."

"I rang up on Monday to say I wasn't coming here," he replied.

"But you must understand, Mr Beeston. You didn't tell me you were taking your holiday."

"Why, pray, do I have to do that?"

"Well, Mr Beeston, in future I would very much like to know so I can adjust my budget!"

Comprehensively writing the day off, by mid-afternoon the Monday Table would become the Monday poker school, which very seldom concluded before midnight, sometimes lasting until 4 a.m. the following Tuesday morning.

"Evans was host to a very serious game of seven card stud," says James Halliday, "given the amount of alcohol with which we were all similarly handicapped. Sometimes others would join in. The wine kept on flowing, but mostly we drank beer."

Although the stakes were never vast, it was quite conceivable that any one of the players might walk away from the table a couple of hundred dollars lighter.

Personality is supposed to reveal itself at poker. According to Beeston, Evans was all over the place. "He would sometimes bet very highly on a pair of twos or something like that and would keep pressing on, not believing the others would have something better than his pair, or ace high. He was a great bluffer. Halliday was much the better player, far more serious and systematic."

Sydney wine man Nick Bulleid, now a brand manager with Penfolds, used to play poker with Evans in the Hunter Valley. He classifies Evans as "the most incredible bluffer, the sort of poker player who would end the night blitzing everyone and being the biggest winner, or else the biggest loser. He would take outrageous risks and was totally erratic."

Lunch at Bulletin Place was often a game in itself and Evans would frequently use James Halliday, John Beeston, Tony Albert and Neville Baker, who were always happy to participate, as part of a sideshow he would put on for dignitaries visiting the Tasting Room.

"I remember David Wynn once telling me he was bringing to lunch Lord Harewood, the boss of English opera," he says. "He asked for a table of their own, so his Lordship wouldn't be bothered by the other people. I told him he won't be bothered."

"But he's very particular," Wynn persisted.

"For Christ's sake, David, either bring him or don't. I'll put him at the end of my table, so no one will annoy him." Come lunch time, Beeston, Halliday, Albert, Baker and Evans were all playing wine games and obviously enjoying themselves.

Looking down the table, Harewood demanded, "What's going on down there? You seem to be having more fun than I'm having up here!" So Harewood shifted down to Evans' end and joined in the guessing games.

In 1974, the Australian office of Coca-Cola rang, saying the boss of Coca-Cola was coming to Australia and wanted to have lunch with Evans.

"But he wouldn't know me from a bar of soap!" Evans replied.

"He does. He's read your books and we'd really like you to invite two or three of your friends over. Put on the very best wines, the very best Australian, the very best French – it doesn't matter how much it all costs, we're very happy to pay. There will be the President of the World, the President of the Pacific and the President of Australia, but the boss doesn't want to talk about anything to do with Coke. He'd just like a boozy lunch with some wine people."

Thinking it could be fun, Evans called in Halliday, Beeston and Albert to meet the American, who, as it turned out, was an interesting and charming man. "We had a good time and showed him a lot of good Australian wines," says Evans, "and then started playing guessing games."

By around 4 p.m., Evans declared: "I think we have come to the last wine. I propose that whoever is furthest away from picking this wine buys a magnum of champagne for the table." Beeston and the others nodded their approval. "We won't talk about where it comes from," Evans continued, "we'll just talk about the vintage. Whoever is furthest away from it buys."

The wine was opened and it was extraordinary. Halliday began, saying it could be '45, could be older. One of the Americans said it could be '64, another said '53, then someone else said '37. It came back to the global President, who said, "There is no question about it. It's a '21."

"I took off the wrapper and it was a 1921 Clos de la Roche," says Evans. "The whole table, self included, were very impressed." Then the President of the Pacific, said, in broadest American, "Well, I gotta tell you, I didn't know that you had... I mean I knew you had a great palate, but I didn't know you had *such* a great palate, because, man, you *knew* that wine was a '21, you didn't even argue about it, you just *knew* it."

The World President said thoughtfully, "Well, I reckon this Evans is a pretty nice fellow. About an hour ago he asked me how old I was. Then about half an hour ago he called this man over to the table and just whispered and whispered, then sent him

off to do something. I reckoned he was making a gesture. I reckoned he was going to serve me a year of my birth. And as it turned out, I was right."

The table were even more impressed. Then the President of the Pacific turned around, saying: "Well, that is fantastic, how shrewd you were!"

The big boss leaned over and said, "And don't forget that. That's why I'm the goddamn President!"

"That was typical of Bulletin Place," Evans laughs. "It has five thousand of those stories. It was an unbelievable agglomeration of people, an incredible meeting place of souls. People came automatically to our place, like Harry Secombe, Jimmy Edwards, the Earl of Snowdon, Freddie Trueman, André Kostelanus and Arthur Hailey. Diplomats and ambassadors would drop by regularly. One of our guests was one of the richest men in Japan who happened to love wine and food. I never even spoke to him; we would just nod to each other."

"All the great chefs visited when they were in Australia – Bocuse, Girard, Troisgros – and we would introduce them from the floor. All the great wine people – Louis Latour, Gerard Jaboulet, whoever was in town made sure to come by. And because you were able to go downstairs to buy a bottle of wine at retail price to bring back upstairs, we had fantastic wines all the time. Some people would even drag up three Lafites!"

The pace was frantic, but Evans had the stamina to match. One day he asked Annie Tyrrell what was listed on his day's itinerary. She told him no one was expected for lunch. "Thank God for that," said Evans. "Just fix me a cold beef sandwich and a glass of champagne."

Raising money for the 1980 America's Cup Challenge with Sir James Hardy.

The phone rang. It was a French winemaker. "I don't have anyone for lunch today," said Evans. "But if you would like to come in for a glass of champagne at 12.30, I'm just having a beef sandwich."

Another call, this time someone from the Napa Valley. "Yes, well fine. There are a couple of us, a bloke from France, me and a beef sandwich. Fine."

"Then a ballet dancer rang, saying he was a great friend of so and so's, a wine lover and was in town to appear as a guest artist for the Australian Ballet. Lunch would be nice."

"Well, I'm having this beef... Stuff it, come round and have lunch!"

There were now six. "To cut a long story short," Evans continues, "there were fourteen of us to lunch that day. They all phoned and were coming from overseas or interstate, or were locals like Beeston, who rang in and said, "Hello Evans, what are you up to? I'm not lunching with anyone today, Evans, and I think I will probably come over'."

Those were the days. "We sold more Krug than anyone else in Australia from that tiny room," boasts Evans, with not inconsiderable pride, "more so than any of the great hotels, restaurants and clubs. The same could possibly be said for Bollinger, Pol Roger and others. We drank an enormous quantity of champagne, it was *the* drink. We lived life to the full. I'd knock off a bottle every day before lunch with somebody."

Deeta Colvin dropped into Bulletin Place one day, meeting Evans for the first time. "Do you know anything about champagne?" he asked. She replied in the negative. "Then you should start with the best. It's Krug and I shall open a bottle of it."

"In 1984, my last full-time year at Bulletin Place, the champagne bill for internal consumption, my parties and give-aways was $30 000. No wonder I didn't make a profit!"

Rudy Komon occasionally made a call to Bulletin Place where, true to his old form, he enjoyed putting the staff through their paces. Anders Ousback (now a well-known caterer and wine writer) had been an employee of Bulletin Place for a short time when, walking past Evans' office, he was summoned by his employer. "Rudy, you would not have met my young trainee," said Evans. "This is Anders Ousback. He has been here six months."

Rudy Komon turned to Ousback, saying, "We are looking at a wine. Tell us what you think of this," pouring a miserly half-inch of wine into a glass and handing it over.

Ousback looked at the wine, smelled it and said, "It's a Bordeaux."

Komon: "Yes. Commune?"

Ousback: "St Estephe."

"Yes. Château?"

"Well, it's not a First Growth.

"Of course it's not a First Growth! There aren't any First Growths in St Estephe, Ousback. You should know that!"

"It's a second. It's a Cos... it's a Montrose."

"Yes, absolutely right. Vintage?"

"It's umm, it's pre-war."

"Which war?"

"First World War."

"Yes, correct."

"This century."

"Yes, that's right."

"Can I taste it now?"

"Yes, all right. Have a taste."

Taking a sip Ousback said:"It's not a 1910 or 1912. It's difficult... First decade?"

"Yes."

"1908 Montrose?"

"Yes, very good."

"Thanks, Mr Komon. It was very nice to meet you."

Anders Ousback then reveals that what Rudy Komon did not know was that Evans had rung down to the cellar a couple of hours previously, saying that today was Mr Komon's sixtieth birthday. "He was born in 1908. What '08s do we have in the cellar?" There was only the one, a Montrose, which Evans requested to be decanted and brought to his office.

From that moment on, Rudy Komon always showed to Anders Ousback the utmost respect. He never once realised the whole situation was a set-up.

The Tasting Room at Bulletin Place ultimately generated such business that an auxiliary dining room was urgently required. And since Evans couldn't be in two places at once, the second room would have to run autonomously, without the advantage of his personality.

The Beef Room began in the early 1970s. It had a simple but always popular and successful set menu of roast beef and yorkshire pudding. Prices started around $5 per head and orders were simply taken for beef cooked rare, medium or well done, thick or thin, with salad or vegetables. An old sideboard groaned under its burden of different breads, fruits and coffee, and a 20-kilogram slab of cheddar which was slowly whittled away until replaced by another. Later, optional entrées or desserts were added to the menu.

The Beef Room was more of a business luncheon place. Most of its patrons would select wines from a short blackboard list of predominantly Australian wine which altered daily, although a certain proportion would venture down to the cellar to fossick around for a special bottle.

Another project Evans initiated while at Bulletin Place was the Bulletin Wine Club, established in 1970 as a fledgling prototype of the modern direct-mail wine operation. In a special advertisement placed in the *Bulletin*, Evans would review a couple of wines for sale, receive cheques and coupons from interested readers and then organise delivery of the wine.

The club operated from what was initially a dingy, squalid little liquor licence in Leichhardt, Sydney, and was managed by another of the Evans protégés, John Parkinson. Having received orders for 800 cases on its first weekend, it quickly expanded into a sound and viable business. Parkinson remembers his eagerness to take the job with Evans, despite being paid around a third of what he previously took home as a wine waiter.

The club materialised with all the customary Evans haste. "We're launching in two months," he declared, which meant that not only did the Leichhardt cellar need instant restoration into an operable condition, but without any wine to sell, some had to be found — and quickly.

So Evans and Parkinson embarked on a frenetic tour of Victoria and South Australia, Parkinson a little awed by the respect and affection shown to Evans by the winemakers they visited, all aware of his recent work on their collective behalves at the Wine Information Bureau.

Evans took to his tasting with typical gusto and velocity, requiring only two hours to taste the hundred wines Guenter Prass and Mark Tummel had set out for him at Orlando, all the while discussing, debating and giving notes to John Parkinson, whose task it was to collect and store the information as fast as Evans could glean it.

Down the road at Tolley, Scott and Tolley, where Wolf Blass was still winemaker, Evans and Parkinson were shown wines direct from the barrels. Evans immediately recognised volatile acidity in the first wine. "That's a TST wine," said Blass, even then in the process of setting up his own wine company. "But that's a great wine!" exclaimed Evans when shown the second. "Yes, that's my wine," nodded the entrepreneurial Wolf Blass.

"They were heady times," says Parkinson. "Evans was at his peak. The trips we went on were a hundred miles an hour, involved a great deal of energy, but also a great deal of humour and fun."

Tasting the Barolet collection at Bulletin Place in the early '70s, flanked by
Tony Albert and Oliver Shaul.

Throughout his working life, Evans has chosen to employ young people to work for him, those with a potential that he felt he could nurture. When he first took on the youthful Anders Ousback at Bulletin Place he told him frankly: "You will work very hard, you'll get paid nothing, but I'll teach you wine."

He was correct on all three counts, says Ousback. Annie Ellis says Evans was an especially generous employer – apart from financially – for whom it was great to work. She says he made sure everyone had a particular role, so they could all combine well as a team.

If not immediately, material rewards would follow for many. According to John Beeston, if you worked for Evans it was a virtual guarantee of a job in the hospitality industry. Many restaurateurs and hoteliers would hire Evans employees, even if they were still very young. The knowledge spread.

All Evans' employees, from his secretary to bottle shop manager, were encouraged to attend his weekly or fortnightly tastings of new releases, as long as they were prepared to be interrogated on each sample. People like Annie Ellis, Anders Ousback, John Parkinson and Helen Guy, also with the Bulletin Wine Club, were presented with an enviable opportunity to learn fast about wine. Evans was a thorough teacher, not satisfied until each of his 'students' understood every conceivable aspect of a wine, from its background to its present and future.

It was also expected of the bottle shop staff that they would decant and check every great wine taken upstairs to the dining rooms. On some days they spent entire afternoons in awe and contemplation of several glasses of fifty-year-old reds from Bordeaux.

The wine tastings Evans regularly conducted for the public during lunch times and dinners at Bulletin Place were popular and instructive, even if a little unpredictable. Saturday lunchtime was a regular slot, at which keen wine tasters parted with their money in return for soup, cheese, wine and Len Evans.

Nick Bulleid first met Evans in 1973 at one of his Saturday lunch time tastings of classic Australian wines. It began with a Great Western fizz, then a Leo Buring Rhine Riesling and a Lindemans Hunter Semillon and an Orlando Rhine Riesling. The reds were Grange and a fabulous '56 Skeleton from the Woodley's Treasure Chest series. "They were fantastic tastings for a young upstart coming into wine," says Bulleid.

In 1974, noticing that Bulleid had become a regular at his tastings, Evans invited him to join the monthly in-house Bulletin Place tasting panel, whose regulars at the time were John Hennesey, who took over from Annie Tyrrell as manager of the cellars, John Parkinson, James Halliday, and on occasions, Anders Ousback.

Evans didn't like them to become too headstrong too quickly. He once put a Wyndham Estate Sauternes in front of Bulleid and Parkinson and asked them for their opinions.

"Well, look at it," said Bulleid. "It's absolutely bleached water-white, reeks of sulphur dioxide and shows no fruit whatsoever. It's appalling."

Evans turned on them. "You young upstarts!" he blurted. "What do you think you know about young sauternes? If I took you to Coutet, or Rayne-Vigneau, or even Yquem, you would see wines which you would think have no fruit whatsoever. You would proclaim about their level of sulphur dioxide and you would probably say that they were over-oaked. You would say that they were an appalling wine. Who are you to say what a young sauternes is like?"

"Well, sorry. What do you think this wine is like?" requested the chastised and humbled Bulleid and Parkinson.

"It's bloody awful!"

"It was everything we said it was," says Bulleid. "But he wanted to prove a point at our expense – that even great sauternes start off very awkward while very young."

The notes from those tastings were collated and roneoed into a little in-house newsletter, the *Wine Buyer*, which Evans circulated to Tasting Room Members in return for a small subscription. "It was run on a Menzies democracy," says Parkinson. "Most of the time he already knew what he was going to write, but occasionally a thought would pop out from one of his juniors that he might decide to use."

The *Wine Buyer* ran its course over three or four years as a highly influential publication, until partly superceded by the *Wine and Spirit Buying Guide* (which ended its days as the *Wine and Spirit Magazine*), although one did not evolve into the other. During its time, however, *The Wine Buyer* was the only written word, apart from his *Bulletin* wine column, where people could access Len Evans' opinion.

Len Evans was the first consultant-editor of the *Wine and Spirit Buying Guide* which started in September 1975, before John Parkinson, recommended by Evans to initiate the magazine, was given full responsibility as its editor in late 1975. Parkinson quit the post in 1980 to become a consultant to a number of Hunter Valley wine companies, re-entering the direct-mail wine industry on a part-time basis with Cellarmasters in 1982, fully joining, in 1986, the organisation whose Australian office he now heads.

Even in the mid 1970s there was little variety in Australian wine and Evans would quickly run out of new samples to review in the *Wine Buyer*. Penfolds only sold a few reds, Seppelts its Imperial Reserve and a small number of table wines. The large wine merchants like Doug Crittenden would buy large volumes of wine for their own house labels. Evans was happy to review the wines of other competing merchants who, like Crittenden would receive a huge response. The *Wine Buyer* sold large volumes of Crittenden's Seven Oaks Riesling, irreverently referred to by Evans as "Seven Pokes", and introduced many new customers to his shop.

Evans' own selection of wine inside Bulletin Place's cellar was remarkable in the extreme. Allocating a splendid lockable area of the cellar for his museum, Evans began to buy the contents of some magnificent old cellars, including the rump of Tony Nelson's, full of marvellous old vintages of great wine. They were further augmented as Evans called up old favours from top wine companies for special batches of rare museum wines. If only I was older!

Halliday remembers buying a '44 Great Western Burgundy from Evans with its original black label, and bottles of old Woodley Treasure Chest wines dating back to the 1930s and '40s.

Maintaining a cellar of that quality had its problems for, as time passed, it became increasingly difficult for Evans merely to pick the eyes out of the Australian and European wine industries without taking commensurably optimistic quantities of their lesser products. Overstocked, Bulletin Place nearly came unstuck once or twice this way.

When Bulletin Place and Rothbury occasionally stumbled over hard times, Evans wasn't above bringing in for sale large chunks of his own wine cellar to subsidise them, from old Mildara reserve bins including the '58 Hunter Coonawarra blend, '63 d'Arenbergs, the '59 Rosehill Hermitage, old Woodleys Treasure Chests, the '65 Draytons, all major old Australian wines.

"How can you do this?" Anders Ousback would ask.

"It's either the family, the business or the wine," replied Evans. "So it has to be the wine. I can always replace it."

When Evans found himself in hospital after his heart scare in 1976, Bobby Patterson, then his manager, informed Peter Fox, Evans' close friend and a regular customer of Bulletin Place, about what Evans describes as one of his typical liquidity crises. He had again bought too much wine that had to be paid for. Fox lent her $25 000 provided that Evans was never to find out, and there was to be no security and no interest charged.

Bobby Patterson let Evans in on the secret after a month or two, and later on Peter Fox become a forty-nine per cent shareholder in Bulletin Place, basically, according to Evans, because he enjoyed it so much. He paid Evans $45 000 for the stake, which his wife, Jenny Fox, retained until Evans eventually decided not to renew the building's lease.

Those who know Len Evans agree unanimously that making money for itself never really interested him. "He has tended to spend money as fast as he has earned it, if not a little faster," says James Halliday. "He vastly enjoyed buying wine and drinking it, but when it came to the hands-on business of selling, he never really wanted to get his hands too dirty."

Evans sold a lot of wine on the strength of his own conviction. He never promoted or wrapped up a wine he didn't believe in and he still doesn't. Look at the rather unflattering descriptions he's given some recent Evans Family wines and you'll see. I would never buy a Gamay described by its proprietor as "medicinal", but since that's the way Evans saw it, that's what he wrote.

Early in the days of Bulletin Place Evans bought almost fifty cases of Lindemans Bin 3475 1968 Hunter River Chablis, a phenomenal quantity of wine in those days. He gave it a huge review in a newsletter before it went on to become a very famous wine, collecting shelves of trophies. Evans' belief in it sold it out in two days.

Because he removed himself from the wine cellar's day-to-day affairs, often tripping over to Petaluma or Rothbury, it didn't do as well as it might have. "He was notorious for delegating the business to wildly enthusiastic people like Anders Ousback," says Halliday, "desperately in love with wine, but in terms of the hard yakka of running a business, perhaps not as efficient as others."

By the late 1970s, finding the cellar's needs too great to handle alongside his other interests, Evans sold a majority interest in the Bulletin Place wine shop to a syndicate headed by Chris Hayes.

Evans fondly remembers Bulletin Place as enormous fun, a seven-year party until 1975, when his involvement began to wane. "I wasn't putting the energy into it that I had been, and was doing more and more other things like Rothbury, which began to take up more and more time. I was getting other consultancies which became more important to me, I was evolving as a wine man and judging wine more and more. Therefore it lost a bit of its impetus."

In 1985, after managing his affairs from Bulletin Place for sixteen years, Evans moved his family and the focus of his activities from Sydney to the Hunter Valley, too great a distance away from Bulletin Place to commute, although it continued under Sally Cleaver's guidance.

Trade then suffered once Bulletin Place found itself surrounded on all sides by major construction sites and, once the Macquarie Place entrance was closed off, business really fell in a hole. Evans' lease expired at the end of June 1989. Aware that an increase in rent was imminent, he met up with the building's owner, who had personally enjoyed the club concept at Bulletin Place. Evans suggested that he become a partner in Bulletin Place, to understand the parameters of the business and charge its rental appropriately. Although the idea looked likely for a while, the owner later withdrew.

At the time, Evans' annual rental was $60 000, five times the rate of twenty years before. After the building's fate had been tossed around like a football by the National Trust, the Heritage Commission and the Sydney City Council, it was finally resolved that it had to be renovated.

Air conditioning, the installation of which Evans had vigorously objected to on the grounds that it was not in keeping with the character of the building, fire escapes, lifts, and other modifications together costing around a million dollars were all insisted upon. Evans' rent shot to a stratospheric $250 000, far beyond the serviceability of a food and beverage business of that nature.

Quite cheerfully, he says, Evans washed his hands of the entire affair. That was in mid 1990 and, at the time of writing, nothing has happened to Bulletin Place since.

Evans stripped the place bare, keeping what he wanted and selling the rest. An era was swept to an end. "I've no regrets," he says. "It was a lovely part of my life. Bulletin Place was a constant fun rort, but I also worked hard there." Halliday disagrees, saying Evans was so passionately attached to that building that losing its lease nearly broke his heart. "He recognised it to be a very beautiful and central feature of his whole make-up." To Keith Dunstan, it was one of the great tragedies of Sydney that Bulletin Place ceased to operate under Len Evans' charge.

Based there, Evans had been responsible to varying degrees for the two dining rooms; the wine shop; establishing Rothbury and Petaluma, the French and American wine properties owned by the Evans Wine Company; writing his many wine columns; raising money for charities; instigating countless schemes and rackets; and tending to his various consultancies, which had included several major wine and food conventions for up to 4 500 people.

"You should never go back to things," he says. "I believe that once it was over, it was over. I would have found it really difficult to go back and get it happening again. I don't like resurrecting themes. I'd never start a Rothbury again. I'd do something else in a different direction, with a different appeal."

James Halliday who, apart from Evans, knew it as well as anyone else, says there is no question that Bulletin Place was the single and greatest wine centre Australia has ever known, and its greatest fulcrum of activity for both Australian and imported wine.

*P*utting Wine in the Press

It is a sly little traminer which you might find rather
droll. Do you think I can tempt you?
L.P.E., to another occupant of The Hill, the
Sydney Cricket Ground, clutching
two cans of beer.

There are many who believe that Len Evans has been the best wine writer Australia has enjoyed. He was certainly the country's first regular wine columnist and its most prolific and influential wine writer from the early 1960s until the mid 1980s. Then, as he focused his interests and energies elsewhere, he was happy to hand over the mantle to the pack of other writers emerging from the wings – James Halliday in particular – which his own writings and enthusiasm had helped to generate. There is little doubt that Evans' impact while Australians were just beginning to turn their thoughts to wine has yet to be approached by anyone else.

Long before Len Evans began his career as a wine writer he had become a well-known contributor as a humorist for the *Observer* magazine, which ultimately became the *Bulletin*. He had already established himself as a television and radio script-writer of rare wit and quality, although few would realise he was one of the writers for the satirical *Mavis Bramston Show,* considered by many who watched it to be years ahead of its time.

Later, Evans became notorious around Australia as one of the personalities on the *Would You Believe* television show, in which writer Frank Hardy, Cyril Pearl, comedienne Noeline Brown, actress Jackie Weaver, (now Senator) Michael Baume and Evans would attempt to outdo each other with the most incredible lies. Finding the dual pressures of script-writing and hotel life at the Chevron becoming excessive, Evans gave away his writing in favour of hospitality. Golf had made way for writing several years before, as Evans navigated his way through the myriad of possibilities his talents had given him.

When Walter James published *Barrel and Book: A Winemaker's Diary* in 1949, it was the first book written about wine in a non-technical sense since those by Hubert De Castella in the 1890s. Apart from Max Lake's books and the occasional magazine article, there was very little written for the public about serious wine appreciation until Len Evans turned his attention to it.

In 1962, he considered it a shame that there was not a regular wine column from which he could learn more. Discussing this issue with Hertha Nolte, who looked after the Chevron's public relations, he was encouraged by her to approach the *Bulletin* magazine himself.

Opportunity knocked when Peter Hastings, the *Bulletin's* editor, dropped in to the Chevron for lunch. "I asked him why he didn't have a wine writer" says Evans, "and he asked me what, exactly, a wine writer was. Once I told him, he suggested I jot down a few thoughts and give him what I considered might be a typical wine article.

"I wrote the article, signed it and waited for the publication day. When the wine column finally came out, I was horrified. There, instead of my own byline was an article by this "Cellarmaster". But when I looked at the words more closely, I realised they were my own! I had become "Cellarmaster". Peter Hastings had invented the "Cellarmaster" byline, put the logo there and, as a result my name was never mentioned for years. This way I became the first regular wine columnist in Australia."

"I went straight to my General Manager, Frank Christie, to apologise," says Evans, "because I had very strict ethics about this sort of thing. Of course I was writing in my own time – and today you wouldn't think anything of it. Christie said he didn't mind, as long as Peter Hastings accredited the article to Len Evans, Beverage Manager, the Chevron Hilton.

"I proposed this to Hastings, which of course he totally ignored. But by this time Frank Christie had forgotten all about the issue anyway. 'Cellarmaster' went on."

Evans doesn't think his first article was all that good; no reflection on the first wine he ever recommended in print – Penfolds' Traminer-Riesling, which he predicted would go on to win a gold medal. It did, more than once. It was a blend of roughly four parts traminer from Minchinbury (near Penrith, New South Wales) to five of Rhine riesling from Modbury (South Australia). Evans described it as one of the more consistent hock styles.

He says, "'Cellarmaster' created quite a stir, you know, especially in Melbourne which was, without any question, a more sophisticated market than Sydney at the time. For a long time no one there knew who "Cellarmaster" was, but they assumed, of course that it would be a Melburnian!"

The famous Evans byline had become widespread by the end of the 1960s, but Evans' own name came to be associated with the column more and more, especially with the launch of the books *Cellarmaster's Guide to Australian Wines* (1966) and *Cellarmaster Says* (1968), which identified quite clearly who was the initially anonymous "Cellarmaster". Both books were anthologies of the best of the columns, edited and fashioned into guidebook form.

The Evans phenomenon snowballed, catching the media by storm. Suddenly each publication wanted a wine critic of its own, so the number of columns he contributed to increased dramatically, especially once he had moved to the Australian Wine Bureau in 1965. To spread himself out in a blanket of pseudonyms was the only answer. Evans became "Bacchus the Elder", "Henry VIII" and the "Compleat Imbiber" to name but a few. "I was writing so many articles under different names it was unbelievable," he says. "But I don't know how many articles I wrote, for I've never kept them."

From the outset, Len Evans, through his actions and writings, helped to shape the pattern of drinking wine in Australia. If he championed a cause strongly enough, the chance was it would get a healthy boost. On the other hand, when he bemoaned an inadequacy loudly and eloquently enough, which he is still utterly unafraid to do, sooner or later people tended to get the message.

His influence and direction were felt from his earliest writings. It is ironic to think that in 1963 Evans wrote that "If Penfolds keeps up with Grange Hermitage, they could well dominate the quality red wine market for many years to come." Evans was an early supporter of winemaker Jack Mann's Houghton's White Burgundy, which was first believed to be made from semillon with a slight additive of tokay. Later, the semillon was found to be chenin blanc, a similar-looking vine. Aware of its well-known patronage by politicians, Evans described it as "big and very full, parliamentary in character and interminable in discussion"!

Jack Mann, as Evans recalls, was one hundred per cent Western Australian. The only trouble with Western Australia, he once said, was the water. "We have to purify it with a little chablis, you see."

In the early 1960s, one of Evans' "Wines of the Month" in the *Bulletin* was another Houghtons wine, the Verdell, a white table wine made from the verdelho grape which, until that time, was generally made into a fortified dessert wine. After all, it was originally a Madeira grape. Despite Jack Mann being dismissive of his own wine, Evans found it "extremely interesting, having tremendous flavour and richness, and a very spicy aromatic quality". Exactly the words one might use to describe a good vintage of Moondah Brook Verdelho, a modern Houghton's wine made with the same grape which, with the excellent and more sophisticated Sandalford Verdelho is today recognised as a multi-trophy winner and one of Australia's unique white wines.

Another Jack Mann wine enjoyed by Evans was the Houghtons Rosé, still arguably one of the top three in Australia. In the early 1960s he anticipated a great future for rosé wines in Australia, if only people would wake up to it. Sadly, they're still sleeping.

Other wines he was keen to recommend were the Coonawarra Cabernets from Wynn ("worthy of much praise") and Orlando's rather downtrodden Barossa Spaetlese Rhine Riesling, which remains today one of the best value-for-money cellaring Australian white wines and a personal favourite of mine.

By now one of the few individuals in Australia with a genuine understanding of world wine, Evans was in a position to offer constructive advice concerning the development of classic Australian styles. "When Australian rieslings get more fullness and richness in the middle palate," he wrote, "they will dazzle the world." In *Cellarmaster Says*, Evans declares, "Rhine riesling will make the best hock-style wine in the country, despite the marvellous traminer-riesling blends and straight traminers of Penfold's. The traminer will be a most welcome addition if it becomes more freely available, and I do hope we see more of it. But, as in Alsace, it will eventually play second violin to Rhine riesling."

Again, this was correct. We did get the traminer, but most of it was planted in all the wrong places. Those correctly sited vineyards, like Delatite Dead Man's Hill (Mansfield, Victoria), Capel Vale (Bunbury, Western Australia) and Orlando Flaxman's (Eden Valley, South Australia), eloquently make Evans' point for him.

Evans has championed the cause of Australian cabernet sauvignon ever since he began writing, even though it was extremely rare at the time and took people like Max Lake to give it the spotlight. He also acknowledged that a little cabernet can go a long way, and that the richness of shiraz can be used to supplement the occasional deficiency on the cabernet palate.

In 1968, he recorded in the *Bulletin,* "I'm convinced that cabernet is most useful as a blender. There will undoubtedly be many Australian straight cabernets of high quality in the future, but generally speaking, I find cabernet a little too positive in this country. The tannin is too harsh and the palate too thin. The variety can best be used by lending its great flavour and firmness to softer, rounder, perhaps less flavoursome grape types."

Enter, stage left, merlot and cabernet franc, circa 1980. Evans was again ahead of his time. The story of the Petaluma Coonawarra red blend, principally cabernet sauvignon and merlot, still many years from that article, confirms how right he was.

Evans also predicted that new varieties would play a significant role in Australia. Witness chardonnay, sauvignon blanc and pinot noir. He also forecast the improvement of winemaking technologies and resulting improvements in table wines. While brandy was still an immensely important segment of the Australian wine industry, he predicted less pressure on the making and selling of brandy, enabling more grapes to become available for fortified and perhaps table wine. Radical stuff at the time it was written; again right on the button.

Evans also attacked our personal habits, kicking and cajoling us into the twentieth century. In the early 1960s, he used the *Bulletin* to bemoan our abuse of champagne styles, "frozen almost to the point of no return, shaken to achieve the biggest pop, gurgled into large saucer glasses the quicker to dissipate the all-precious bubbles, years of tender care guzzled in a moment of unthinking self-indulgence".

Bemoaning the above situation he then told us how, recommending that "it should be drunk classically… slowly, appreciatively, from long-stemmed tulip-shaped glasses that retain aroma and flavour, and let the bubbles ride gently to the surface. I like it best as a dinner party aperitif, served chilled but not frozen, instead of the omnipresent sherry." While Barossa Pearl was then far from his mind, that was neither the first nor the last time that the then statutory Australian sherry moved into Evans' critical sights.

Another time, he vented his frustration at the infanticide of our habitual drinking of robust Australian wines before they were ready. "I can see no reason why the major companies should not make the bigger wines and sell them right away to the public. Why not state on the label, UNFIT FOR DRINKING NOW, LAY DOWN FOR 1968." Back then, you see, back labels were almost twenty years away. Sadly today, they're awash with more hype than fact.

Evans played an important role in getting wine to be served with meals on domestic Australian flights. In the *Bulletin* he records that while flying between Sydney and Adelaide, when asking for a bottle of champagne he was informed he was flying on a domestic airline. "I pointed out that a domestic champagne would be fine," he says."Sorry!" "Just a bottle of red then." "Sorry!" "White?" "Sorry! Sorry! Sorry!"

At the time, he was travelling interstate almost every month, and wrote that, alone, he "could justify the service single-throated"!

Demonstrating that most of the international carriers which visited Australia served wine, some of it Australian, he concluded the broadside in typical Evans style. "Mr Ansett, your dinners are a triumph of the packagers' and printers' art. The sugar is by Industrial Sugar Mills, the biscuits by Arnott, the butter by York, the cigarettes by Kent, the Decimal Currency Guide by Desmal, the Old English Processed Cheese by Kraft. And the wine is by Nobody." Shortly afterwards wine was indeed served on Australian domestic flights.

Evans has long championed the use of regional and varietal names to describe wine. Even in the early 1960s his writings revelaed a no-holds-barred hostility towards the "time-honoured dishonesty" of generic labelling. It played a role, he agreed, in encouraging people to try wine for the first time, but with the increasing sophistication of the wine market (and we are discussing the 1960s, it must be remembered), Evans saw no use in naming Australian wines with the regional names of their intended European counterparts.

He was most aggressively against those names newly introduced to Australia in plagiaristic fashion. "There are now at least two Liebfraumilchs on the market, one of which even copies the famous Blue Nun. There is, apparently, a firm that has registered the name of a famous German Vineyard and consequently could be selling wine under this name. Finally, a sparkling wine, made from Muscat Gordo, is called Asti Spumante. Does this mean that soon we will have a Barossa Château Margaux or a Hunter River Vosne Romanée?"

Later, Evans recounted that while the liebfraumilchs continued to exist, the nuns had nevertheless "got themselves to a nunnery". In a fine example of improvement for the collective good, his commentary encouraged Stock Distilleries to alter the name of their spumante to "Gala Spumante", thereby initiating one of the most successful brands of that style of sparkling wine yet known in Australia.

Evans once discovered a particular Australian wine sporting foreign nomenclature, which also claimed on its label "Show Award Wine" and "Vintage Wine". Miffed by these fallacies, he rang its maker, telling him that the only honest thing on his label was the statement "Produce of Australia". "What rot!" the winemaker replied. "What about the 26 fluid ounces?"

In the mid 1970s, Len Evans began contributing occasional articles to the *Weekend Australian*, whose regular wine columnist was then John Stanford. Although delivered in the inimitable Evans style, his pieces were largely information-based, like those of James Halliday, who also began submitting there on a freelance basis.

In 1977, the group were lunching with Les Hollings, the Editor-in-Chief of the *Australian*, when Evans said he would rather contribute a "bits and pieces" column, as he had once done before in the *Sunday Mirror*'s "Fare Thee Well". It could include a recipe, a joke, followed by a wine review, then perhaps a story. "Why don't you call it 'Indulgence'?" he was asked. That's how "Indulgence", one of Australia's most memorable columns, was born.

"Indulgence" commenced in 1978, evolving into a very large piece each Saturday, doing precisely what Evans had suggested. As much a forum for public contributions as for those of Evans himself, it became a sort of noticeboard, to which highly intelligent and literate people with expertise in a wide variety of cultural and artistic disciplines could submit ideas, word plays, stories, jokes and outright lies around Evans' own themes. It was clever, funny, topical and self-perpetuating.

Sometimes, when perhaps lacking a story or theme, Evans became it himself. At a Queen's Birthday fireworks party in 1976 at Brokenwood Winery in the Hunter Valley he experienced his angina attack. Sensing the limits of mortality, three years later he took his health to heart and decided to impose a strict diet on himself, although the standard concept of quietly going about the business of losing weight was utterly foreign to Len Evans. Through "Indulgence" his diet was made a public event. He initiated a competition for people to nominate the precise weight he would lose over his nominated six weeks of diet, for which the twelve most accurate entrants would receive an autographed cartoon of Evans in pre-and post-diet condition, while the winning entrant was also awarded a free dinner for four in the capital city of his or her own State.

Requesting that people donate from $1 to $10 per pound lost, Evans set out to raise money for three charities: The National Multiple Sclerosis Society of Australia, The Federation of Autistic Children's Associations of Australia and the New South Wales Society for Crippled Children.

Many thought he would never do it. Robert Mondavi, famous Californian winemaker and industry statesman, burst into Evans' Sydney office brandishing a copy of the newspaper, fearing the worst for Australian wine consumption.

Commencing at 14 stone 8 pounds, Evans ultimately weighed in at a London retail store weighing 13 stone 3 pounds 12 ounces. Days one to fourteen were recorded in *Indulgence* to single-digit calorie detail, describing Evans' continual frustration at his unaccustomed adoption of the word "no" throughout a myriad of tempting lunches, dinners and tastings.

A typical daily entry was: "*Eleventh day*: tasting started at 8 a.m. on an empty stomach. Fifty-plus wines followed by a range of Château Tahbilk reds, going back to 1964, some which opened very well indeed. Then to lunch with the Sammy Club and to chat with Michael Parkinson, the guest speaker, "a legend in his lunch time". Lunch of fresh grilled sardines, boiled vegetables and two glasses of white. 300 cals. Tie up all work and fly to Adelaide to look at new winery. Dinner at The Fish House, excellent – half a crayfish tail and a small fresh flounder and salad. With a glass and a half of wine about 500 cals. Throw in the crusts of rolls picked at, through sheer aggravation/deprivation and was still under the 1 000."

Days fifteen to twenty-eight were recorded less precisely as enthusiasm waned, while the diet itself began to suffer as Evans wondered more and more what was the point of it all.

Writing in the *Weekend Australian*, he said, "I won't reveal what I had for lunch that day [of the weigh-in in London], but I could have taken on Robert Morley as a rival eater."

The diet raised nearly $6 000, Rudy Komon being the greatest contributor, paying $1 825, tallied at $10 per pound lost. Nick Bulleid was sufficiently moved by Evans' much-publicised anguish to put something down in the form of a limerick:

The cheek of old Evans astounds.
His presumption, likewise, knows no bounds.
For while his girth wastes away
We're expected to pay up
Our dollars in exchange for his pounds.

Bulleid believes that beneath the facade the diet, albeit totally out of character, was diligently adhered to. "His heart trouble slowed him down and revealed something I thought I would never see in Evans. For the first six months, he was absolutely shocked and chastened by the whole thing."

Then, suddenly, Evans realised that, although he was healthier, he was utterly miserable. "My specialist says that if I keep on doing as I am now, then I could live for another thirty or forty years. But if it's like this, I don't want to."

The diet was off and he started drinking again, believing, as Bulleid recalls, that although he might shorten his life by a few years, he would do everything in his power to make them good years. A decade later he took precisely the same approach after a single heart bypass operation.

"Indulgence" successfully occupied much of the back page of the *Weekend Australian* until 1981, when Evans was "poached" by the *Women's Weekly*, where he wrote weekly columns for four and a half years, while making occasional television appearances on Channel Nine, and continuing to pursue the "Cellarmaster" column for the *Bulletin*, all media outlets owned by Kerry Packer's Consolidated Press.

"When the late Geraldine Pascall – bless her heart because I liked her – took over "Indulgence" in 1981 (when Evans moved to the *Women's Weekly*), she said she would be much more severe than I had ever been. I asked her why. She said because it would make her reputation. And of course it did."

When he returned to the *Weekend Australian* in 1986, Evans was disappointed to discover that people thought the "zing" had gone from "Indulgence", so he moved from the back page and wrote the "Hunter Diary" column until 1990.

"I had a very happy association with the *Weekend Australian*," he says, "and I enjoyed writing for their readers, with whom I had a terrific relationship and a lot of fun."

After the "Cellarmaster" books, Len Evans' next published work on wine was the *Australia and New Zealand Complete Book on Wine*. First published in 1973, it was an original work of excellent quality and was reprinted a number of times. It is a large compendium-style volume, constructed around Evans' own tasting notes of hundreds of Australian wines and, today, it remains the best ongoing record of many. James Halliday regards it "a benchmark of the time which stood way ahead of anything else, tremendously influential and important".

Victorian wine personality, educator, wine judge and wine director of Rémy Australie, Colin Richardson, says that around the time Evans released the first edition of his book he was "bigger than Quo Vadis". "You could hardly escape him. Evans was being quoted on everything, on radio and television, and in print. If he said a wine was good, he made it. To get a good guernsey in that book was all you needed. It was the most comprehensively detailed book on wine I had ever seen."

Inside the copy he presented to John Beeston, Evans inscribed: "Beeston, I love you. This is the Bible now. Len."

Evans conscripted other wine people to contribute, including a terrified Anders Ousback, who clearly remembers the summons to Evans' office, where he was told: "I am doing a book on wine for Hamlyn. I want you to write a section on the care and service of wine."

"But I had low marks in English at school," said Ousback, "I didn't like English and I can't write."

"I need 5 000 words."

"I can't do it."

"I am not troubled if you think you can do it or not," Evans stated. "I would like you to do it and I need an outline by next week showing what you'll actually be writing."

"But Mr Evans…"

"Thank you, Ousback."

"I went through so much angst that week," remembers Ousback. "But from that article I was commissioned to write a column in *House and Garden* and so began writing. I never would have done so but for that, and always would have maintained the idea that I could not write." Since then, Anders Ousback has become a highly regarded wine writer, has published short stories and is currently working on a novel. Evans knew exactly what he was doing. Much of his legacy is found in the people he has encouraged, pushed or bludgeoned into realising their own capabilities.

There have now been five editions of Evans' "big book", the last appearing in 1990 and titled *Len Evans' Complete Book of Australian Wine*. All together they have sold around 170 000 copies. John Parkinson, part of whose responsibilities at Bulletin Place involved researching Evans' columns and books, was heavily involved in the preparation of the second edition, which he largely compiled under Evans' direction.

His publishers talked and effectively pushed Evans into the publication of that final edition, itself a total re-write by other writers under Evans' editorship.

What of the modern brand of wine writing? Evans is not much impressed, but doesn't entirely blame the writers themselves. "There isn't much editorial encouragement for wine writing today, but there is a great deal of incest in the wine-writing industry. Most of them write for themselves," he observes.

What Evans finds missing in modern wine writing is the expression of the essential joy of wine, the sort of enthusiasm he so effectively and infectiously transmitted through "Cellarmaster" and "Indulgence". One highly proficient wine writer was once told by Evans that he was "plain bloody awful". "You are writing like a scientist," Evans told him. "You're too clinical. Enthuse more, tell them what a great drink it is." Valuable advice, and it made its point.

"Not a lot of wine writers today are good writers, and there aren't enough people around wine with lots of fun or a lot of wit in them," he says. "But we do have the best information being knocked around by certain writers, by Halliday in particular."

"James Halliday is a very good friend of mine and a fine chap. He has done well at Coldstream Hills because he's a very good winemaker with certain wines. He has made a very big thing of entering shows and he's won a lot of gold medals, but his contribution to Australia is easily greatest in the areas of wine writing and research. He is clearly the most important wine writer in Australia today."

Evans believes that too much time is spent acknowledging the wine industry's so-called leaders and great characters, without enough real assessment and opinion. And he thoroughly deplores the popularistic style of "I got pissed yesterday" wine journalism.

"The English are still the best wine writers. Cyril Ray is a fantastic writer on wine. Auberon Waugh is a very good writer. I don't think he's a wine writer, but he's a fine writer with very good feeling. Oz Clark, Robert Joseph, Jancis Robinson, Jane McQuitty and Anthony Rose are very good and of course, Hugh Johnson and Michael Broadbent have written some of the most important books on wine in English or any language. It's a shame we haven't got more of them."

How is Len Evans regarded by his peers? Melbourne writer, Keith Dunstan, whose skills and experience have taken him to the very top of the journalistic tree, says the quality of Evans' journalism was invariably excellent. "Len is a very imaginative and funny writer. As you can see from *Cellarmaster Says*, it still stands up as good stuff to read even now."

In his early days, Evans would dress up the McLaren Vale winery of d'Arenberg in print from time to time. Its wines also won a number of show awards and as a consequence, just walked out the door. In a *Bulletin* piece I find typically amusing, Evans says he once observed that the winemaker, d'Arry Osborne, was inclined towards formality during vintage. "He wears his old dress shirts as wine-making gear and this is said to give elegance to his reds."

At the time, Evans didn't see himself so much as an educator, but more as an instigator. "I was so enthusiastic about the product, and I wanted everyone else to know about it," he says. "Mine was all a fairly all-up-front, enthusiastic, gushy style of writing. I think I became a better and tighter writer later on. I believe in enthusiasm. I don't think for years that I felt other than that I was sharing some of my enthusiasm with a whole lot of other people."

Colin Richardson says that no one since has had anywhere near the clout Len Evans had in the early 1970s when wine consumption was rocketing. "He was the ideal man in the right place, at the right time."

"He has certainly been the most influential man in the game, in his writing and his personal contacts," echoes Dan Murphy, himself an early Australian wine writer who started a weekly column in Melbourne's *Age* newspaper in 1967. "He's probably the best writer we had, with an incredible ability to make things interesting." According to James Halliday, Evans towers over every other writer since the mid 1960s. "He is head and shoulders in front of anyone else and has always been able to write extremely well." Keith Dunstan reflects that Evans wouldn't merely suggest you ever bought anything, but he had a way of forcing you to do things he recommended.

Evans was not only the first to tell people about wine, but to let them know they could enjoy it. It was his style, described by John Beeston as "racy but never Ocker", that enabled Evans to communicate to suchwide-ranging audience.

Halliday believes Evans had several tiers of reader and that the broadness of his approach and reach was quite exceptional. Some, he suggests, were people who didn't really want to learn about wine, but who were amused by his stories and the way he presented it; others were occasional drinkers who suddenly had their attention caught; then there were serious learners who hung on every word; and finally the complete wine experts who used him as a yardstick for their own opinions.

Halliday stands up Evans' wine columns as the four-minute mile of wine writing – someone had to be the catalyst, to show it could be done. "He has set the pace and the standards. For others to survive or flourish they have needed to do as well." Brian Croser believes Evans to be technically the best wine writer Australia has ever had. "He is a man of opinion. His use of language is the best there is and his personality shines through. It's a shame he is not writing more now." Former editor of the *Wine and Spirit Buying Guide*, John Parkinson agrees, saying that no one has had his finger on the pulse of Australian wine to quite the same degree.

I have yet to read writings on wine by anyone else which so effortlessly move from reference to fact to opinion to description to conclusion, all with a style and flow of which most writers would be deeply envious. If I was told to read a selection of wine literature I would make sure a healthy percentage wore his byline.

Len Evans has earned the right to give his opinions. Speaking as a wine writer who has studied wine making and contributed hundreds of wine articles over seven years, I am certain that he, unlike far too many who attempt it, has the right to deliver any opinion he wants to about wine, wine people or wine institutions. He knows it better than anyone else I have met and I rest easy with the integrity of what he says.

The impact of nearly three decades of Len Evans' participation in the wine and food media is both phenomenal and ongoing. His occasional contributions today, written only when the mood takes him and when moved by a particular issue he feels compelled to address, reveal what the Australian wine reader has missed since he chose to discontinue his regular serious wine comment.

"He created the genre, the expectation, the general ambience which has seen more written in Australia per capita and per newspaper spread than in any other country in the world," James Halliday acknowledges. "That is part of the reason why

Evans, Mick Morris (centre) and John Stanford on a Wine Press Club weekend in Rutherglen, May 1980.

the average Australian wine consumer knows one hell of a lot more about wine than the average American, the average European, most certainly the average French and, possibly, the average English wine consumer too."

Nick Bulleid says there's no doubt that Evans paved the way for every subsequent wine writer. "When he started, wine was what poofters or deros drank from paper bags. Evans helped change the attitude. He probably did as much for wine writing in the "Indulgence" column in the *Weekend Australian* by just talking about wine in a convivial setting and telling us how good it was to drink. He would talk about wine as part of a memorable occasion, but would never forget it's only a drink; even if it was a '45 Mouton."

Len Evans considers the thirty years since he began writing about wine the most exciting time of change in any industry in the world. "Thirty years ago," he recalls, "Australia was steak, eggs and bread and butter, or perhaps a filet mignon with a glass of porphyry sauternes or a glass of beer in one of the better restaurants."

One day Evans was in McLaren Vale, a South Australian wine township when, at 1.32 p.m. precisely, he went into the pub for lunch. Immediately he was told, "Lunch is off".

He protested, "But people are still eating."

"Lunch is off. It finished at 1.30 p.m."

More protestations: "Surely you have some food – perhaps a salad or something?"

Eventually Evans conceded defeat and wandered off down McLaren Vale's main street for a cold pie and a warm Coca Cola. While sitting on the kerb he penned a story about it.

When, some time afterwards, "The Barn", McLaren Vale's fine restaurant applied for its licence, its owners used Evans' article to prove there was a need for it. Today, Evans smiles proudly and states that one can now eat very well in Coonawara, McLaren Vale and the Hunter Valley, each of them once virtually bereft of civilised dining.

"There's no doubt that Melburnians were ahead of the Sydneysiders in their eating and drinking," he believes. "The change since those days has been incredible. Sydney's first really continental restaurant was only opened in 1956. Now there are hundreds and thousands of them."

As Australian food became more diverse and interesting, so did its wine. Today, there are around 10 000 different wines made each year in Australia, still a mere fraction of the world's output, but an incredible increase nevertheless. To identify a well-made wine from the popular varieties down to its vineyard and vintage year now takes an unbelievable degree of skill and a far greater proportion of pure luck.

During a television appearance Evans made in the early 1960s, the presenters revealed five masked wines, including a Hamiltons Ewell Moselle, Houghtons White Burgundy, Lindemans Cawarra Claret and a Penfolds Dalwood Hermitage. To the amazement of those with him, he picked every wine. "But there were only a few dozen table wines around in those days," he says. "There is no way in the world you could do that today." Remember that the next time you're put on the spot at the Beefsteak and Burgundy Club!

Such was the momentum behind Australia's push for more and better wine that, in 1968, Evans predicted a shortage of the sort of Australian wine that would interest the readers of his *Bulletin* column, forecasting an increase in the consumption of imported wine in response. The prices of local wines were rising and the red wine boom was devouring wines barely weeks after their release. The personal cellar trend, in which everyone was expected to have their own wine collection, was in full swing.

The wine media, Evans in particular, wielded enormous power in those times. He remembers the aftermath of an article he wrote about d'Arry Osborne. Not only did it sell out all the wine he had written about, but it almost sold out the Osborne's entire supply of bottled red wine stocks.

"Halliday can still sell out a wine, more or less," he says. "But he can also push a wine like he did a Rothbury semillon, give it an enormous plug and not sell a case."

There are constant dangers associated with recommending wines, especially to those you know. When visiting the cellar of a serious wine-student friend and having tasted a number of Spanish and Australian wines, Evans noticed a pile of a particular white in the corner. He questioned how his friend could possibly get through all those bottles, especially since the wine had well begun losing its freshness and delicacy, possibly even becoming flat and coarse.

His host exploded: "But you recommended it! You said you liked it, so I bought twenty dozen. You should do something about it. Why don't you also tell us how much to buy?"

Evans: "Ye gods, the responsibility…"

Another danger, Evans discovered, was to omit the occasional elementary fact. One time he was enjoying a cold beer when "a *Bulletin* reader with a dry red eye" confronted him with the news that a red wine he had recommended had gone off.

"I closed my eyes," said Evans, "the better not to see him with." Yes, he was told. This reader had bought a bottle but now it was full of "stuff".

"Sir," said Evans. "That was probably the crust. Didn't you try it?" "How could I," came the reply, "with all that muck in it?"

It turned out that the wine had thrown a crust in response to storage in Tasmania's bracing climate. Evans was almost too ashamed to repeat the story to his readers in the *Bulletin*: "I have never written about crusts because I assumed you knew all," he confessed, before delivering a concise explanation and a lesson in decanting.

Whereas he has been only too pleased to help those he admires, Len Evans has always felt uncomfortable with the critic's ability to destroy the livelihoods of wine makers and restaurants. "For whatever reasons, if a bad restaurant still attracts a set of customers, no one has the right to destroy its business. Perhaps its customers are equally as bad."

Writing in his "Fare Thee Well" column in the *Sunday Mirror*, Evans once delivered a scathing review of a restaurant in Bondi Road, but believing he was doing the right thing by the restaurant, deliberately omitted its name from his article, merely saying what street it was found in.

"It was a catastrophic evening the day I dined there. I couldn't believe it when afterwards I found out what had happened. The owner had found his Maitre d' making love to his wife and so had gone at them with a cleaver, seriously wounding them both. He then killed himself.

"For some reason, or else because they had no idea what had actually happened, the staff still opened the restaurant that night, with the second cook as Maitre d' and the third cook as someone else. It was a total disaster."

Weeks later, he received a letter from a restaurateur, writing on behalf of four restaurants on Bondi Road whose trade had shrunk by over half since the publication of Evans' article in the *Sunday Mirror*. The letter asked him to name which restaurant he had reviewed, and what, as a group, they could possibly do to get things back to normal.

"I then realised with horror that by not mentioning the name of the restaurant, I had destroyed all their livelihoods. So I had to go to each of these four fairly indifferent bloody restaurants and do a flattering review on Bondi Road restaurants, in which I had to praise them well beyond their worth to get their trade back," he says.

"So I don't think critics should play God. It is not the job of the writer to demand change. The writer is a fairly insignificant person today and is far more interested in this kind of hypothesis than the public. The public are the people who run the wine industry."

In Len Evans' opinion, the court case of leading Sydney food critic and publicist Leo Schofield concerning one of his restaurant reviews, had more to do with Schofield's actual style of writing than the precise nature of his criticism. "I call Leo's the 'baroque' school of food writing, versus my berocca style of wine writing. Leo is a great bloke who has done a power of good for Sydney."

"Of course I've felt compelled to criticise things from time to time, such as the practice of using foreign names on wines and not serving wine in the air. But although it doesn't make reputations as easily, it's much more difficult being a nice critic. It's far harder to establish your credibility by taking the 'pro' course and not panning somebody. Knocking is so easy."

When assessing Evans' credibility over his thirty years as a critic it would be foolish to ignore those who claim his involvement in his own wine interests – principally Rothbury and Petaluma – sufficiently coloured his written opinions, to whatever degree his critics are motivated through fact, prejudice or jealousy. As I have previously suggested, you don't get as big as Len Evans in a small, introverted industry without attracting an inevitable degree of criticism, some of it extremely well delivered. Incidentally, as far as Evans is concerned, this criticism is entirely ineffective, since the only yardstick by which he judges his own performance is his own, and possibly that of his closest friends.

Peter Doyle, who numbers as one of his best friends, says the one thing Evans never did was to plug his own wines, unlike a number of other wine writers who would almost appear to be under contract to certain wine companies. "Len never ever promoted his own," says Doyle. "I told him he was the worst wine writer in the world for not doing it, but he promoted everyone else's. That's the sort of genuine writing he did."

Peter Doyle is not the first person involved in the wine and food industry to suspect that most wine writers have some form of hidden agenda.

Not to dismiss the issue, Evans continues to have his critics. Tongue in cheek, he was once awarded the *Wine and Spirit Buying Guide*'s "Most Unpredictable Advice Award", for recommending a Rothbury Estate Individual Paddock wine for being "one of the best wines around".

More pertinent is Brian Croser's view. "Evans is brutally honest. He has never written up a Petaluma wine when it has not been good. He writes about the companies that are doing things – but to an extent most of the people who are doing things in this industry are his friends anyway, although of course there are others who are that he hasn't written so much about. If that's bias, that's bias."

Discussing any possible bias in Evans' writing, Colin Richardson says it's an easy criticism to make, which could be levelled at anyone. "I don't believe either that Halliday just writes about the Yarra Valley, or that Dan Murphy only ever wrote about the wines he was selling. It's just not true. I don't know what motivates those who suggest it."

Biased or not, there is no doubt that by championing whatever Australian brand he has chosen to oversee, Evans has helped to pave the way for the rest.

Peter Lehmann, one of the best-known figures of the Barossa Valley, once confronted Evans, saying: "Christ, you push the Hunter!"

In reply, Evans asked: "Do you do anything but push the Barossa?"

Lehmann: "But you're different!"

"Why should I be any different?" Evans asks. "I am nowhere near as involved in the Hunter Valley as someone like Murray Tyrrell is; I never have been. I have been interested in other wine areas as well."

That's not entirely fair. He is Len Evans, and the point behind this book is that he occupies a unique place in Australian wine. And for anyone still in doubt, I am one of many who have witnessed him being brutally critical of the Hunter Valley and his own wine.

At the end of the day it is rather simple. If you trust Len Evans, have bought the wines he has recommended, absorbed from him a conception of what quality in wine really signifies, and have simply been entertained by the man, consider yourself fortunate. You will have enjoyed many a good bottle, come to appreciate something others regard as intangible, and you will have laughed yourself hoarse. No other single person could have done that for you.

The
*I*ndulgence Factor

I have been just saturated with fine wine in a single meal.
L. P. E.

*L*en Evans has no peer as the master of the grand wine occasion. No innovation of his was grander than the Single Bottle Club, which works a little like a mathematical equation: mix one measure of Evans' obsession to drink the best of the best wine ever made with superlative food; two parts his passion to do things on an unprecedented scale; three parts his fanatical impatience to extract the utmost out of every moment and four parts his generosity and insistence on doing the very greatest, most indulgent things imaginable in the company of his friends; divide it by the number of half-glasses you can extract from a very old and ullaged bottle of wine, and you instantly arrive at the formula for the Single Bottle Club.

The dinner which is now understood to have launched the Single Bottle Club took place on 4 February 1977 in the Tasting Room at Bulletin Place, in honour of famous English wine màn, Michael Broadbent. The twelve present were Murray Tyrrell, Simon Seward, Ray Healy, Max Lake, Rudy Komon, Peter Fox, James Halliday, Hermann Schneider, Dan Murphy, Michael Broadbent, Malcolm Fraser and Len Evans. The wine stewards for the occasion were two Evans protégés, Anders Ousback and John Parkinson. You can see for yourself why I have reproduced the menu and wine list.

Menu		
Turtle Soup	Very Dry Oloroso	1796
Sand Crab	Le Montrachet (Domaine de la Romanée-Conti)	1972
Tahmoor Quails	Clos de la Roche (Barolet)	1921

Beef Medallions with Truffles	Château Haut-Brion	1929
Raspberry Soufflé	Vouvray Liquoreux (Marc Bedif)	1921
	Château d'Yquem	1921
Nuts and Muscatels	Quinta do Noval	1931
	Seppeltsfield	1878

Old Wines Tasting

Rudesheimer Apostelwein	1727
Château Villemaurine	1898
Château Ausone	1894
Château Lafite	1893
Château Peyrabon	1878
Château Lafite	1874
Sunbury Hermitage	1872
Château Gruaud Larose	1825
Château d'Yquem	1888

A snapshot over the shoulders of wine steward Anders Ousback (standing upright) of the 1977 dinner. At left Peter Fox has his head turned towards the camera, Max Lake is partly obscured by the candlestick, Michael Broadbent is at his left, Malcolm Fraser is taking a sniff and Len Evans is taking time out.

I just cannot imagine what it would be like to drink 1 591 years of wine at a single dinner. Yet at this dinner it was nearly only 1 341.

Wine Steward Ousback, who would have done anything to be present that night, was for some years a self-confessed extremely clumsy person. He well remembers Evans' build-up as he introduced the evening's star, the 250-year-old German half-bottle.

"We are now going to open the 1727 Rudesheimer Apostelwein. This is the great wine from the Bremer Ratskeller..." he barked on as Ousback slowly drew the cork. "And now Ousback is opening the 1727 Rudesheimer Apostelwein..."

At the news of this climactical announcement, a man standing with his back to the tasting table suddenly turned around, his coat catching one of the tasting glasses, knocking it over, and shattering it noisily on the tiled floor. At this loud, theatrical moment everyone's eyes turned instantly to Ousback, all anxiously anticipating disaster.

The only one in the room to know the wine was safe, for he had only just finished decanting it, Ousback spoke to his hushed audience: "Oh I say, shall we open up the 1728?"

"It just seemed like a line at the time," he says today. Legend now has it that Anders Ousback deliberately dropped an empty bottle to create the effect, but as usual, the truth is funnier.

One of the consequences of the first Single Bottle Club dinner was that Evans was publicly criticised for paying around $450 each for some of the bottles of wine he opened that night. Rising valiantly to his own defence in the *Bulletin*, he wrote: "Pay $450 for a bottle of wine! The man must be mad. Probably, but it's my money, and I don't criticise the gamblers and the questers for the Admiral's Cup and the racehorse owners and the status seekers, all of whom, to me, spend their money other than I would. But it's their business. I just wanted to taste the wine."

Another critical reaction to the early dinners was of its possibly sexist nature – no woman being present. At the time, in the late 1970s, Evans responded that there were no female palates in the country good enough to invite, although one feels that argument would no longer apply. To his knowledge, Single Bottle Club member Tony Albert says the issue of women has never been discussed, and the club has no stated policy, although men would naturally be less convivial and relaxed if women were also invited. "That would not stop us approaching one of the leading English women wine writers, should she be in town at the same time and should a vacancy be available," says Albert.

The Single Bottle Club gradually drifted away from the Tasting Room at Bulletin Place, the accepted and natural venue for its early dinners. For several years now, members other than Evans have taken the responsibility of hosting them, which involves provision of venue, food, theme and several great bottles, although Evans remains the major supplier of wines. One such host was Malcolm Fraser, Australian Prime Minister from 1975 to 1983, who held the 1982 Single Bottle Club dinner at The Lodge, the prime ministerial residence in Canberra.

Despite the effort and expense involved, there are so many potential hosts now eager to put on dinners that they have begun to share the hosting. Nearly every variation of the themes, constructed around the great wines of the world, has been attempted, invariably with phenomenal success.

"The group is always good," says Brian Croser. "Perhaps it lacks the joy it used to have and maybe it's a touch pompous, but perhaps that's required when people are paying their airfare and bringing along a treasure."

Such is the quality, age and breeding of the wines presented, that club member and celebrated Melbourne restaurateur Hermann Schneider now admits to a feeling of apprehension before the Single Bottle Club Dinners. "You could enjoy any one of these wines enough singly," he confesses. But is it overkill? Tony Albert doesn't think so, "not given the experience of the nucleus of the Single Bottle Club, who are very used to tasting great wine".

Perhaps the Single Bottle Club will run out of inspiration, finally exhausting its possibilities. I hope not. Its dinners represent the pinnacle that a love for wine could lead you towards, even if their scale and impact are hard to imagine. Perhaps being a member is like being part of the Australian cricket team – one needs that sort of level to aspire to. Besides, to be perfectly frank, I would love to attend one! Who wouldn't?

Of course the essential driving force is again the spirit of Len Evans. Could it live beyond him? Much as those who have participated in them may wish otherwise, it is empirically certain that Len Evans' birthday parties will not. Evans has always made something of his birthday, but typical of the man, in a spirit of extraordinary generosity.

Anders Ousback was first exposed to this phenomenon while working at Bulletin Place. Summoned again into the office, Ousback was pinned down again by his employer to see that all was under control for his birthday celebrations the following week. He meekly suggested that perhaps it was a trifle presumptious to think that things weren't already being done, to which Evans quickly snapped: "The birthday isn't for me, it's for you lot."

Evans' open admiration of Napoleon as a great leader and legislator is no secret. Both were, or in Evans' case, are, small people, something not wasted on those who know and respect Evans the most.

For several years the Tasting Room was entirely without decoration until Tony Albert returned from France saying to Evans, "I have with me a lithograph. You can't have it unless you put it into the Tasting Room."

It was the famous Edwardian portrait in which Napoleon sits, staring gloomily into the sun. Evans welcomed it, and so it hung by itself in the Tasting Room for at least two years, facing Evans as he looked down his table.

On one occasion Evans went away for several weeks prior to his birthday. Taking advantage of his absence, Anders Ousback organised a photographer to super-impose a press shot of Evans' own head, taken with just the right sort of quirky expression, onto a photograph of the original lithograph. The result, which looks almost genuine, was substituted for the original on the Tasting Room wall on the day of Evans' birthday, directly in front of the spot from which Evans would address the throng that luncheon.

Everyone knew about it except Evans, and when he rose for his speech of thanks, the picture was very much in his line of vision. Right in the middle of speaking, he glanced at it twice, went back to the speech, looked up again, decided he couldn't go on and emitted a short, sharp expletive of the most unprintable kind.

The room exploded into laughter. So too did Evans, once he saw the joke.

For those of us whose birthday lasts merely a single day, it is perhaps difficult to comprehend how Evans' fiftieth could take the form of a three-day festival, for which it was expected that invitees would take holidays from work. Evans was instructed by a Bulletin Place employee: "You're not going anywhere for these three days unless I'm behind the wheel."

Day one celebrations included two black tie parties at Bulletin Place conducted by Sally Cleaver.

Day two was courtesy of Peter Doyle, and it nearly killed him. "I supplied a picnic on the water over at St George's beach," he says. Evans was shipped there by his friends on board Alan David's junk and Doyle's brief was to supply the seafood.

In the early 1980s, it was a trend for the wine companies in Sydney to hire at least one very attractive lady as part of their sales team. These ladies began an informal group known as "Ladies of the Vine". Doyle hired an old-fashioned sailing yacht and invited around twenty of these women for the voyage, all to be dressed in particularly flimsy, scanty pirate uniforms and armed to the hilt with bunches of gladioli. Then he set sail with his leggy band of buccaneers hidden below.

Doyle takes up the story. "Evans was sitting majestically up on the for'ard of his boat, drinking champagne and watching this old yacht bear down on him. The old yacht kept on bearing down, with Len now standing up and waving, calling 'This way!'

"We came up alongside and the girls burst out from below in their costumes, throwing garlands of flowers all over him. It was a debauched afternoon. The only thing that saved it was the Single Bottle Club Dinner that night."

That dinner, discussed at more length in the chapter "Len Evans on Wine", included the 1646 Tokay, the oldest wine Evans has ever drunk. It was expected that Doyle and others would front respectfully and healthily for this wine and the memorable bottles of 1909 Coonawarra and 1872 Craiglee Claret from Sunbury in Victoria which were also opened that night.

"I remember drinking six hundred years of wine and refusing to have a pee," Doyle recalls.

Day three began with an airlift by helicopter to Berowra Waters Restaurant, where Gay and Tony Bilson put on lunch. "I didn't go," Peter Doyle confesses. "I was too bloody sick." Helicopters then ferried the guests back to Darling Harbour, where boats took them out for a picnic on Sydney Harbour.

The grand finale was a Chateau Petrus dinner and tasting that night, which covered all the great years from 1943 to 1975, including the outstanding years of '45, '47, '48 and '49. One of the wines required for the dinner was the 1955 vintage, ultimately unearthed in England by Anders Ousback.

Ousback had written to Evans saying that although he knew the requirement was for two bottles, he had nevertheless found an Imperial, the single equivalent of eight. Evans pondered the problem, but Tony Albert offered a solution: "I think you had better buy it whatever the cost. We shall need a drinking wine in the middle of dinner."

Evans' sixtieth birthday took place in the Hunter Valley, at "Loggerheads" and Rothbury, losing nothing by comparison with that of a decade before. It was a

Rabelaisian weekend, beginning on the Friday night with the 1990 Single Bottle Club Dinner.

Guests and their partners, a party of about one hundred, had been instructed to dress in Edwardian style for the following day's sports – croquet, golf, half-tennis and petanque, all played on the lawns at "Loggerheads" and on its adjoining short golf course. Participation was mandatory, but guests were also distracted by an endless variety of live music, from Scottish bands to jazz groups and choirs. At one point, the entire Hunter Valley Hunt stormed through for a salute – horses, bugles, beagles, red jackets and all.

Bollinger flowed ex magnum morning, noon and night, and throughout a grand ball in Rothbury's Great Cask Hall, complete with a 19-piece ensemble. An incredible and ever-changing buffet presented seafood, then many roasted meats, and finally fruits and cheeses.

Things continued apace on Sunday, finals day, when the many sporting trophies were hotly contested. Highlights were a fly-over by sky-writing biplanes and a cameo performance by the French's Forest Big Band.

Although they were not strictly wine-related events, it would be remiss not to describe the famous Christmas parties thrown by the Evanses at their Greenwich home throughout the 1970s. Christmas parties were another very big thing with the Evans family. Once you were invited, that was it; guests were never issued a second invitation, but regardless of how they felt after their own Christmas luncheon, were expected to attend come hell or high water.

The younger Evans generation would dispense champagne until the guests, numbering about two hundred, had arrived. The night's highlight was invariably the floor show staged by Len and Trish Evans, herself a singer of some note, with outstanding support from Bob and Jan Oxenbould, John and Roslyn Rourke.

Dressed fancily in feathered hats and boas, the ladies would make a grand entrance down the staircase. The show would start around 11 p.m. or midnight and last for an hour, brilliantly and hilariously sending up whatever was topical at the time. "We wrote them ourselves, and some were actually pretty good," admits Bob Oxenbould. Everyone I've spoken to agrees.

At its conclusion, the entire gathering would join their voices, always nostalgically ending with "Land of Hope and Glory" and almost taking the roof off. Much the merrier, guests would begin to leave around 4 or 5 a.m., already impatient for next Christmas.

Once they were relocated in Bulletin Place, the Christmas parties went up a notch in scale. "Evans would bring in live sheep," says Peter Doyle, "or camels the following year. They were great parties, but drove his staff mad. If he told them that he wanted an elephant out the front for this year, they had to get an elephant. It didn't matter how difficult it was."

Those Bulletin Place parties, suggests Bob Oxenbould, were a direct extension of the amazing Evans creations at the Chevron's Silver Spade, which he had virtually managed to turn into his own personal restaurant. "He would save all the chipped wine glasses throughout the year for Christmas day so, after the toast, everyone could stand up and smash their glass upon the floor. We were then stranded in a sea of broken glass, completely terrified we would fall over."

Playing
*P*oker with Wine

Wine should never be taken too seriously.
L. P. E.

*I*t was only natural that Len Evans would turn his competitive instincts to wine, although many outsiders wrongly perceive the Monday Table, which began at Bulletin Place in 1969, as a serious institution. Noses and palates have been put out of joint for centuries as people come unstuck playing guessing games with wine. But in the manner to which you are probably becoming accustomed, Evans took the concept of guessing a wine's identity to a new dimension, refashioning the wine options game to his own improbable scale.

Today there is even a board game version of wine options. Evans has also refined a mass options game to the extent that he can simultaneously challenge two thousand wine-crazed Americans at the New York Wine Experience to correctly guess, with a little suggestive leading from himself as master of ceremonies, the puzzling identity of the mystery wine in front of them.

Len Evans was not singly responsible for the evolution of the Options Game, although it would never have occured without him. There came to be three regulars who joined Evans at the Monday Table; Tony Albert, who met Evans in 1966 at a Chevron Fine Wine Auction; James Halliday, who was friendly with Albert from college and university days; and John Beeston, whose capacity to lunch there has become the stuff of legend. Neville Baker, another habitual client of Bulletin Place, occasionally became a fifth member of what people came to recognise as the "Bulletin Place Front Row".

Tony Albert puts it slightly differently: "We were the front row; Evans the Captain and all the other positions."

"In its purest form the Options Game is a rarefied form of oenological poker," James Halliday explains, "at its lowest, an undisciplined and noisy rabble vitriolically criticising the chairman's [Len Evans'] rulings on the admissibility of questions, while in the next breath turning on the wine so lovingly [albeit deviously] brought by another of the school."

"It was basically a very irreverent and crazy game," says Albert. "No reverence was shown towards Evans or each other. "We would regularly insult the others and never take the thing too seriously."

Over a period of time, as the participants came to know backwards the contents of one another's cellars, and as they became increasingly capable, the competition inevitably became more hard-fought. Also, as James Halliday's profile in the wine media evolved to greater proportions, the friendly rivalry between him and Evans became more obvious. But it never became an issue, says Tony Albert, who as an ex-officio arbitrator, made sure the game didn't become too grave and retained its sense of humour.

So how did an Options Game at the Monday Table proceed? Each participant had his own pigeon-hole down in Bulletin Place's cellar and would deftly secret masked bottles into it, often weeks before the particular event. To prohibit the bottle's shape from becoming a variable in the guesswork, and since many of the wines had thrown a sediment, they were all decanted into identical bottles, each engraved with a player's initials.

Each player started with $4 in 20¢ pieces, which Evans would collect in bundles from the bank. A coin was surrendered to the kitty for every question wrongly answered, the winner at the end of the game being the one with the most coins still in possession. The losing 20c pieces were invested in Opera House Lottery tickets.

In the early days there were barely any rules governing the questions. Halliday remembers that he and Evans would begin by asking outrageous questions, such as "was the 1875 vintage of this wine served to Bismark on a certain occasion?" the results of the most esoteric, yet industrious research.

Those determined as non-palate questions were eventually outlawed. Halliday says that every question must have been "capable of being answered on the basis of taste alone, on the completely invalid assumption that we have perfect memory recall and total knowledge of every wine ever made in the world".

For quite some time, there was no limit placed on the number of questions that could be asked per wine, resulting in embarrassing, if not quite volatile moments, especially as wines from the nineteenth century would not infrequently appear at the table.

Halliday recalls that, in 1969, Evans produced a dark brown-green, unctuous and incredibly explosive sticky riesling. His first question was, "Is this wine younger or older that 1875?" They pondered it, some saying younger, some saying older. Those saying younger were correct. "Is this wine older or younger than 1880?" he then asked. "Poker comes immediately to the fore quite apart from anything else," says Halliday, "and we all said it's older."

"No," said Evans. "It's younger."

They went on in five-year progressions until the wine was ultimately pinpointed to its correct vintage, 1959, by which time, beams Halliday, there was a huge pile of money on the table, and a look of extreme pain and anxiety on everyone's face!

This quickly led to another change of rules, limiting the questions to five and the adoption of the convention of no more than two vintage questions per wine.

A conventional game might go a little like this. The first question might relate to the wine's region or sub-region. For instance it might be asked of a red wine whether it was a Medoc, a Pomerol or a St Emilion, recognising that each person at the table would instantly pick it as a Bordeaux claret. The answer: a Medoc. Those who guessed otherwise would forfeit 20¢.

The next question might relate to the districts within the Medoc: is it a St-Julien, a Pauillac or a St-Estephe? A Pauillac. Then, a first-growth, second or less? A second. Then it has to be Pichon-Longueville-Baron or Pichon-Lalande, the only second-growths in Pauillac. Pichon-Lalande. Is it from 1947, 1948 or 1949? Answer: 1947.

The wines and the results of each were entered into a scoring book, which charted the history of the decade. A winner was nominated each Monday, and the Mondays were logged into series of ten, the cumulative score being carried from week to week. From the losers, the series winner received both a case of champagne and much indignation.

Making the games more interesting, the Monday Table then decided to introduce themes for each week, such as Bordeaux days, pre '45 first growth days, Burgundy days, Great Burgundy days, or old Australian days. The range of wines was quite remarkable; its standard, says Halliday, frankly astonishing. Realistically, the game could never be repeated today with wine of that quality. It is extraordinary that those four people who shared the same obsession for the best possible wine with the means to drink it, happened to be together around 1970–75, able to indulge at a time when wine prices would permit. The Australian dollar was particularly strong against sterling, with a fixed exchange rate of just $1.29 per pound. It was an extraordinary period, with first-growths from 1945 costing only $30–$40 each!

Halliday says the Options Game often brought to the surface the roguish side of Len Evans. "We had one of these so-called 'great' days, which could be first-growth Bordeaux, Yquem, Romanée-Conti, Chambertin or that sort of thing.

"One time Evans brought along this Bordeaux and, after getting a couple of questions right, we all crashed dreadfully, because it turned out to be the 1962 Ducru Beaucaillou. We were at him like a rat up a drainpipe, because being a second-second-growth, it was clearly not a great wine.

"He defended his position to the hilt, pointing out that at the auctions of the time it was bringing in more than any other second-growth. Not first-growth prices, mind you.

"He said it was a very famous wine in London and everyone was talking about it. We regarded it as a deviate incident, and remembered it for years after."

There is a delightful story about Evans and two cases of red Burgundy and one of the world's very greatest wines, La Tâche, vintage 1948, which Evans, Halliday, Albert and Beeston had collectively bought at a Christies auction in London. They used Bulletin Place as a clearing house, from which the wines would then be divided. When the time came to collect the La Tâche, it simply wasn't there. "No one could work out what happened to it," says Halliday. "The fortunes of war," he shrugs.

"Evans had a habit of putting on Romanée-Contis at Options Games because I kept on getting them right," says Halliday, "down to the château, the property, the vineyard and the year – which sometimes I would get wrong. But the fact they were Romanée-Conti I would always get right, which would always get up his nose. With typical Welsh stubbornness he kept on producing Romanée-Contis and I would keep on getting them right."

About four years later, during an Options Game, up came '48 La Tâche, to the immediate and injured cries of "Evans, where did this bloody '48 La Tâche come from?"

Evans immediately feigned shock, horror, ignorance. "I promise you it just turned up. I really have no idea, etc. etc."

"About two months later," Halliday continues, "another wine comes up. I smell it and the questions go on. Half way through the game I say to Evans, 'Evans, this is not '48 La Tâche. It had better not be another bottle of '48 La Tâche'!"

"Sure enough, it was." Further cries of outrage, injury, theft, misappropriation. "Another couple of months go by," says Halliday. "Another wine comes up. It's the '48 La Tâche again! You bastard, Evans!" Then he said there was no more. "That's all I can ever find. If it is the stuff that went astray, you've shared it with me, and I haven't really taken it from you at all."

But there would always be another bottle. Even if it wasn't La Tâche, Halliday, Beeston and Albert would be tricked into thinking "Are you doing this to us again, Evans, or not?" "By the rules of the game," says Halliday, "while you are not allowed to deliberately deceive by intonation or subtle hints, he would of course put into my mind that it was '48 La Tâche when it wasn't. It could have been '49 La Tâche or some other DRC wine of around the same time which tasted similar. It became an absolute cause célèbre," Halliday says, "and he milked it for all it was worth, revelling in every moment."

Great efforts were made by all players to unearth wine of unlikely character or origins. Early on John Beeston caused tremendous consternation and annoyance by producing a second-picking Brown Brothers Graciano, made after one of the north-east Victorian frosts. Thereafter it was unanimously agreed that wine of that nature was ruled out, except for Deviates' Day, when anything was possible. Halliday once infiltrated a Fijian wine made from bananas, which led to another changing of the rules, which were eventually pretty well formalised by the mid 1970s.

Guests of a certain proficiency in wine were welcome to join the table. One was John Parkinson, who would spend hours contemplating the ideal Options Game wine. One day he left Sydney extremely early, drove like a demon to get to Tyrrells in the Hunter Valley and found there a very old Mount Pleasant wine blended from two different vintages. Rushing back just in time, he found himself in huge trouble later on – his wine was simply far too devious!

To give an idea of how devious Deviates' Day could actually be, James Halliday described the events of one such day in his *National Times* column, on 27 December 1981.

"Evans graciously admitted his wine was [as we all guessed] an Italian sweet wine from the north of Italy. Question one: 'Is it from Verona, Alto Adige or Friuli?' Friuli of course. Then followed agonised wonderings through unheard of appellations of Friuli leading to an 'easy' question four: 'Is the grape variety picolit, tocai or sauvignon?' Only Beeston, who has an encyclopaedic knowledge of matters devious, got it right. Albert and I, students of human nature, cursed ourselves for not following Beeston's lead and answering picolit.

"They made mincemeat of my cabernet-cinsault blend from Lebanon. All went to that well-known property Château Musar, stumbling briefly over the year (it was a '69). It served me right; I will have to go back to that Russian champagne I produced a couple of years ago."

On that day, Tony Albert produced one of the most extraordinary wines ever served at an Options Game and had the questions to match. According to Halliday, it went a little like this.

"Question 1: 'Does this wine come from on the first hand Bulgaria, Romania or Cyprus; on the second hand Turkey, Lebanon or Israel; and on the third hand Russia, China or Japan?' The middle group was correct.

"Question 2: 'Which?' Answer not, as we supposed Israel, but Turkey.

"Then into the nuts and bolts of the main Turkish viticultural districts. 'The Aegean Thrace or South East Anatolia?' Straws were clutched, coins tossed. Then to the jugular: 'Is the wine Buzbag, Trakya or Koroglu?' It was that well-known Turkish Buzbag."

Deviates' Day aside, the players became rather good, perhaps getting only one or two questions wrong all day. An average winning score out of twenty would tend to be four or five mistakes, with the worst performer having eleven to twelve mistakes. "We all had our golden moments," says Halliday.

Brian Croser regularly engages Evans and friend in Options Games and was present for several Monday Tables. "There were always a lot of inspired guesses," he says, "and more cellarmanship than was recognised. They knew one another's cellars and virtually controlled the importation of wine of extreme quality. If they didn't inspire the arrival of some wines, they smelled them out on arrival. Although it was somewhat restricted, tremendous ability was still required."

Croser remembers a period of around five years at Bulletin Place when Evans would bring out a magnum of Paul Jaboulet La Chapelle Hermitage 1961, the epitome of a great Rhône Valley red. "The first question he would ask was: 'Is this from the Hunter Valley, Coonawarra or the Rhône?' For five years straight James

Halliday and I always answered 'The Hunter'. He loved that; the idea that the great old Rhône could look like an old Hunter or an old Coonawarra."

Yet others would claim their revenge. Evans once picked a Mildara Hunter-Coonawarra blend of 1958 as a French claret. "The fact that I'd made the same mistake for the past five years didn't make it any better," he says, although he does remember the wine's maker, the celebrated wine judge Les Ekert doing precisely the same thing, much to his own embarrassment.

Hermann Schneider never really enjoyed the Options Game. "To me it was just poker," he says. "They all played together so many times and worked off each other."

Evans insisted that he organise a Melbourne team for a Test Match between Sydney and Melbourne, but Schneider always replied, "If you want a competitive wine tasting, fine, but not the way you play it."

In 1973, two or three years later, Evans' opportunity finally presented itself. Through Keith Dunstan's column, Peter Joyce, President of the Wine and Food Society of Victoria, challenged Evans saying later: "It is beyond dispute that the palates of the Wine and Food Society of Victoria are superior in every aspect to those of any other group, State or conglomeration of people."

The NSWOCGTVVV75 (the New South Wales Options Club Grand Tour Victorian Visit Vintage 1975) defeated at the hands of Victoria. Back row: John Beeston, James Halliday. Front row: Neville Baker, Len Evans, Tony Albert.

Triumphant, Evans rang through with the news. "Schneider, since you didn't have the guts, I have accepted a challenge. Peter Joyce has formed a team. The venue will be Two Faces Restaurant (owned by Hermann Schneider). I trust you and want you to collect the wines. I want a great dinner at the end of the night, loser pays all. But you know we can't lose."

Schneider said that if Evans wanted him to officiate, it would only be on the condition that all was to be done in writing, there were to be no vocal answers. "There was no chance to lead the witness by playing off each other, since they knew one another's strengths and weaknesses so well, and no collaboration," he says. "Otherwise the system was the same."

This was eventually agreed upon, much to Schneider's surprise, and he was promptly installed as Master of Ceremonies. He enlisted Doug Crittenden as referee, who would have been in the Victorian team had he not been recently discharged from hospital after a hernia operation, to help him select the wines and frame the questions.

The Sydney team was easy to select – the Bulletin Place Front Row, the options elite of James Halliday, John Beeston, Tony Albert and Neville Baker. Max Lake was appointed honorary team doctor. Pitted against them were Peter Joyce, Joe Sullivan, David Thomas, John Cunnington and Peter Walker. Bookmakers had the Sydney team firm favourites at 5-1.

Preparations could hardly have been more disparate. The Victorians were typically dour, diligent and abstemious, training sessions aside, taking the whole thing seriously and going early to bed. Confident the Victorians would be a complete pushover, the Sydney team trained themselves heavily before turning their journey to Melbourne into a grand drinking tour. Bottles of French Champagne were opened on their arrival at the Melbourne Hilton, where they stayed with Frank Christie, Evans himself luxuriantly ensconced in the Presidential Suite.

Come midday before the grand event, it was party time at the Presidential Suite, with a swanky buffet of champagne and caviar. By 3.30 p.m., when Hermann Schneider left the rowdy Sydneysiders to set up the restaurant, the beer was flowing and the poker just beginning.

The teams arrived at Two Faces at 7 p.m., the Victorians entering quietly and individually, smartly dressed in dinner suits. A Bentleigh limousine then pulled up noisily outside, and into the restaurant swaggered a very cheerful and cocky Sydney team, all attired in spangled Edwardian blazers with New South Wales waratah badges sown over their breast pockets. Underneath were the letters NSWOCGTVVV75, standing for the "New South Wales Options Club Grand Tour Victorian Visit Vintage 1975".

The teams were put to order, the substantial silver trophy bought by Hermann Schneider put on display, and the palates finally put to the test. The blind tasting included approximately a dozen wines.

"In those days there weren't many obscure Australian vineyards to choose from and any overseas styles had to be pretty authentic," says Doug Crittenden, "so everything was really pretty straightforward."

Nevertheless, some difficult wines were unearthed. For each question, cards were handed out, answers recorded, the cards handed back and correct answers read out.

Sydney lost on the first wine by four to one. By the third wine, once the possibility that they could actually get rolled began to dawn, their sweat was clearly visible. As Keith Dunstan observed, the match see-sawed all the way through, until they came to a mystery wine, which nobody could identify too well – Reg Egan's Wantirna Estate Cabernet Sauvignon, from the district of Wantirna South, located in one of Melbourne's outer suburbs.

Sydney lost by a whisker, 129 points to 125.

Evans was fuming: "We will never forget this, Crittenden!" and, using the analogy of Pearl Harbour, "We will remember Wantirna South! You have put up this cheap, nasty little suburban wine which we have never heard of – it's a perfect example of Victorian perfidy!"

To an extent he had a point, for while there were four Victorian wines in the tasting, there were none from the Hunter. "You wait till you come back to Sydney – we'll spring a Dubbo Cabernet, a Back O'Burke Shiraz and a Colloroy Chardonnay!"

Evans has never forgiven Hermann Schneider for the Wantirna Estate, yet the funny thing is that while he blamed it, Sydney did not actually lose on that wine! Actually, he has never forgiven anyone about it, not even the wine's creator, Reg Egan!

"It was probably one of his biggest defeats," says Schneider, who remembers that Evans was terribly bitter and Halliday had turned white. "Dinner was flat, an absolute fizzer." Keith Dunstan was one of the few who thought it hilarious.

The English, too, were taken by the revelry and nerve of a full-blooded Options Game. While in England, Evans was invited to dine with Michael Broadbent, who had made an Australian evening of it by also inviting Anders Ousback and Murray Tyrrell. The other two guests were Andrew and Mrs Lloyd-Webber. "We are going to have that Options Game you like to play," said Broadbent. "What do you think of that?" he grinned.

The first wine was poured. Murray Tyrrell was on Broadbent's left, so he began: "It's German."

Evans was next: "Mosel."

Ousback: "Bernkasteler."

Lloyd Webber: "Oh, so you think it's German, do you?"

Back to Tyrrell: "Bernkasteler Graben."

Evans: "Obviously '64."

Ousback: "Shipped by Tarnish."

Broadbent: "Blast!"

The second wine was poured. Murray Tyrrell: "Obviously a Pomerol."

Evans: "It has to be Petrus."

Ousback: "1964."

Bang! The second wine was out of the way. Australia was on a roll, England enjoying it less and less. It was even more infuriating for Broadbent because his three Australian guests were obviously entirely carefree in mood, constantly joking and laughing. Ousback has since admitted that they were also incredibly lucky, experiencing one of those rare streaks of fortune akin to a cricket batsman having two consecutive lives in the 'nineties. But Michael Broadbent wasn't to know.

Steeling his resolve, Broadbent then gritted his teeth: "You'll never get this," he said, a dead give-away on a masked wine, for you immediately know never to pick an obvious one.

Tyrrell began: "It's Pauillac."

Evans: "Lafite."

Now a pause, Ousback was painfully aware of his duty not to let the side down. "Well, yes it is Lafite."

"But you'll never guess the vintage," baited Broadbent, looking directly through Ousback.

Anders Ousback's birth year, 1951, was a rotten year in Bordeaux. It also happened to be the year that chapitalisation (the addition of sugar before the end of fermentation) was first allowed in the area, and he considered the wine reeked of added sugar, and was "pissy and thin".

Taking an absolute punt, Ousback: "'51."

Broadbent was furious. So annoyed in fact that he walked to the sideboard, came back with a brace of brimming decanters and plonked them on the table. "All right," he said. "Stuff you all. That is 1893 Musigny and that is 1882 Chambolle something or other."

Had the roles been reversed, Evans would have loved to see someone getting them all right upon right, thinks Ousback.

Vengeance was eventually Broadbent's for when, on another occasion, he invited Evans to dinner, the wines he chose for an Options Game were a Hanzell Chardonnay 1959 (from California), an Auvergnal Gris 1944 (try Hungary), a Château Musar 1974 (this time Lebanon) and a Bussaco Tinto Reserva Especial 1945 (Portuguese, obviously), a wine only ever sold from the hotel attached to the vineyard. Evans says it cost him $14 in 20¢ pieces.

The beauty about the Options Game, especially when played on a grand scale, is that anyone can win, regardless of their wine knowledge or palate, provided of course they are neither colour-blind nor possessed of a palate awaiting a transplant.

The dinner to launch the Hunter Valley Wine Week at Melbourne's former Dorchester Restaurant was attended by an audience of wine people and politicians, including the then Australian Prime Minister, Malcolm Fraser, and also Tony Street, then Minister for Industrial Affairs, plus their spouses. Messrs Fraser and Street both fancied themselves a little at the steering end of a glass of wine.

As he was wont to do, Evans conducted an Options Game at the dinner's conclusion, at which neither of the two politicians distinguished themselves. Neither did Murray Tyrrell, James Halliday, Dan Murphy, Colin Richardson, writer Robin Bradley nor winemaker John Ellis.

"The winner of the second game, who answered correctly every question about a Saltram Eden Valley Cabernet Shiraz of 1971," says Evans, "was the First Lady, Mrs Tammy Fraser." How Evans quite managed that result is still beyond Colin Richardson, for although it was never made obvious, he is convinced from the moment the game began that Tammy Fraser was destined to win.

That, ladies and gentlemen, is the genius, the style and the humour of Leonard Paul Evans.

The Grand Vision

Long before he had the means to do it, Len Evans had publicly trumpeted his ambition to control a wine company of the highest quality which spanned three continents — something which had never been done before. His friend and financier, Peter Fox, had the money to fund the grand vision and the will to spend it.

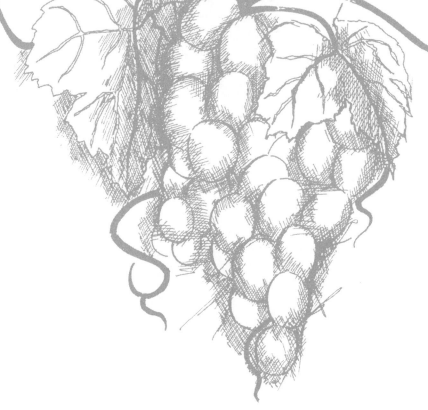

The
*D*ream of Rothbury Estate

It's ironic, I suppose, to be so proud of a company that has
yet to recover its losses, yet I could not be more so.
L. P. E.

Rothbury Estate is Len Evans' own progeny, a Hunter Valley based winery founded according to classically grandiose Evans concepts and ideals. For the first time since its initiation in 1968, it is now financially secure, a major achievement in itself. Its story is unlike that of any other Australian wine enterprise.

In 1968, Murray Tyrrell had the idea of subdividing part of his excess land in the Hunter Valley to encourage small private syndicates to establish their own vineyards. He should have realised that by discussing it with Len Evans, the concept would mushroom.

Less than a year later, Rothbury Estate, the most visionary, idealistic and grandest project of its kind ever seen in the Hunter Valley, was up and running with Evans as its Chairman, Murray Tyrrell its Vineyard Manager and Gerry Sissingh, lured away from Lindemans, its winemaker.

The original Tyrrell concept was to attract an army of qualified professionals, skilled in areas other than wine, by offering a combination of tax advantages and the aura of the "wine lifestyle". It would also guarantee the Tyrrells Winery an additional source of grapes.

However, the Evans dream for Rothbury extended at least two dimensions beyond anything Tyrrell or anyone else in Australia for that matter, had yet conceived. The grand Rothbury vision was to make a single estate red and a single white wine, from shiraz and semillon; grown, made and bottled at Rothbury, whose name alone the wines would wear. There were to be no varietal names on the label, no "white burgundies" or "hermitages"; just "Rothbury Estate" plus the vintage year. Rothbury would not even make or sell a sherry, then still the biggest-selling wine in Australia, becoming the Hunter's first winery not to do so.

Rothbury didn't need to sell its wine through retailers, they thought. Evans never had much time for the wine retail industry, believing it took out more than it put back. Rothbury would instead deal directly with the public, initiating its own club and tasting society.

In addition, Rothbury would become the crossroads where wine and those who celebrated it would meet. It would emphasise purity and pleasure, charting its own way where no winery had gone before. It was wine's very own Starship USS Enterprise, with Captain Len Evans at the helm.

Alongside Evans and Tyrrell, the original founders of Rothbury Estate were Dr Alan Burgess, Dr John Burgess, Peter Davidson, Alan Grainger, Ted Gowing, Rudy Komon, John McDowell, Frank Mills and Bob Sanders, an assortment of accountants, orthodontists, radiologists, department-store owners, broadcasters, dentists and surgeons. Although the original shareholders still await their first cent in dividend, all of them, the deaths of Alan Grainger and Rudy Komon withstanding, maintain and actively participate in their investment.

The syndicate began to develop Rothbury Estate in 1968, at the very height of the red wine boom. Two years later, there were 55 hectares of shiraz planted on the red clay slopes around and behind the winery site with 36 hectares of semillon on more lightly textured soils. Red plantings were then considered to be paramount, but later on the whites were to save the day.

The Rothbury syndicate's original intention was to grow about a hundred hectares of vines, but amid the financial euphoria and clamour of the late 1960s, countless requests from other investors led to the formation of three associated vinegrowing syndicates, Herlstone, Homestead Hill and Brokenback. The majority of those who participated in these separate vineyard syndicates still remain among the 2 000 or so other Rothbury shareholders.

The Brokenback vineyard, planted to 108 hectares of vines, has as its backdrop the spectacular Brokenback Range on Broke Road, just past the Tyrrells' property. Homestead Hill was purchased in 1970 by its own syndicate, which planted 46 hectares of shiraz and 12 hectares of semillon between 1970 and 1972. The Herlstone Hill Vineyard covered 67 hectares of vines.

The four syndicates were amalgamated in 1974, and a successful share issue was made to the many other wine lovers still waiting to become part of the Rothbury

Celebrating of things to come at Rothbury, in its early days.

adventure. James Halliday believes Evans' flair was instrumental in its conception and its success. Once wine enthusiasts became minor shareholders in the promising wine company, they were eligible to receive special shareholders' prices on wine and access to special private binnings of top quality reserve wines, a concept many would even today find difficult to resist.

Four million dollars was spent on Rothbury Estate as its vineyard size soared past 400 hectares. Prior to 1960, the total plantings in the Hunter Valley amounted to only 360 hectares. Although only a mere fraction of these original Rothbury vines now remain, the company's winery, sited just off Broke Road, Pokolbin, should stand proudly for centuries.

The locals called the winery the Pokolbin Opera House. Designed by leading Sydney architect Keith Cottier to Len Evans' own ideas and concepts and awarded the prestigious Blackett Award in 1970 for outstanding excellence in industrial design for architecture, the Rothbury Estate winery was erected in the nick of time for the 1971 vintage.

The winery is a beautiful and stylish concept, built in two halves apparently pushed together, housing superb functional spaces. Its main central feature is the Great Cask Hall, which seats over 200 people for a meal under its magnificent vaulted timber ceiling, safeguarded by sixty-two looming and sentinel-like 4 500-litre wine casks. Keith Dunstan says the impression made by the hall is so ecclesiastical that on entering he has to make a conscious effort not to cross himself! A choir loft which perches high above the seated throngs is regularly used by madrigal singers and musicians. In 1989, the winery was extended to accommodate an additional 5 000 French oak barriques.

That the complex should turn out so splendidly was hardly a surprise to Doug Crittenden, although he remembers Evans being "a little hostile" when he declined to become a Rothbury shareholder. "Len was always very enthusiastic about his next project," he says. "Anything he says, he does it, regardless of scale. He always achieves what he sets out to do." But on first seeing the drawings, it did cross Crittenden's

Trish and Len Evans at a fancy dress dinner at Rothbury.

mind that Evans was getting a bit carried away. Its first vintage, the worst in Hunter Valley memory, was a real trial for Rothbury, a year of incredible deluge. Luckily, the sun came out in 1972.

Complete with a new label designed by the distinguished Australian artist, Fred Williams, Rothbury was ready to roll. In its early days, most Rothbury wine was sold direct to its shareholders and to members of its club and direct-marketing arm, the Rothbury Estate Society, publicised through a monthly newsletter, the *Rothbury Pressings*. Today the society, which was established in 1973, has over 45 000 members.

By offering quality wines at lower prices, wine educational dinners, jazz festivals, operas and other musical events, cricket weekends, and the inevitable but brilliantly staged, Rabelaisian feasts, the Rothbury Estate Society captured an important niche in the market of genuine wine enthusiasts, and continues to identify with them and meet their needs today.

However, by consciously avoiding the conventional means of wine distribution in favour of its direct selling approach through mailing and cellar door sales, Rothbury has probably given the broader wine industry reason, if not justification, to downgrade its wines.

Melbourne's largest wine retailer, Dan Murphy, recalls that at one stage he found himself unable to promote Rothbury wine through the *Vintage Club Magazine*, the monthly publication distributed through his own wine club. Fully aware that many of his own members were also members of the Rothbury Estate Society, he was unwilling to advertise identical wines being offered at a better price through Rothbury's newsletter.

Although Rothbury retains its emphasis on direct mail today, it's wine is now available in the trade, competitively fighting it out on the retail shelves.

From the outset, Rothbury's winery was well equipped, but occasionally, even with the best machinery available, problems did inevitably occur. On one occasion, an hydraulic oil leak from a Bucher-Gayer press found its way into a wine. Evans remembers that it became a personal challenge for Gerry Sissingh to remove the resultant pungent oily character.

"He used to fine this wine, play with it, settle it and attempt all sorts of things," he laughs. "The funny thing was, that whatever he tried, he could not get that character out of the wine. And yet he persisted. He would put it at number seventeen in blind tastings, number two in tastings, he would serve it after he'd given you a chilli sandwich, he'd do anything he could to try and flog this bloody wine. And it never worked.

"But one day a Melbourne wine merchant arrived and wanted to buy some bulk wine. We showed him this wine at $4 a gallon, that one at $3 a gallon and another wine for $2.75. Oh, and that wine over there is only $1 a gallon.

"So he tried the one costing $1 a gallon and said 'Hey, that has rather a nice flavour. I like that one; it's got real Hunter character. I'll buy that one'."

The merchant bought the lot at $1 a gallon, then sold it for less than 70¢ a bottle, promoting it as a unique Hunter Valley wine. When he sold out he called back to see if Rothbury had any more! Little wonder the Hunter has had problems with its profile in Melbourne!

In the aftermath of the 1971 vintage, another Sydney-based syndicate of professionals, scientists and wine enthusiasts began to plant their own vineyard.

Brokenwood made its first wine, a Hermitage, in 1973, using a corner of a shed lent to them by Evans at Rothbury, using their own equipment. The grapes were picked into garbage bins and conveyed to Rothbury, again courtesy of Evans, in the back of his Bentleigh Continental. "I suppose that's why we have been charging such exorbitant prices ever since!" exclaims John Beeston, one of Brokenwood's founding partners.

Made from eighteen-month-old vines, but given such de luxe treatment, the wine turned out very well, drinking today as a typically idiosyncratic, but ageing Hunter red.

Three years later, another Brokenwood partner, Nick Bulleid, was learning the ropes by working as a cellar-rat at Rothbury. Evans asked him with half a tongue-in-cheek: "Mr Bulleid, how much are you paying us for this winemaking course you are getting?"

Evans was both a frequent host to and guest of the Brokenwood partners. Bulleid remembers him on occasions showing up at about 2 a.m. looking for a game of poker. "If no one would turn on the lights and play poker with him, he would stand under the verandah and yell abuse at those of us inside," he says.

As I have hinted, it was anything but plain sailing for Rothbury. Its original shareholders still await their first dividend, much of the vineyards have been uprooted, and only after some major crises has it stabilised onto a sound and viable course. That Rothbury even exists today is testimony enough to the sheer tenacity, pride and fighting spirit of Len Evans.

While some of Rothbury's problems were unquestionably of its own making, driven as it was by its initial idealistic obsessions, its fate would have been only marginally more comfortable had it originally shown the pragmatism it now displays. Simply speaking, had someone put a curse on Rothbury, it could hardly have been more effective.

In addition to the problems faced by every other emerging and over-geared wine company – of high interest rates and the mushrooming of small wineries from different areas which competed for interest and for market – Evans has listed those he rates as Rothbury's major setbacks, namely: the planting of excessive areas of shiraz in the excitement of the red wine boom without foreseeing the end of the demand; the planting of too many vines on soils which could not sustain them; excessive faith in the true estate concept "from own vineyards to bottle" and the concurrent abuse of the term "estate" by other wineries which brought in fruit from other places; that Rothbury was the wrong size, being too big for boutique status and yet too small to compete in cost efficiencies with the major wineries; a dreadful run of drought from 1980 to 1983; and the wages explosion of the mid 1970s, which was ultimately responsible for the re-financing of the company.

Rothbury began by planting wildly uneconomic vineyards with all the wrong varieties. But to examine each of Evans' reasons in turn, no one else predicted the end of the red wine boom, either. It died just as the many vineyards established in the Hunter at the end of the 1960s were coming into production, all driven by red wine's seemingly impregnable popularity. The Hunter Valley was not the only Australian wine region to find itself laden with thousands of tonnes of red grapes or gallons of red wine it was unable to sell.

If the time taken to plant a vineyard, wait for the vines to produce a crop, make and then mature the wine for sale is taken into account, Rothbury didn't have any wine to sell until 1973/74, by which stage the pendulum had swung firmly to white. By 1975, the white wine explosion was in full force, leaving Rothbury no choice but to make lots more white wine, and quickly at that.

Nobody else thought to test the different Hunter soils for their productivity. Some are so poor they are unsuited to growing almost anything. Much of that land planted in the Hunter should never have been planted to grapes, certainly not without drip irrigation or a hotline to heaven. In the past, if winemakers didn't have enough fruit, they would simply plant more vines, since land was so cheap. If you could exist on three quarters to a tonne per acre, you would probably survive. No one knew very much about the relationship between the Hunter and wine economics at all, and no one really cared.

Murray Tyrrell, heavily involved in the establishment of Rothbury and its vineyards, didn't suggest trialling the vineyards first. Why should he have? Everyone made the same mistake, witnessed also in the speedy liquidation of Hermitage Estate, whose vineyard soils soon proved totally inadequate for a commercial wine operation.

The average yield of the Rothbury Vineyard fell to a measly 3.7 tonnes per hectare and in the tragic 1981 season, dropped as low as 1.25 tonnes per hectare. Some vineyards cropped less than 0.3 tonnes per hectare, producing a crop worth around a third of what it cost to grow.

Today, only 16 hectares of the original 91 hectares of grapes remain around the Rothbury winery. Only 89 hectares are retained at two of the original vineyards which, after improved vineyard trellising and management, have begun to show a return – when the Hunter's fickle weather permits.

It is perfectly true that Australian wine companies have abused and happily continue to abuse the term "estate" and the implicit suggestion that wines sold with "estate" labels were indeed grown, made and bottled on a single property. Sadly, there is no regulation to prevent them from doing so, provided the claimed origin of the wine, as given on the label, is a minimum of 80 per cent correct.

Australian wine is, however, among the most travelled in the world by the time it is eventually given a cork and a label, something the local market has been accustomed to for decades, even if only through its ignorance of the fact. If Evans and his team were attempting to foster a renewed Australian consciousness of the "estate" concept by acting in a responsible and literal fashion through their use of the term, they were expecting too much. The rest of the wine industry would hardly be likely to take immediate notice and mend its ways.

In retrospect, it is easy to see that Rothbury has always been the wrong size. It is easily out-gunned in price whenever the large companies decide to fix it in their sights, so it has little option but to compete on quality. Yet, to remain viable, Rothbury must sell far more quality wine than any "boutique" or small winery. Evans and his board have recognised this for years, and their efforts to float and expand Rothbury are a direct consequence.

Anyone who tells you the Hunter Valley is an easy place to grow grapes is a fool. They're not my words, however much I may agree with them. Its climate is fickle, it tends to experience much of its annual rainfall when it least wants it – at and around vintage – and it is prone to regular drought. Struggling to find its feet, Rothbury Estate experienced four such successive years from 1980 to 1983.

"If it's not drought, it's vintage rainfall," bemoans James Halliday, a partner of Brokenwood for many years. "It's a dog of a place to grow grapes. The Hunter would not exist if not for the tremendous strength of the Sydney market and that long 100-year bond which connects the two. Yet, despite all these things we can put our fingers on, the Hunter has this curious ability to grow wonderful grapes in certain years and in certain styles."

Three complete schedules of re-financing were needed to cement Rothbury's future. Halliday says it would have been all too difficult for many people. "Take Evans' ability to enthuse and fire up people like Daniel Chen, a hard-headed Chinese businessman, whom I had never seen at a wine function in my life. Somehow, Len earned his respect and attention and now he is an essential part of the saving of Rothbury."

In 1976, well-known squire of the Melbourne country fringe, Sigmund Jorgensen, laird of the Montsalvat art community at Eltham, was Evans' guest for lunch at Bulletin Place. Throughout the day he was aware that Evans simply wasn't himself. Try as he might, Evans could neither relax nor stop fidgeting. The next day Evans invited Jorgensen to the Hunter Valley, which the Victorian was glad to accept, although, once again, it became clear that Evans had something on his mind.

On the way, Evans made his customary pit stop for a bottle of Krug, but his attitude, however much he tried to be friendly and forthcoming, was unusual. By now Jorgensen was feeling quite uncomfortable, for nothing seemed to trigger Evans' customary bonhomie. They arrived at Rothbury and went into the office, Evans becoming more tense and Jorgensen feeling more awkward by the minute. Finally, the phone rang. Evans' countenance immediately brightened, he instantly became his old self and, like the baron of the castle, he summoned his minions, the local Hunter winemakers, over for lunch.

"It is a great celebration!" he cried down the telephone. "Bring the best bottle from your cellars, I've got Sigmund Jorgensen here and we're going to have an enormous lunch!"

This was indeed several years before Jorgensen' star began to shine as the owner-proprietor of one of Melbourne's classic restaurants, Clichy, and so the Hunter winemakers, Jorgensen happily concedes today, had little reason to know him from a lump of dirt. Lunch was an incredible affair. Champagne was opened, great wines uncorked and superb food was lavishly presented. A classic Evans affair.

The telephone call that changed his mood, as it transpired later, was to let Evans know that Rothbury had found more financial support and would live to fight another day. "Instead of publicly using that to justify his party," laughs Jorgensen, "he used me as the excuse!"

In 1977, a large reorganisation of Rothbury shares took place, which led to the interests of Len Evans and his friend, financier and partner, Peter Fox, taking control of the company with Daniel Chen. Fox then acquired around 12 to 12.5 per cent of the capital. The major lender, the Australian Industry Development Corporation, which was at one stage the major operator of vineyards in the Hunter Valley, retired its funds in 1980, when a further 1 000 or so members of the Rothbury Estate Society elected to become Rothbury shareholders.

In publicly listing his reasons for Rothbury's early and ongoing difficulties, Evans chose not to include the death, in December 1981, of Peter Fox, his very close friend and financial supporter, although all who knew Evans then say the effect was devastating. Although the financial impact of Fox's death was shattering to Rothbury as a business, the personal toll it took of Evans was many times greater.

Fortunately, he was able to absorb and pay for the Fox shares, once again drawing heavily on an ingrained tenacity and drive that most individuals could never have mustered, while most of the wine industry waited expectantly for Rothbury to fall. Evans acknowledges a huge debt to both Mick Cameron, a chartered accountant who represented Sir John Proud, a member of one of the original Rothbury syndicates, who was instrumental in holding it together, and to Daniel Chen and his son Eric, who were always central to its recovering stability.

Until the 1992 float, the previous floats were worth approximately 25 per cent of the company, the Evans and Chen families controlled the remainder of the shares, 30 per cent and 24 per cent respectively.

Peter Doyle obviously enjoys the idea that Rothbury was started by a "heap of prudes". "I always call them that," he winks. "They wanted absolute purity of wine and Len, along with all the others would pontificate about it and scorn the Wyndham Estates and the other commercial winemakers who made traminers and other wines for the masses.

"But I do notice now that the wheel has turned, and today Rothbury itself makes wine for the masses. Commercialism has reared its rotten, ugly head. Len has turned. His ideals are still there, but now they have had to play second fiddle."

No one could question that the ideals with which Evans and the rest of the Rothbury syndicate commenced were loftier than the Australian market was ready for. However, in changing Rothbury's focus from the idealistic to the realistic, Evans hasn't lost hold of those ideals in many respects, even though many of the clauses of the original Rothbury creed have, through economic necessity, fallen by the wayside.

Rothbury is no longer a true estate, it is no longer exclusively Hunter Valley, and it's a long time passing since it relied exclusively on shiraz and semillon.

Now that wine has become an everyday beverage in Australia, which is precisely what Evans and the rest of the wine industry were hoping for, the raw enthusiasm that fuelled Australian wine in the 1960s and 1970s has largely evaporated. Rothbury and other companies like it must now produce good volumes of affordable wines for everyday drinkers to enjoy. The changes at Rothbury are a legitimate response to the industry's changed circumstances.

Rothbury altered its course towards chardonnay and pinot noir, moving into the mainstream of varietal wines from several regions, even to the extent of buying a vineyard of sauvignon blanc at Marlborough, at the northern tip of New Zealand's South Island. Quality, however remains a genuine issue.

Cowra is one of several smaller wine areas dotted in a line from Wagga to Orange, just inside the barrier of the Great Dividing Range. Essentially a warm to hot climate, it is best known for its typically peachy, creamy and melon-like chardonnay, whose youthful tropical flavours ultimately prelude complex honeyed and toasty characters with bottle age.

Cowra chardonnay first captured nationwide attention with the remarkable 1980 Cowra Chardonnay released by the Riverina College of Advanced Education at Wagga Wagga, New South Wales, coincidentally made by Brian Croser, Evans' associate in Petaluma. Cowra was also the source of fruit for the early Petaluma chardonnays which, from the 1990 vintage onwards, have been made exclusively from Adelaide Hills fruit.

The next great Cowra wine was made only a year later – the Rothbury Estate Cowra Chardonnay 1981, made in the first year that Rothbury sourced fruit from the region. The Cowra style immediately clicked in the market place. Only a year later Rothbury purchased 36 hectares of mature vineyard there which, after graftings and further expansion, now stands at 44 hectares.

That single purchase was certainly the best thing Rothbury ever did, in terms of its survival, cash flow and export, and today Rothbury's future is very closely bound up with its Cowra Chardonnay, its major product line and flagship. It is ironic that Rothbury is no longer dependent on Hunter shiraz and semillon, but on another variety and another region.

Evans enjoys his adopted wine. "You need to cellar wines from cool climates for years to get the sort of depth this wine has in its youth. And then, after a few years in the bottle... Just look at that 1981! Bloody marvellous!"

Everything that pleases Evans most in his Cowra Chardonnays – flavour, richness and persistence – are undeniable. And although they've not the subtlety, finesse or elegance of premium cool climate wines, they do suit many foods and are simply a joy to drink.

Rothbury Estate remains one of the lower Hunter Valley's best producers of white wine, especially semillon, whose style at best evokes memories of the great un-wooded Lindemans whites of the 1950s and 1960s. Many commentators believe Rothbury to be the leading contemporary maker of the Hunter Valley white wine. Although it is accepted that the great Rothbury semillons of the past came from uneconomic vineyards that have since been grubbed out, careful attention to style in the well-equipped Rothbury winery continues to make excellent ageing semillon in good years. The 1972 Rothbury Semillon is a wonderful wine still at its peak and others from the 1970s are also in great shape. "Benchmark stuff," according to Nick Bulleid, who says that some from the 1980s are developing just as well.

When Evans claims the Rothbury Cowra Chardonnay is probably the best value chardonnay on the market today, he's not just being bombastic. His baby, however, is a 100 per cent barrel-fermented Hunter chardonnay, made in a big malolactic style especially for markets in the United States and United Kingdom. Responding to forlorn calls from home, some has since been allocated to Australia.

The Rothbury Chardonnay Reserve is what James Halliday calls a Dolly Parton wine; a massive peachy, toasty style with huge richness and flavour, meaty structure and depth. In time Evans hopes to develop the style further, to develop the chardonnay breed. "Length is one of the great things I'm after," he explains. "More length, more richness on the afterpalate and more nuttiness."

Evans acknowledges that reds have never done as well at Rothbury, "although there are some '74s and '76s you would just love." John Beeston has a soft spot for the 1973. The main problem has been lack of depth and weight, tending to produce thinner, faster-maturing wines. But things have suddenly changed with Rothbury shiraz.

"In 1987 we decided to adapt the style," says Evans, "but the vintage wasn't good enough for us to put into practice the new ideas. 1989 gave us an opportunity, and the 1989 individual vineyard wine, named after Rudy Komon, is a magnificent Hunter." It's one of three extraordinary Rothbury shirazes made that year from Hunter fruit; the others are labelled as the Rothbury Hunter Shiraz and the Reserve Shiraz, the wine ranked as the Top Australian Shiraz at the 1991 Gault Millau Wine Olympics in Bordeaux.

James Halliday says it's interesting how they've suddenly unlocked the door, "especially since 1989 was not a flash vintage. It was one of the wet years".

What's more, having tasted the 1990 version, he says they've done it again. "It's a marvellous bloody wine. Very, very interesting. I'm assured that it's 100 per cent Hunter Valley, although the wine is not by any stretch of the imagination a traditional Hunter style, with all that strong oak. It's much smarter winemaking than anything else they've done. It will be fascinating to see how the wines develop in the longer term. I've yet to get to the bottom of it, but for my own interest's sake I will one of these days…"

The red revolution continued in 1991, which Evans says even betters the 1990. "I'm very happy with the change in our red situation," he says, "making richer, heavier red wines, with tremendous depth of flavour and character. The last three years have all been acclaimed at a very high level."

It's typical of Evans' obsession that he is determined to make classic pinot noir in the Hunter Valley. Would he bother if he didn't have such a crush on Burgundy? "Of course not! Why would you? And that's a perfectly valid statement which justifies itself. It's that sort of love of Burgundy engendered in Murray Tyrrell by Rudy Komon and I that kick-started the whole chardonnay and pinot noir thing rolling in Australia. Tyrrell's never had the recognition he should have for that."

Halliday says it's classic Evans to think that everything is possible if you set your mind to it. "In the same way he's growing gamay around his house," he jibes. "I think he would do better with other varieties, but it's a free world!"

Evans is first to admit that by and large, Hunter pinot noirs develop with time into lovely, soft-flavoured wines, not necessarily very Burgundian or even very pinot noir, but very drinkable Hunter reds, often hard to identify as pinot. "The 1983 Rothbury is beautiful, the 1986 is lovely. But who's prepared to wait for them these days?"

Halliday says, "You can't knock it, but you are better off using other varieties in the Hunter. In the longer term, once all the chips are down with pinot noir and people's understanding of the style, you won't see it made in the Hunter. Evans knows how to make pinot. They've tried all the techniques at Rothbury, even including washing the casks out with brandy spirit à la the alleged Domaine de la Romanée-Conti technique." Imagine the expense, but I for one applaud the sheer energy and enthusiasm of this definitive Evans obsession.

Len Evans launched the Rothbury Ribbon Dinners in March, 1973. Based on the famous French wine association, the Chevaliers de Tastevin, the Rothbury Ribbon Society became a tasting guild which regularly meets, banquets and helps encourage its membership of enthusiasts to aspire to and then progress to a higher level of wine knowledge.

Hardly an elitist club or hierarchy, the society comfortably caters to those with different abilities. Novices are presented a White Ribbon and then may progress to Green, Red and ultimately to Purple, by which stage one can infer that the person on the other end of the palate has some idea of what he or she is talking about.

To move to Green Ribbon status, aspirants are required to pass a basic test of identifying five grape varieties, and by the Red Ribbon stage they have started towards the identification of particular wines. Purple Ribbons require exhaustive tastings and written identifications of wine with comments on style and quality. In early days, Evans failed more than half the applicants for Red Ribbons, and the pass rate for Purple Ribbons is still respectably low.

Nick Bulleid's first Ribbon Dinner was the sixth one ever held. Thanks to the alphabet, he and John Beeston were the first to be awarded their red ribbons, although of the six or seven who received the award that night, one was James Halliday. Rudy Komon made grandiose presentations of the ribbons, each attached to a small pewter "tastevin" or tasting cup.

Bulleid openly admits that he failed to pass Purple on the first two occasions, and James Halliday ultimately became the first ever Purple Ribbon holder. As far as Dan Murphy was concerned, the Rothbury Ribbons created enormous competition in the world of wine. "If you were really serious about it, you had to get the Purple Ribbon. To do it you had to be mighty good; it was like being a Master of Wine (the highly rated classification given by the English wine trade)."

According to Bob Oxenbould, the Ribbon Dinners saw the Evans showmanship at its best. "He would always flambé the desserts. He'd call up a couple of people from the audience, put aprons on them and then out would come the fresh strawberries and the peaches. Evans always insisted on being in charge of the flaming. Most people just make a little flame, but with Evans in typical form – "Pppiouuwwwggghhh!" – a mountain of flame, up to the top. Flames would go everywhere, eyebrows would be singed…" Little wonder that Evans estimates he can cook enough seafood flambé for 250 people in fifteen minutes!

Peter Doyle remembers the night Evans nearly burned down Rothbury's Great Cask Hall. "He is the untidiest cook in the kitchen," he says. "To go in where he has cooked is a bloody nightmare. Evans should cook in the middle of the Pacific Ocean, then the mess he makes would be washed away. It's all because of his flamboyant throwing.

"On this particular evening the brandy didn't just flame, it exploded, covering twenty people around the hall with exploding flame, singeing girls' hair, dresses and everything. Rothbury was dead lucky to survive. If he built it, he was going to be the first one to burn it down!" Knowing Evans, it wouldn't have been cheap brandy, either.

Still standing, the Great Cask Hall has witnessed countless other banquets, numerous parties and has fed and watered thousands of people in a style to which only one person was ever really accustomed. Often people were expected to arrive in fancy dress, black tie or evening gown, regardless of where in Australia they might have departed from. Melbourne wine historian David Dunstan says that in Evans' ideal world, everyone would always wear black tie. He once had to change into his in the toilets at Sydney airport!

The underlying Elizabethan current bubbling through Evans' veins would again majestically surface, or else the theme might be Edwardian, Victorian or Medieval fancy dress. Frank Christie remembers that the dinners, like those at the Chevron, were bigger and brighter than anyone else's.

Himself a chorister of note, Nick Bulleid rates Evans with a good voice which he isn't afraid to use whenever the mood takes him, i.e. often. "He has a powerful voice which carries well and could have been worth training. He loves singing, dancing, letting his hair down and playing ridiculous games around the table. Those dinners were Evans being himself."

Nevertheless, Evans takes his role at Rothbury seriously. "As Chairman I'm responsible for the dreaming, the scheming, the long-range thinking," he explains, "and I look after the very important relationship between the Board and the shareholders." Dennis Power has since taken responsibility for Rothbury's business management. "There have been accusations that Rothbury has been run as a fiefdom," Evans realises, "but nothing could be further from the truth. It has always been run very much with the interests of the shareholders at heart. There's never been the need for a vote around the board table – everything is decided by consensus."

Rothbury Estate's present vineyard holdings in the Hunter Valley amount to 141 hectares, 40 planted to chardonnay, 37 to semillon, 44 to shiraz, 11 to cabernet sauvignon and 9 to pinot noir. The winery crushes around 2 500 tonnes each vintage, making around 180 000 cases of wine, estimated at around 0.34 per cent of Australia's production.

With its moves towards a public listing, Rothbury has begun to take more charge of its own destiny in its distribution. Evans recognises that the company needs to become larger, either by making more wine itself or by acquiring and/or amalgamating with others. At the time of writing, the success or otherwise of this venture is unknown.

He admires the way Rosemount has performed overseas, establishing its own people and presence on the ground in the United States. Evans' intention is to put together two to four Australian wine estates under a single group banner to establish a single, large Australian-owned distribution capability in the United States and Europe. He is looking to join Rothbury in this way with wineries from different areas, possibly from Coonawarra, Western Australia and the Yarra Valley.

All considered, it's fair to say that Rothbury is possibly already a stronger brand in California and London, where its wines are recognised as being very international in character, than back home in Australia. Len Evans aims to sell 50 000 to 70 000 cases of Rothbury overseas each year, and is already shipping 40 000.

If he achieves it, all credit to Evans, whose continual and energetic push towards classic styles has helped shape the nature of all Australian wine and put it before leaders of international markets. It's only fair that he should get some benefit in return through his own conception, Rothbury Estate.

In the *Wine Atlas of Australia and New Zealand 1991*, James Halliday writes that the Rothbury Estate is Len Evans' most tangible contribution to Australian wine. Evans is as deeply committed to it as ever. "It's ironic, I suppose, to be so proud of a company that has yet to recover its losses," says Evans, "yet I could not be more so."

*P*eter Fox and the Golden Years

Garlic, BO; I'm back in France!
L.P.E.

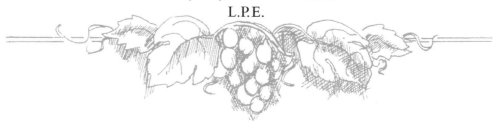

*L*en Evans' grand vision was not confined to Australian shores. His dream was for a worldwide wine company of the highest quality, with properties in France, the United States and Australia, all of which required funding. Typically, he was able to source the monies he required through a friend who shared his ambitions with him – Peter Fox.

Len Evans was doubly fortunate to meet Peter Fox. Not only did the Sydney-based entrepreneur and tax minimisation specialist genuinely become one of his closest friends, but Fox was prepared and able to use his dollars to turn Evans' almost fanciful dreams into life-size reality.

On a separate plane to their friendship, the two formed a unique and symbiotic relationship of shared ambitions and no complications, as Barry Humphries might have said. Len Evans recognised that through Peter Fox's means he could achieve his goals, while Fox clearly needed to share in their realisation and in the euphoria that surrounded them to fulfil an important need of his own.

Peter Fox, himself a wine enthusiast, met Len Evans in the mid 1960s, becoming like many a regular patron at Bulletin Place. Evans remembers their first ever financial transaction. "Foxy recommended to me some shares I asked him about, as an acquaintance. A week later they sold for about half their former value! It always amused me that our business relationship started that way."

Sharemarket predictions aside, the friendship between Fox and Evans grew stronger and stronger. As described in the chapter about Bulletin Place, Fox salvaged Evans' business there in 1976 with some much needed funding, while Evans was in hospital recovering from his heart scare. Fox later became a 49 per cent shareholder in Bulletin Place and in 1977, 12 to 12.5 per cent shareholder in Rothbury. Then, together, they formed the Evans Wine Company.

The grand concept behind the Evans Wine Company was classically full-scale Evans, of great emotional and personal interest, but still eminently practical and feasible. Well thought out and commercially sound, the idea was to develop high quality vineyards in Australia and overseas, concentrating on France and California.

Winemakers could be moved from site to site and Evans could experiment with, adopt and marry the best techniques and philosophies of each region.

Taking the standard multi-national approach, the scheme would work one way or another by balancing currency rates. Each location could be used as an export sales base for the other foreign wines.

The company bought a Coonawarra vineyard in 1977 and one in Clare a year later. As described in the next chapter, the Evans Wine Company was an early source of funding for the important Australian label of Petaluma for which Evans continues to serve as Chairman.

Shortly afterwards, he and Fox acquired the Fordwich vineyard in the Hunter Valley, then consisting of 100 acres of semillon, shiraz and trebbiano which was grafted to chardonnay, before they began to look overseas for a château, beginning with Château Suduiraut in Sauternes, France.

Suduiraut is the next most prestigious château in Sauternes after Château d'Yquem, embellished with a magnificent château and gardens designed by Le Nôtre, who also created those at Versailles. English wine merchant Kit Stevens, Master of Wine, alerted Fox and Evans that it was for sale. The starting price began around 3 million Australian dollars or 15 million francs, but kept going up and up.

Having made five visits there between the two of them, Evans and Fox found the owners impossible to deal with, using every ploy conceivable plus others that stretched the imagination, to inflate the property's value beyond reality.

"We argued about the furniture, the curtains, the carpets, the wall-hangings and even the light-fittings, all of which put the price up," says Evans, still visibly exasperated by the experience.

"Then the eldest daughter said we couldn't possibly want the museum of wine, since we couldn't expect to take away her father's life's work. I reminded her that M. Fonquernie only took over the château after most of the museum wines were made. The old father turned round to the daughter saying 'He's got you there!'.

"We finally assembled all of the people involved in Suduiraut together – the old man, the old woman and the eldest daughter, representing the other two daughters. Each of them thought he or she was the negotiator. In complete exasperation, when I finally realised we weren't getting anywhere, I said 'I am going to give you a price. This price will stand until the end of the month. To whom should I give this price tomorrow?' The three of them immediately said 'Moi'.

"Peter and I went outside. We stood there in the gloom of Château Suduiraut. Night was falling, there was a faint drizzle and we both had our Burberrys on. A duck on the pond then gave out the loneliest, most mournful quack I've ever heard in my life. Peter turned round to me and said, 'Ask them how much they want for the flaming ducks!'

"There's no doubt that had we bought it for 25 million francs and moved in the next day, that duck would not have been there. They never really meant to sell the château and the eldest daughter still runs it today."

Fox and Evans used to stay in Bordeaux with an Englishman, David Robson, at his particularly attractive petit château, Château Rahoul, in Graves. Eventually Evans asked Fox: "Why don't we buy this one?" Some $600 000 later, financed through Fox's company, Adelaide Holdings, it was theirs. "Then we bought Padouen in

Barsac and in 1978 became very much the centre of Australian wine activity in France," says Evans.

Built by Guillaume Raoul in 1646, Château Rahoul fitted the Fox syndicate very well. It has a splendid residence which underwent various transformations in the seventeenth, eighteenth and nineteenth centuries. David Robson, its owner since 1971, had carefully modernised and renovated the house, cellar and vineyard.

The château is surrounded by park-like gardens, shaded courtyards, storage cellars and outbuildings. Its vineyard is planted to 11.5 hectares of red vines (merlot 80 per cent, cabernet sauvignon 15 per cent and malbec 5 per cent) and 2.5 hectares of white (semillon), producing both dry red and dry white wines, with a maximum capacity of around 5 000 cases of red and 500 cases of white.

Evans anticipated that, by introducing modern equipment, more new wood for maturation and Australian winemaking techniques, Rahoul could make a better wine. He found its winemaker courtesy of Kit Stevens, who introduced Evans to Peter Vinding-Diers, a Dane who had previously worked in South Africa and Bordeaux.

Their first vintage was in 1978, a small, high quality vintage which made a wine that exceeded all Evans' expectations, although he didn't interfere much that year, giving Vinding-Diers a chance to show what he could do by himself. As a young wine, the 1978 Rahoul had a high colour, a good fruity nose, plenty of flavour and a fine, astringent finish.

The following year, Brian Croser was seconded to act as consultant to the red wine making, and to teach Vinding-Diers how to make dry whites. The 1979 vintage was very large although its quality was quite high. The merlot was good, but since the cabernet was a shade thin and under-ripe, the '79 red was leaner and lacked the flavour and power of the '78. The year 1980 was disastrous for dry red in Bordeaux, the rain bucketing down to such an extent that pickers lost their footwear in the soil.

Although Château Rahoul was only classified as a "Petit Graves", it won an unprecedented seven gold medals during its brief ownership by the Evans Wine Company. Once it started winning its awards and bringing recognition to the area, Evans noticed that its stocks amid the local district of Portets rose dramatically. Until then it had commonly been referred to as the "United Nations" place up the road, where the winemaker was a Dane with an English wife, the owners Australian and Welsh, and which played host to visitors from all over the world.

In 1982, the year that the Evans Wine Company was forced to sell Rahoul, it was one of sixty-seven châteaux which applied for "Grand Cru" status. The other sixty-six were rejected. Rahoul's application was put on hold to monitor subsequent vintages, but in 1984, two years after the Evans Wine Company had moved on, it received the honour, becoming the first Château in Graves to be newly given a "Grand Cru" status or "Appellation" since 1957.

Located in the northern part of the commune of Barsac, Sauternes, Château Padouen is a farm-style property of 11.5 hectares, 9 of which are planted to 80 per cent semillon, 15 per cent sauvignon blanc and 5 per cent muscadelle, which produce around 2 000 cases of wine. Its present house was built in 1703 as a hunting lodge.

Evans and Fox picked it up for $300 000, although to do so they encountered similar problems as when negotiating for Suduiraut. More experienced this time, they insisted that settlement covered absolutely everything but found on arrival that the light bulbs had been removed!

Evans' objective was simple. He wanted to make a really great wine, so he immediately rang the changes. The vineyard was picked five times and on each "pass" only those parts of bunches, fully rotten with noble rot, were chosen.

Offspring of a long, dry season, the 1978 wine had plenty of flavour and was quite heavy and "liquoreux", although Evans would have preferred a greater infection of noble rot. In 1979, Evans seconded Australian friends who visited around vintage time to sort the grapes on tables after picking, in so doing re-introducing an ancient winemaking practice which then left the local officials speechless.

Four large white tables were used to divide the entire crop into two discrete sortings for the entire vineyard, one at the normal ripeness of around 13 degrees Baume, sufficient sugar to make a full-bodied dry white, and the other at a very respectable botrytis-affected 19 degrees, superb for sauternes.

As the gossip of Padouen's high sugar levels coarsed its way through the vineyards of Bordeaux, a Government inspector, a certain M. Franc, watched in astonishment as the sorting process took place. "The levels are perfect," he said. "But it's easy to see how you done it – you're cheating!"

The 1978 vintage Barsac won a Gold Medal for semi-sweet wines at the Concours des Grands Vins in Macon in 1980, the only Gold Medal to be awarded at the competition. The 1979 dry white, given a grey label and the cheeky annotation "P" on its label, after the "Y" dry wine of Château d'Yquem, collected a Bronze Medal.

Today, despite his success at Padouen, Evans reflects that the vineyard was too low-lying ever to make the great wine modelled on Yquem that he had dreamed of.

Well before its currency was floated, Australia's wine embassy in Bordeaux certainly was. "Have you ever fed and watered an Australian visitor in the heart of a wine district?" asks Evans, still smarting years after catering for the likes of Primo Caon, James Halliday, Brian Croser, former Brisbane restaurateur Gino Merlo, and planeloads of other renegade hordes of vacationing colonials. "The champagne bill alone would sustain an average-sized vineyard for a year. Ah, the cost of free labour!"

Château Rahoul, splendid house of many rooms was the mandatory staging house for dozens of wandering ambassadors of pleasure, including Maggie McKenzie, Geraldine Pascall, Patric Juillet of Le Café, Anders Ousback, Paul Lloyd, Nick Bulleid, Geoffrey Roberts, David and Margaret Levin of London's Capital Hotel, and Billy and Sonia McMahon, to name but a few.

Guests were welcome on the understanding that it was not a hotel, and for their hospitality, sufficiently indulgent to question the adequacy of the word "generous", a little help was expected around the house, garden, vineyard or cellar, depending on the skills and predilections of each particular guest.

Former wine writer Sarah Gough, presently with the Victorian family wine company of Brown Brothers, was "chatelaine" at Rahoul for eight months from March 1980. For maintaining house, gardens, guests, her sanity and the château's equilibrium, she was paid a small allowance, given board and lodging, plus a once-in-a-lifetime chance for a young Australian to manage a French château.

Three of her first house guests were Rudy Komon, artist Fred Williams and his wife. After they had been there three days, Peter Vinding-Diers called Evans in Australia with the news that his three guests wanted to stay longer.

"Let them stay as long as they want," Evans magnanimously pronounced, clearly under the impression that his stock of ten dozen bottles of Deutz champagne maintained by Kit Stevens would outlast any onslaught of which even Rudy Komon was capable.

Three days later a worried-sounding Vinding-Diers was on the phone again, saying they were still at Rahoul, and still drinking Evans' champagne. Evans still showed no outward sign of concern.

Another week later Vinding-Diers rang to say they had gone. His guests had been very entertaining and very generous, he told Evans, but they had drunk the château out of champagne, and had made a significant impression on the stocks of 1945 Château Rahoul red and the remainder of its cellar, whose devastation Sarah Gough had been powerless to prevent. Evans met Rudy Komon off the plane at Sydney, saying, "You have drunk all my champagne."

"And what else is it for?" asked Komon.

Since Evans was entertaining there shortly afterwards, a sequence of frantic calls followed to the French wine houses, desperate for stock. Months later Evans was proudly able to hang a large gouache of a nude woman by Fred Williams on his office wall at Bulletin Place. Underneath was scribbled the note "Thanks for the drink".

One of the perks for those who invested in the core Fox business, Adelaide Holdings, was to stay at Rahoul without paying board. So in addition to the international wine people, the guests for whom Sarah Gough would play host, consisted of an utterly unpredictable and eclectic group of Australian investors and movie personalities including well-known actors and directors. Fox had a stake in the successful Australian film *Breaker Morant*, so on one occasion Gough was invaded by a crowd fresh from the Cannes Film Festival.

Most of the time, says Sarah Gough, her visitors had either just arrived in France, in which case she was predictably intimidated by their expectations of classic gourmet cuisine and plenty of it; or were on their way out. She seems to have preferred those on the way home, who would simply stop in at Rahoul to dry out, and to whom a perfect repast would just consist of dried bread and Vegemite taken from a supply regularly topped up by other antipodeans on walkabout.

On one of his two visits to France in 1980, Evans publicly teased Sarah Gough, much to the amusement of the rest of the household. "You must be bored out of your mind at night," he laughed. "Give me a signal and I'll be straight up." Frowning slightly, Gough was not at all certain of her new employer's intentions.

Rising early next morning, she took coffee into the master bedroom where, in the centre of an enormous kingsize mattress lay an Evans-sized mound, completely covered in towels and jumpers.

Gough asked: "Mr Evans, were you cold last night?" "Bloody freezing." She then remembered that all the spare blankets were stored in her room. "What do you think you would have done if I'd knocked on your door last night?" he asked. "You would have jumped out the bloody window."

"Evans was a tremendous host as long as people contributed and put some effort in," Gough says, remembering his reaction when one house guest for vintage would play sick in the morning to avoid working in the vineyard. Later the same morning she would then make her way to a two-or three-star restaurant for lunch, to review in a major Australian newspaper." "Evans would go right off," says Gough, "and his eyes would turn from blue to steel grey."

The atmosphere at Rahoul was electric as its owners and visitors were swept along by the giddy euphoria and pace of the times. As ever, Peter Fox was happy to step back from the limelight, allowing Evans to assume control. "Len would then walk in and create," says Gough. "Today we will make bouillabaisse!" Fish, shellfish and crabs would all be boiled up, leaving a wreckage of pots and pans, with stray morsels and remnants of fruits de mer strewn all over the kitchen, across benches, tables and floors in the most "godawful mess".

His creative urges momentarily satisfied, Evans would then round up those eager to explore for one of his many expeditions, leaving the catastrophic scene behind for others to attend to. One wonders if he would have got away with it had the results not been so good.

James Halliday was a guest-come-worker for the 1979 Rahoul vintage. "We had a fabulous time," he remembers. "We'd take it in turns to cook and would go off to the Bordeaux markets to find incredible foods. I once bought some veal shanks for a glaze for roast whole baby lamb, which you could buy new-born. The shanks cost four times as much as the lamb. The French were horrified when they realised their beautiful veal was to be treated in such a fashion."

On one memorable day, the troupe went to the famous restaurant Michel Guérard at Eugénie-Les-Bains for lunch. Their next stop was Biarritz, the Atlantic seaside town, for dinner at the Café de Paris, which in 1945, had bought a fabulous wine list from a famous Bordeaux restaurant, Le Chapon Fin, and paid next to nothing for it. One glance at the wine list was motivation enough to book into the nearby Palace Hotel immediately.

It was deemed necessary to work up an appetite for dinner and the tables of the tattered old Biarritz casino, a fading run-down reflection of glories past, were open and beckoning. Once inside, the group was spotted by a small man dressed in battered white tuxedo, looking to all intents and purposes as if he had stepped straight from a Somerset Maugham play, who decided to attach himself to them. Recognising the individual from his days at the Chevron as a much-jailed con-man, Evans even remembered his name, but played along with him most of the night just for fun.

The Café de Paris had expanded its wine list, adding to it the classics from the great years between the Wars, with a variety of '45 and '49 clarets and a spread of '62 Domaine de la Romanée-Contis, the greatest of burgundies. So the group decided to have the simplest possible meal and "to drink themselves to an absolute standstill". This didn't present much of a difficulty and when they ordered their third bottle of Sauternes at the end of the meal, says Evans, the entire staff spontaneously assembled at the balustrade near their table and burst into warm applause.

Despite the galaxy of wines opened and consumed that night, the food bill was still 20 francs more than that for wine, so incredibly cheap was it to drink! Great 1928 and 1929 clarets only cost between $A10 and $A20, the 1937 Rieussec just $A16!

Although Evans became passionately involved in the traditions and lifestyle of French wine, California was his third and most obsessive frontier. To him it represented the opportunity to move into a new wine industry, becoming part of it from its earliest beginnings.

With Robert Mondavi's help, in 1978, Evans and Fox found and bought the Weaver Ranch on the Silverado Trail in California's Napa Valley, just below the famous Rutherford Winery, and where Round Hill Winery now sits. Of the 12 hectares on the ranch, 7 were already planted to cabernet sauvignon. Completing the property was a modern ranch home and a garden ringed by a tall natural forest.

With Brian Croser, who would have been Technical Director to the worldwide company, Evans designed a beautiful winery and administration centre, utilising the olive groves in the front of the property and the lake on the site. He was keenly looking forward to flying the Australian flag there.

The Chairman of Rothbury and Petaluma keeping an eye on his product.

In December 1981, aged forty-three, Peter Fox was killed when his Ferrari ran off a road, presumably at high speed. His companies were then finding the going extremely tough, fighting the economic recession of the 1980s, but Evans is certain that had no connection with his death.

Personally, Evans had a disastrous year in 1982. He was instantly confronted by the almost insurmountable challenge of holding together the assets of the entire Evans Wine Company. Although the receiver for Adelaide Holdings valued its assets at more than 8 or 9 million dollars, Evans had to deliver 5.3 million dollars very quickly. Down the company went into liquidation, Evans losing everything he had in the venture, including Rahoul, Padouen and the Weaver Ranch.

"With Dennis Horgan's help we found the approximately 2 million dollars required for Petaluma", says Evans, "and we were able to absorb and pay for the Fox shares in Rothbury, but we couldn't find the money to save the two châteaux and build the Californian one."

Without question, his greatest loss in France was that which Evans had yet to grasp, but to which he had become so close. Together with Fox he had negotiated to within a hair's breadth of buying the entire Alexis Lichine company, which included the whole of its large commercial wholesale operation and huge Bordeaux warehouses, its stock, money in bank, and two châteaux, the cream of which was Château Lascombes, the famous second-growth in Margaux, plus shares in the Somerset Wine Company in America and Georges Duboeuf in Beaujolais.

Letters of intent had been exchanged with Lichine's owner, Bass Charrington, for 27 million dollars, the money virtually borrowed and buyers almost sorted out for the wholesale side of the operation, which was of no interest to either Fox or Evans. Château Lascombes would have been theirs for less than 10 million dollars.

"How big a punt is this?" Fox had once asked Evans, prior to the 1981 vintage. "If we have five dud vintages now, we are in big trouble," Evans had replied "If we have five reasonable vintages we can get through, but if we have a dud vintage, a couple of reasonable vintages and a couple of good years, we are home and hosed."

Look what happened – 1981, 1982, 1983 and 1985 – the greatest run of vintages since the 1940s. With the escalation of château prices that subsequently followed, they would have bought Lascombes for a song and then could easily have sold half of it for between 20 and 30 million dollars.

"It would have been the biggest coup of my life," Evans reflects. "It is the project that I regret leaving most. I would have loved very much to have done Lascombes."

To their credit, Bass Charrington, who were very keen for Evans to take it, honourably held the offer open for six months after Fox's death to allow him to find the backing. But the task finally proved too great. If, in 1982, I had known as much financially as I do now, we would have kept all those properties," he says today. "We would have gone public and would have a more flourishing business than we do now. But that's all hypothetical. I didn't know. I probably trusted other people too much. I don't think I was as tough then as I probably am now."

"I was always the schemer, the dreamer, the entrepreneur wine man while others were the finance people. I have certainly become more financially adept in the last ten years. As you get older you realise what you're good at.

"We had a dreadful time," Evans remembers. "I tried to hold Adelaide Holdings together, I got onto the Board to try and help them, but there were a lot of hawks around. It was a nasty story."

Evans remains grateful to James Halliday, who contributed freely of his time and legal expertise to help him through a difficult predicament of immense legal and financial complexity.

Brian Croser is convinced that, had Evans succeeded and the Evans Wine Company existed today and was financed properly, it would be extraordinarily successful, one of the world's great quality wine companies.

Although the episode was a catastrophe for Evans, he remains realistic about his losses. "Rahoul was not on the best site, soils and aspect. We enjoyed France very much, but the vineyards were simply not good enough to produce great wine. Rahoul is what it is. It's not a first-growth property and never will be, the *terroir* imperatives in Bordeaux do work."

Even more than Rahoul and Padouen, Evans' greatest actual loss was California. He regrets enormously not having set foot in the Napa Valley. With Croser he had really worked it through, but as Croser says, the project was stillborn, whereas in other ventures Evans had already experienced satisfaction of having achieved.

"If I could now choose where I would like to go," Evans speculates, "I would honestly say that I would rather finish back in America than France, unless we got some really worthy part of France – either a great-name vineyard, in Burgundy, Bordeaux or Champagne, or else a totally new challenge, well apart from the normal recognised regions. But I would love to go back to America, to establish an Australian foothold in America."

"He spoke more about California than France after Fox's death," says Croser, "and spent more time trying to get it out of the hands of the receivers. In retrospect, he was dead right in his ideas."

As the reality dawned on Evans that his dream with Peter Fox was finished, he was understandably and obviously devastated. It was the severest imaginable dual loss – a great, genuine friend, and the opportunity, which, as Sydney social identity Diana Fisher says, represented a stepping stone he thought to be rock-solid. "And then it was gone."

His friends, especially those in Sydney, were an immense support to him. After Fox's funeral, Albert, Halliday, Beeston and a few others accompanied Evans back to Bulletin Place, where at lunch they sat down in silence to taste the range of Domaine de la Romanée-Conti '76s, recently arrived from France. "Then we threw our glasses against the wall," says Albert. "It just seemed appropriate."

"Len came up very well in the end," says his friend and Melbourne restaurateur, Hermann Schneider. "His quality emerged as he came to terms with the situation." "Being Evans," says Nick Bulleid, "you just had to get on with it."

Brian Croser says that Evans could sense that Peter Fox had been experiencing real difficulty. "His heart was going out to Fox and his death was shattering. He always felt that Foxy should take it easier on himself, rather than rushing around at the speed he did."

What sort of individual was Peter Fox, and what was his relationship with Evans? A large, quiet and unassuming man, Fox had a pleasant, dry sense of humour that might sometimes take time to show. His apparently disinterested gaze, through sleepy green eyes, was entirely misleading. He would happily play second fiddle to Evans, perhaps appearing to slide out of a conversation, although his rapier-sharp mind would never miss a tick. He was even-tempered and gentle. Peter Doyle never heard him raise his voice in anger. Fox was also a champion water-polo player who still played competitively until the time of his death.

Regarded by several who knew him as a real artist and a very creative person, Fox was a brilliant accountant, very quick to grasp a situation, whose core business was tax minimisation in the days when tax schemes were much in play. He never flouted the law and John Beeston, formerly a solicitor, suggests that many of his ideas would still be quite operable today.

Without question, Peter Fox got much of his pleasure watching Len Evans doing what Evans does best. "Peter had a great love of wine and a good palate," says Evans. "We got on so well because he enjoyed my life so much. We went around France together and he loved it. He enjoyed buying and going on buying trips. He absorbed the whole ambience of wine and wine people, wining and dining and staying in good hotels.

"He also did marvellous things. He was a very generous, kind man, a very sweet man. I never heard him say a bad word against anybody. Recently I looked back at the eulogy I gave at his funeral. It was rather nostalgic, for what I said then was very true."

Fox was devoted to Evans. Halliday agrees it was a personal friendship which led him to invest money in the various Evans activities. "He was never as committed to wine for wine's sake as we were, but was extremely interested in it," he says. "He was always welcome at the Monday Table, although he didn't always come, and he attended all the Single Bottle Club Dinners.

"There was nothing that Peter wouldn't do within his capacity for Len," Halliday continues, "and no amount of financial support that he wasn't prepared to give." Frequently involved in difficult and highly risky ventures, Fox looked to Evans as a means of finding pleasure from what he was doing.

Anders Ousback is in no doubt that Fox's funding ability was just the icing on the cake for Evans. "Peter saw in Len someone with imagination and flair and without money. He was a patron to Len in the real sense of the word. Obviously the bottom line was important, but not the whole story."

Flying to London together Evans and Fox were both served a glass of Dom Pérignon, which they accepted without ordering a meal. By the time the plane refuelled in Bahrain, they were informed that they had drunk the aircraft out of Dom Pérignon, but "Would they mind La Grande Dame instead?" As Anders Ousback recalls, "Evans and Fox had sat talking for twenty hours. There would be very few people Len could be bothered to sit with and talk to for even half that time".

A man of great vision, Fox was always running other ventures concurrently with the Evans Wine Company, forever hastening to the next challenge. Only months before his death he had bought "Boomerang", his harbourside home, for $2 million, a price Evans then considered as madness. However Fox was convinced that the value of harbourside homes would rise beyond all belief within ten years, and he proved to be quite correct.

Fox also bought into part of Noosa, which was subsequently auctioned off for fire sale prices, before realising many times the value Fox paid, as people came to recognise its true value.

"He wanted to build an empire," says Peter Doyle, "but, like many empires, the brakes fell off and it went too far. The whole world was on fast track. People were making fortunes and no one was losing fortunes."

However, the entrepreneurial Peter Fox met the recession head-on and over-geared, without a sufficiently sound cash business to replace the very profitable tax avoidance business that had not only established him, but made him a wealthy man.

He enjoyed the extravagances and spoils that money could bring. His home at Elizabeth Bay, where he played host to grand parties and dances, had a cinema. Every June he would throw a party at Bulletin Place, with a theme that reflected his activities over the past year. Once he became involved in the film industry, his theme was "Back to Hollywood", and every guest was expected to arrive as a Hollywood identity. A sculptured ice fountain flowed all night with pink champagne.

"The fact that we were able to put on a different party every year is a testimony in itself to Peter Fox," says Bob Oxenbould. "There were dozens of marvellous, lavish nights with something completely different, just like that one."

Evans has met dozens of wealthy people who have since revealed that Peter Fox was responsible for their start. In such high esteem was he held that one individual, after buying a bowling club to turn into a water-polo centre, sold it on the news of Fox's death to channel the profits into a trust for the Fox children.

The final word is Evans' alone. He doesn't think there was ever a man like him.

Peter Fox gave Len Evans the opportunity to show much of the wine world that Australia should be taken seriously. One such gesture, and a typical one at that, was for Evans to conduct, in his ex-officio capacity for Australian wine, a tasting of Australian wines for his friends in Bordeaux. A cross-section of Australian wine was greeted by a posse of château-owners, from de Pez, Carbonnieux, Petrus, Lynch-Bages, Pontet-Canet, plus several shippers, wine makers, wine writers and even one Californian winemaker, with nothing short of awe.

"In France we couldn't do this." "This is the best range of sound wines I have seen from any country" were some of the comments he heard that night. The rieslings, especially a Petaluma 1979 and a Buring '73, were very popular and although their palates didn't understand the Hunter style, the old semillons amazed them for their complexity and bottle development.

The Australian chardonnays received the anticipated favourable response and even the famous Tyrrells 1976 Pinot Noir was popular. One particularly noted taster didn't like it, says Evans, because it didn't taste well backwards! "If you tasted the finish first, you wouldn't know it was pinot," it was revealed to him.

The Hunter reds were popular, especially the famous Lindemans Bin 1590 of 1959, but the Bordelais naturally related better to the cabernets. The last bracket, which included a Wynns '65, Mildara '64 and Penfolds Bin 60A 1962 was "rapturously received".

More importantly, Evans had the vision to transplant Australian winemaking technologies to the traditional French wine culture long before others considered it. He was absolutely convinced that Australian winemaking could show the French a thing or two, and he proved it spectacularly.

For some time, Peter Vinding-Diers has been regarded as one of the shining lights of Bordeaux white-wine making. Whether he cares to admit it or not, he knew very little more than did his confrères when Evans' team arrived at Rahoul. In short, the traditional technique simply involved throwing in sulphur until you could no longer stand its smell. Vinding-Diers has taken much credit of late, but in the late 1970s, he neither knew how to make white wine, nor did he want to.

Brian Croser, who was taken to Bordeaux especially to make white wines, virtually taught Vinding-Diers what he knows about dry white-wine making. Croser is frustrated that Evans has not been given due recognition for foreseeing the value of clean juice, barrel fermentation, good yeast strains and anaerobic winemaking techniques, in making a Bordeaux white from semillon and sauvignon blanc, that shared all the great characteristics of Graves with the good qualities of Australian winemaking. "We took white Bordeaux and re-invented it," he says.

Nick Bulleid describes the 1979 Rahoul white, made from semillon only, as a spectacular wine containing elements of Hunter Semillon although being clearly a French wine. "It was exactly as Evans would have it, I'm sure," he says.

When Croser arrived in Bordeaux he found that, whereas Vinding-Diers was happy to let him do anything he wanted with the white wine, although he insisted that he fermented with natural yeasts from the estate. Having smelled some of the red ferments, Croser offered as a compromise that he would then isolate a pure yeast strain from the vineyard.

After much work he chose the best, called "Rahoul 2", today quite famous in Australia as "R2", and since used regularly at Petaluma and many other wineries. "He was happy and so was I," said Croser. "I had a culture I could trust." That was the only resistance Vinding-Diers ever made to anything Croser wanted to do.

Rahoul's winery itself was dirty and old, served by an ancient and insufficient power system which gave Croser a shock every time he turned on a pump. It had a tiny half-tonne refrigeration unit which was worked around the clock, but at Evans' insistence, did actually boast the only Wilmes airbag press then to be found in Bordeaux.

Evans took his "we can show you lot a thing or two" attitude to Europe well before Australian wine had made any sort of impact in London for its quality, says Croser, and long before the French even acknowledged that we made wine here.

Especially at Rahoul, Evans showed what good winemaking can do, and at Padouen he demonstrated how even a relatively lowly little estate in Barsac, with Yquem-like attention to detail, could make a high quality wine. Neither his vision nor his results were acknowledged at the time.

Again, Evans measures his own achievements in terms of quality, his only ideal in wine. "He is very much the patron of my winemaking ideals," says Croser. "He has never pretended to know anything about the technology of viticulture or winemaking, although over the years he has acquired quite a good knowledge. He wanted to be a user of the technologies to produce his results. Evans always knew what he wanted, and he happened to think I knew how to get there. Yet he is the patron, the final arbiter of taste and quality."

Petaluma
– *T*aster and Technocrat
in Tandem

Expensive and cheap share the same definition. They are
both paying out of proportion to what you receive. A wine
may be costly, but not necessarily very expensive.
L.P.E.

Nestled snugly at its sheltered base in the Adelaide Hills' picturesque Piccadilly Valley, Petaluma is indeed a deceptive winery. With its popular Bridgewater Mill and Croser labels bringing the total production of its own wines to an impressive 60 000 cases, it is hardly an especially small wine company. In addition, its winery also serves as a major regional production centre which processes various wines on contract for a surprising number and range of other Australian wine companies.

Able to source fruit for its wine from the multitude of new Adelaide Hills vineyards it has fostered for local contractors, Petaluma, steered by the vision of its extremely capable major shareholder and technocrat chief winemaker Brian Croser, also owns major vineyard developments in Clare and Coonawarra.

It is a measure of Brian Croser's stature in Australian wine, as well as Len Evans' perhaps unanticipated ability to play second fiddle, that most Australian wine enthusiasts remain oblivious of the fact that Len Evans is Chairman of Petaluma and was formerly one of its major shareholders. Not only that, but he has played a central role almost since Petaluma's conception, a part second only to Croser's in the shaping of the company.

That he continues in such a vital and energetic manner for a company in which his own shareholding has diminished to a token level says much for how closely and co-operatively two of the healthiest egos in Australian wine, Evans' and Croser's, are able to function together. The reason is simple, they are exceptionally good friends, each ready, willing and able to fiercely defend the other at a moment's notice.

Evans takes intense pride in Croser, and Croser always acknowledges Evans' contribution to his success. Evans has the view that Croser, the 1991 President of the Winemaker's Federation of Australia, has probably done more good as a wine industry politician in the last five to ten years than any other individual has done for thirty or forty. "He has been instrumental in the creation of entities like the Label Integrity Programme, the Small Winemakers' Forum, and the Winemakers' Federation of Australia, yet he's another poppy that continually gets criticised."

Height has nothing to do with it. Evans with one of his protégés, Brian Croser.

It is indeed remarkable that Croser, the Australian wine industry's most high-profile winemaker and leading politician and Evans, its visionary, mouthpiece-come-figurehead, are so closely affiliated. If that seems to you to be a case of two very different, yet complementary, talents being drawn irresistibly together, you are perfectly correct.

Evans says he was looking for a winemaker to work with him when he bumped into Croser, whom he regarded as the best young winemaker around. Croser says that the reason he restructured Petaluma in 1979 was to go into business with Len Evans. But I am racing too far ahead.

Funded by its parent company, Adelaide Holdings, the Evans Wine Company bought its vineyard in Coonawarra in late 1977, which is still known today as the Evans Vineyard. In the same year Evans and Peter Fox also bought the Hanlin Hill vineyard in Clare from Bob Clampett.

When deciding who would make the wines from these vineyards, Evans again came across Croser whom he had first met in 1973 when Croser was a winemaker at Hardy's Tintara Winery, and with whom he had struck up an immediate friendship.

Croser was looking for an opportunity, and a deal was done in October 1978 whereby he would join the Evans Wine Company as its consultant winemaker and build it a winery that he would also be able to use for his own labels. Simultaneously, Croser would develop his own Adelaide Hills vineyard. Today the Petaluma winery at Piccadilly is a major and sophisticated production facility many times its original size.

By this stage, the Petaluma concept was gathering steam. Croser had already released, of all things, a Spaetlese Rhine Riesling, 1976 vintage, made from grapes grown in Victoria's Goulburn Valley. In the present Petaluma scenario its second wine was equally bizarre – a 1977 Gewürztraminer made at the Riverina College of Advanced Education, Wagga Wagga where, with Dr Tony Jordan, currently the Managing Director of Domaine Chandon in Victoria's Yarra Valley, Croser had jointly established a winemaking course.

Evans took serious note of this wine, made with Cowra grapes, and rated it the best Australian traminer he'd seen since the old Penfolds Trameahs (made from 100 per cent traminer) from Minchinbury, Rooty Hill, in New South Wales.

Evans still remembers the phone call he received from Croser after the 1979 vintage: "The fruit from your Clare vineyard is the best riesling I have ever seen in Australia. It would take me ten years to get fruit like it."

That was Evans' first riesling from the Hanlin Hill Vineyard, then the highest in altitude in the Clare Valley, and it set the pattern for the Petaluma style. In the 1984 edition of his *Complete Book of Australian Wine*, Evans writes: "It was unlike anything yet seen in this country, as the aroma was intense, the palate quite heavy in flavour and body and the acid finish considerably pronounced. Alcoholically the wine was very strong, a result of the grapes being picked much later than normal and fully fermented out. The considerable depth of flavour, while partly attributable to both the vineyard and the lateness of picking, is also a result of the method of making…" That is the special quality of Croser, and the wine initiated what is now known as the "dry spaetlese" Petaluma style.

By this time, Croser was convinced that his future lay in a closer association with Evans. He was initially attracted to Evans' very broad understanding of wine and his outstanding palate, and James Halliday openly acknowledges that, in the early days of Petaluma, Evans was clearly the number one palate in Australia. It was a perfect match. "Evans recognised Croser's talents, and Croser also saw, through Peter Fox, Evans' ability to introduce capital to the venture," says Halliday.

Later in 1979 it was decided that the Coonawarra, Clare and Adelaide Hills vineyards should be consolidated under Petaluma, and that the Evans Wine Company should invest in the company and complete the winery. According to Croser the quality of the fruit from the vineyards was a bonus. He says he was primarily motivated by the idea of going into business with Len Evans, himself an outstanding supporter of Petaluma since its first releases. He describes Evans then as "the most enthusiastic and knowledgeable wine visionary with whom I had been in contact in Australia, absolutely dedicated to the process of making, selling and consuming the best wines of the world."

After Fox's tragic death and the subsequent readjustment of ownership, a stronger Petaluma has emerged, according to James Halliday, who gave freely of his legal services in disentangling the various wine interests from the other Fox enterprises, and facilitated the introduction of Dennis Horgan as a third partner, replacing Peter Fox as Petaluma's financial muscle.

Brian Croser says that Fox's demise and the forfeiture of the French and Californian properties made him and Evans focus on what Petaluma was really about. "It forged a link between Croser and Evans in adversity and focused us to make sure it would work. In retrospect, as things have turned out, Petaluma has probably developed further as a company on its own, and not part of a global concern."

Until Fox's death, he and Evans each owned 40 per cent of Petaluma, and Croser 20 per cent, although Croser had the rights to buy up to a third. When Horgan ultimately sold out in 1987, after a disagreement on whether or not to go public, Croser was able to dramatically increase his ownership by purchasing Horgan's share. The picture is made marginally more confusing, yet very much more interesting, because, in 1985, the French Champagne house of Bollinger also became shareholders in Petaluma.

Croser and Evans had long decided that Petaluma would aspire to make sparkling wine of the highest quality, so it seemed natural to want a Champagne company to enter and own half of Petaluma's sparkling wine operation. They went to visit Bollinger, which had already expressed interest, Pol Roger and Veuve Clicquot.

"Clicquot were very keen, Pol didn't want to go outside France, and Bollinger continued talking," Evans recalls. "But they didn't want to be half of a sparkling wine company, saying instead that they wanted to be part of Petaluma. We were still very happy with that idea. Bollinger became the house Champagne here!", cries Evans, gesticulating magnanimously towards the "Loggerheads" refrigerator.

There was a time when Evans felt that Rothbury and Petaluma would possibly amalgamate, and that Croser and he would then move on to other things, but Brian Croser has continued his own expansion either under the Petaluma banner, with the highly successful "Croser" méthode champenoise, and also through his development in Oregon with the Dundee Wine Company and its Argyle label.

"I might well do more with Croser again in future if the opportunity is right for us both," Evans speculates. "If a French château management proposition came up

The Chairman of Petaluma and his friends for lunch. Back row (from left): Primo Caon, Wolf Blass, Bob MacLean, Robert Hesketh, Greg Trott, Brian Croser, Michael Hill-Smith, Colin Ryan and Aldo Bratovic. Front row (from left): Peter Lehmann, George Fairbrother, Evans, Max Schubert and Jack Kilgour.

again, I would almost certainly want Croser involved in it."

As far as Petaluma is concerned, Evans has been happy to reduce his shareholding and leave to Brian Croser the final say in all decisions, even from an early stage. "Petaluma is his thing. Croser is now in charge of three labels totalling 60 000 cases – Petaluma, Bridgewater Mill (the second label) and Croser – quite an accomplishment. He's the one who does all the work. I am still very happy to be his chairman."

According to Evans, over the years each has learned more about what the other is good at. They're complementary and synergistic. "We understand better that there is a place for both of us. For one so young, what Croser has done for the industry is quite remarkable. He's a great asset to the industry, and this has nothing to do with his technical side. He is a highly intelligent and constructive man. I'm very fond of Brian, and recognise his great intellectual abilities."

Coming from such different backgrounds in wine it is little wonder that they might take different paths to achieve the same objective. One such example is the Petaluma Coonawarra red, whose stature has risen measurably, vintage by vintage until the making of a remarkable wine in 1988. Evans was all for richness, with a significant amount of it to come from shiraz. Croser sought immediate elegance and focused his attentions on cabernet sauvignon and merlot.

"We have always argued about the red," says Evans. "I loved the 1979, an excellent, rich, complex wine, with its Australian shiraz overtones, and I think he probably got too squeaky clean with the cabernets in the early 1980s. I think it's a fairly public debate among wine people.

"I always thought the red should be a little richer and heavier, which has started to happen – from '85 to '86, '87 to '88. I think the '88 is a ripper wine. The '89 wasn't good enough, so it was discarded and now he's even getting a bit of shiraz back into the wine, for even Croser himself likes that bit more depth now: the richness of middle palate fruit, versus the intense fine style that he personally likes."

In simple terms, they would probably have arrived at a similar result had Croser retained the original Evans preference and imparted his own concepts of elegance into that framework.

Croser recognises that while Evans was not so supportive of the cabernet merlot concept in Coonawarra, once the decision was made, he accepted it completely. In the same way, Evans has always been able to step back from a panel of show judges over whom he was chairman, and let them make their own decision. "He makes a fantastic devil's advocate. He never thinks for a moment about costs or profit. He only thinks about quality, much to the chagrin of our accountants."

Evans obviously relishes his role at Petaluma. "I'm supportive of Brian overall and try to be a good, balanced and constructive chairman. I'm part of putting together the final blends except for the Rhine riesling, which has nothing to do with me. It's a matter of straight conversion of fruit to wine anyway, and doesn't require much blending. I'm much more involved in the red, the sparkling wine and the chardonnay.

"I believe that Petaluma Chardonnay is perhaps the most consistent high quality chardonnay in Australia. The 1988 vintage was very good, '89 better and '90 even better again. I'm very excited by it. A sophisticated, very fine, elegant but deeply intensely flavoured wine is evolving from that Adelaide Hills vineyard."

Another Evans influence in Petaluma has been the introduction of a degree of American oak into the chardonnay. Croser had believed that only French oak was suitable, but has since acknowledged that Evans was right.

Evans is convinced that, as a winemaker Croser has always been a magnificent protector of wine fruit, the fruit of the grape. "Now he is appreciating, as he develops stylistically, that there is a need for other dimensions. You have to be a good scientist to make wine properly. But finally, half the artistry is putting the wine together and deciding what's what, like the blending, or "assemblage", of champagne.

"I still believe very much in Petaluma," Evans affirms. "I think Petaluma has established itself as the number one quality small winery of Australia. I don't think anyone could argue with that. Leeuwin had an opportunity to challenge, Coldstream Hills might yet have an opportunity to challenge, but Croser's dedication and absolute wine integrity will ensure Petaluma's long-term future. The greats are still to come."

James Halliday agrees, saying: "If you asked a majority of people to nominate what they thought was Australia's best small winery – adopting a moderately elastic view of what encompasses "small" – surely Petaluma would be the number one choice.

"In a sense, you can debate how much that is reputation," he continues, "or how much is reflected in the wines in the bottle. You could say with hindsight that the Coonawarras from 1980 through to 1985 have not been as strikingly good as their reputation might suggest they are. But the 1987 and 1988 are truly superb. Brian has been on a learning curve."

I will permit myself the luxury of the final word. Since he broke onto the scene with a truly remarkable Rhine riesling, made for Hardy's in 1975, Brian Croser has been a tall poppy, growing taller every year. We know what Australia does to them.

With the invaluable help of friends and colleagues like Len Evans, Brian Croser has justifiably established Petaluma as an internationally-known brand of Australian wine with a stature comparable to any other, with the exception of Grange Hermitage and possibly the Yarra Valley's Mount Mary vineyard, for the time being.

Petaluma's Rhine Riesling has been exemplary since 1984 and its chardonnay since 1986, although the greatest strides are the most recent. The "Croser" sits comfortably amid the best sparkling wines made outside France and, like several of the leading Australian méthode champenoise wines, seriously questions one's motives for buying any but the best French Non-Vintage Champagne. The Petaluma Coonawarra 1988 is a breakthrough for the region and should demonstrate to a number of Australia's larger wineries that Coonawarra red wine does not have to forfeit structure, colour and longevity to capture attention. But this is a book about Len Evans, who, as I have described and as Brian Croser proudly acknowledges, was instrumental in it all.

Grand Master
of the Grand Lodge

It's an awful thing to say, but I've probably tasted most of
the great vintages of most of the major wines of the world.
L. P. E.

For the greater part of the last fifteen years, Len Evans has held the mantle of Grand Master of the rites and mysteries inside the Grand Lodge that is the Australian wine show circuit. Wine shows involve much tasting, debate, ritual, prestige, competition and high stakes. They are just the sort of habitat you would expect Evans to thrive in, and thrive he certainly has done.

Evans has been Chairman of the Royal Sydney Show since 1978, and, at the close of 1990, retired from the Royal Adelaide and the National Wine Show, Canberra, where he had served as Chairman since 1988 and 1982 respectively. He had been a judge at Adelaide since 1974 and at Canberra since its inception in 1975. Not surprisingly, Sydney, Adelaide and Canberra are regarded in the wine industry as the three most prestigious of the major wine shows.

All Australian wineries are free to enter their wines in shows, although many smaller wineries choose not to. Following the traditional model of the agricultural show, wines are entered into specific classes, determined by either varietal, stylistic or minimum quantity requirements, or perhaps a combination of these. Each "class", which could contain anything from two to 150 entries, is judged together by a panel of three judges, one of whom is designated the panel head. Each judge allocates a mark out of 20 for each wine, the totals are added and a score given out of 60. If a wine scores a total of 46.5 points it is awarded a bronze medal, whereas, if it scores 51, a silver is awarded. To win a gold medal, a wine is required to score a minimum of 56.5 out of 60.

The judges are free to discuss each wine, should it be required, before medals are awarded, enabling some wines to be reconsidered and re-evaluated as the score-counting progresses. A certain degree of horse-trading invariably takes place in some shows, as judges occasionally mark up wines at the request of others, in return for which the others could be expected to be more generous for their preferred wines in return.

Evans' farewell dinner after his final Adelaide Show in 1990, at Chesser Cellars, Adelaide. Back row (from left): John Vickery, Primo Caon, Philip John, Colin Gaetjens, Tim Knappstein, James Halliday, James Godfrey, Brian Barry, Bob MacLean. Middle row (from left): Anthony Rose, Peter Wall, Max Schubert, Jack Kilgour, John Duval, Peter Lehmann, Brian Walsh. Front row (from left): Robert Hesketh, George Fairbrother, Len Evans, d'Arry Osborne, Geoff Merrill and Chris Hatcher.

Two or three trainee, or associate judges, accompany each panel and evaluate the same wines in the same fashion, although their marks do not count towards the points ultimately awarded. The judges I admire are those who pay due heed to their associates and listen to their opinions when fastened in a marking deadlock of their own. Several judges in major shows, who rate their egos higher than I rate their abilities, treat their associates little better than cannonfodder.

Aside from and above the judges who work in these panels is the chairman of judges, whose role is to brief the panel judges in matters of style interpretation and to help break deadlocks of opinion. Able to play a roving role, almost with a licence to influence in any way the chairman also frequently decides to become directly involved in the allocation of medals and trophies.

Depending on the show and the nature of the class involved, the top gold medal of a class may also collect a trophy, or it may have to be evaluated against the gold-medal winners of several other similar classes to battle it out for a single trophy. It all depends on the individual show and its particular system.

The Australian show system is criticised for handing out too many awards, to engulf the market with medal-winning wines. "I say that's great, absolutely wonderful, if it's the case," beams Evans. "If the beer industry had a similar system, or if the cheese industry really had a big system going like that, the public would follow it and buy better." For companies to survive, they would have to produce a better quality, he argues.

"If a public relations company came up with the idea of the show system, they would be regarded as bloody geniuses. It has terrific clout in the market and a huge power for publicity which should never be minimised," Evans believes. "The present system is a tremendously positive vehicle of trends, standards and the interchange of ideas. It has blossomed over the last ten to fifteen years and has done a power of good for Australian wine, which the industry still doesn't really understand."

In the early 1960s Evans was listed as an associate judge for the Sydney show. A year later, through a lucky break, he became a judge when one so nominated called in sick. Chairman of the show, George Fairbrother, was very supportive, although in Evans' opinion the promotion came before he was ready for it.

"There's no question that for several years I was largely mystified by the whole thing. I was good in some classes but not in others. I could handle the whites but found it tougher on things like the fortified wines and brandy. I had to work hard at them", he says.

Although he rates George Fairbrother as his judging mentor, Evans says he was was simply too sweet, too kind and too gentle to be a great chairman. "He was a great character and a great gentleman," he says. "George was an early Roseworthy graduate and a wonderful teacher in a quiet, humble way."

While judging vintage ports at Sydney with Jack Kilgour and John Stanford, Evans came across the most outstanding vintage port he had tasted. He and Stanford both marked it 19.5 out of 20, but Kilgour only gave it 13.5.

"We could not budge him half a point," says Evans. "He said it was a hard, broken wine with no flavour, while all I could see was this magnificent old, wonderfully structured, fine, elegant, marvellous example of Australian vintage port. I showed it

Evans and his show judging mentor, George Fairbrother.

to George Fairbrother, who took one smell and said: 'Jack, I think you'd better look at it again'.

Jack said he wouldn't give it a gold and if it got one it was the chairman's own business. So the chairman duly gave it a gold. The wine turned out to be the famous '45 Stonyfell Vintage Port which Jack had made himself! It was quite possibly the most famous vintage port in Australian wine show history!"

This is one of the many reasons it is impossible to take people seriously when they accuse judges of being able to identify their own wines in shows and point them accordingly. Styles and those styles similar, yes, but not individual wines.

Evans judged at Melbourne a couple of times in the mid 1970s, but couldn't face up to it again. "To me that whole parade of being a gentleman and that kind of thing is too much. It's all right being a gentleman, but it's no good being a dilettante. I couldn't stand it." Evans made his feelings quite clear, and hasn't been asked back.

Doug Seabrook was chairman of the Brisbane show when Evans judged there. "I couldn't stand it either. I liked Seabrook as a person and enjoyed his company, but he was far too autocratic as a chairman, and would often wander off to do his own thing." An interesting remark, for Dan Murphy says that, on principle, Seabrook would never agree with anything Evans had to say.

"I have severe memories of some of my early shows," Evans admits. "I was judging with Doug Seabrook in Sydney and once we weren't on speaking terms.

Copping an eyeful at the Adelaide Show, 1988.

Neither of us would simply budge from our views. I'd find that abhorrent today. If I find judges taking stances I kick both their arses."

When Evans was made chairman at Sydney in 1978, former Lindemans boss, Ray Kidd said he thought Evans had the capacity to become a great chairman. "That was an encouragement to me, for I really had tried hard to be a top judge," Evans says. "But being a chairman was a different thing. A chairman is not merely a co-ordinator of the show – although I think I did that to some extent in shows I controlled – a chairman must put his stamp upon the show."

It will surprise many to hear that Brian Croser, who succeeded Evans as chairman at Adelaide, says that Evans was anything but an autocratic chairman. To Nick Bulleid he is the least interventionist chairman that he has judged with. "He will want to taste the gold medals and top silvers, and hear about any arguments that may have happened," he says.

Croser says that for Evans the foremost principle is the sovereignty of the panel. "He will never over-ride a panel. Whatever decision it makes, right or wrong, the decision will stand. He will stimulate discussion and will create controversy within a panel, by provoking and stirring things up. He may either support an individual judge, or act against him or her, before walking away, leaving them to resolve the difference."

Nick Bulleid says that he will ask afterwards what was decided and only speak up a little more loudly if he considers a real injustice has been done.

Other chairmen will do the same thing, but will then directly recommend other wines for medals, or ask for other changes in awards. Some chairmen are so interventionist they will want to examine all the wines not considered fit even for a bronze medal by the panel judges, and then perhaps demand that one should be awarded a gold. Evans would never contemplate such an approach.

"Gold medals are won, rather than given," he believes. "I try neither to be too feeble nor too autocratic. I have always been amused to have it inferred that I have been autocratic. If you think of the collective egos involved in the wine business, how the hell could anyone be?"

To John Beeston, the Evans style is perhaps a little more dominant than consensus in nature. "He's not a Bob Hawke. He won't stand on your feet, but he will say you're quite wrong, to Halliday, Croser or anyone. He's got no particular favourites."

He remembers the first year, 1976, that Brian Croser, then very much on the ascent, was an associate at the Sydney Show. "He came up to me, looked at the other judges and said: 'What a lot of tired old palates there are here', to which I rejoined immediately: 'Don't forget what those initials stand for – T.O.P.'

"He laughed, and we did the show together, although I judged quicker than Croser did. He was quite furious that someone was quicker and possibly more decisive even than he. He was worse then than he is now. He needed to have his arse kicked for twenty years. I was the only one who kicked Croser's arse quite regularly!"

"At the end of the show, in an astonishingly rare exhibition of humility, Croser said 'I really enjoyed judging with you. What do you think of me?' Considering what we had discussed earlier, I said: 'I think you have a Promising Under-Palate'." Early in his show career, James Halliday, who has since become one of the most important wine judges both in Australia and overseas, was struck by the "incredibly introspective attitude" of the judges taken directly from the wine industry. To him, Rudy Komon, one of Australia's leading wine judges for over thirty years, was a wonderfully eccentric exception to that, as were the Department of Agriculture officer Graham Gregory and Jack Monty. The winemaker judges, he believes, were far too inward-looking.

While serving as an associate judge under Evans' chairmanship at Sydney, Halliday remembers running off to him "in a state of incredible anxiety" with an incredible wine, saying the judges had just knocked it out by pointing it at only 13.5. "They didn't even give it a bronze!" cries Halliday, who thought the wine was extraordinary. Naturally, he wanted to know what was going on.

It turned out to be 1962 Grange Hermitage, a great wine. "One judge had put the claws into it for its volatility and the others had run along with him," says Halliday. Fortunately, Evans saw it Halliday's way. He remembers the wine well enough, and loved its richness, length, "sweet oak finish, taste of violets, truffles and old boots". The wine finished the day being awarded a silver.

Halliday recalls that at one of the early shows in which he participated, a superb (French) 1961 Burgundy served at a dinner after a day's judging was utterly dismissed out of hand as a very bad wine because "apart from anything else it was rebuffed as volatile". Most Australian winemakers then lacked even the most basic understanding of French wine, and really didn't have much idea of styles other than those they made themselves.

Central to the judging itself, according to Evans, are the chairmans' briefings to the panel judges in relation to the precise definition of styles. Of particular importance is the rigid definition of top quality in each category, to facilitate a clearly understood pattern of what judges should look for. Evans, being a genuine wine internationalist with a great expectation of what Australian wine could achieve, was the perfect foundation upon which style definitions could be built. He hates "wishy-washy attitudes where golds are handed out because style is not important enough".

"I've been in situations where five top wines were being debated for gold medals, and the chairman took a quick look and said to give them all gold. I think that's pathetic. It brings the system undone. That sort of approach does nothing for the winemakers and nothing for the show," argues Evans.

As I have described previously, Evans and Croser are extremely good friends, although Croser is being utterly objective when he says that Evans is the best wine judge in Australia. "He is the teacher of wine judges and the forward thinker of what wine shows should be about."

Not content with merely deciding upon the benchmarks, Evans has long since taken it upon himself to broaden the horizons of the judges and associates under him by exposing them to important benchmark styles. He has been an immeasurable influence on judges' accuracy, integrity and ability to interpret style. More than anyone else, he has emphasised the structure of wine, its depth and intensity.

The results are found not only in the medals and trophies awarded and in the many wines discarded, but in the internationalisation of Australian wine, which has taken one who understood the great international wines as well as Evans to accomplish. The wine show system became his vehicle, as he introduced Australian judges to benchmark imported wines, broadening their vision and illustrating how these wines achieved their status. Halliday says Evans' education of judges almost rates with Rothbury as his greatest single contribution to Australian wine.

It is not my intention to suggest that Evans only encouraged those wines which duplicated international characteristics, for as you appreciate more about wine, it becomes apparent that the parameters of quality stretch across international boundaries. What should pinot noir, chardonnay and riesling taste like? What was Australian wine doing that was short of the apex? In a nutshell, this was Evans' point. Australian wine judges and makers had to come to grips with classic wines to be able to see their own local styles in a global perspective.

How did Evans go about the education of his judges? You guessed it – by taking them out to dinner. Earlier he had looked on as George Fairbrother habitually referred to an international wine whenever a dispute over a local wine proved difficult to settle. Seabrook would regularly open a top Spanish sherry or a great Portuguese port when a panel of judges were hotly debating the merits of style of an Australian show entrant. Evans had also been to the occasional dinner after judging sessions when excellent French table wines were brought to the table and discussed.

His touch, however, his real polish, was to put these principles into a classically Len Evans dimension. By taking the judges and associates out to dinner and pouring down their throats great quantities of premium imported wine, he initiated what has since become a tradition in most of the major shows, the Chairman's Dinners. He presented rows of great wines throughout a meal of the highest standard, explaining their qualities, characteristics, and even flaws and putting them into perspective.

Most of his guests were never likely to have tasted wines of this calibre otherwise. Their eyes were quickly opened. Suddenly, Evans witnessed them buying great wines in their own private right, showing them to other people within their own companies and even including imported wines in their company's own in-house tastings, critically comparing their own wines with the imported wines, all the time learning from them. Evans' dinners set the snowball rolling, which to the good of Australian wine, hasn't stopped. He remains largely responsible for presenting the lion's share of the wine opened at the Sydney show's Chairman's Dinner, although the judges and associates themselves are now encouraged to pull their own weight.

After the 1990 Chairman's Dinner in Sydney, held at Bilson's Restaurant, one of the Hardy winemakers, Tim James, serving as an associate judge for the first time, approached Evans. "How long has this sort of thing been going on? This is the best dinner I have ever had," he said. "The wines are so great and I am having such a fabulous time."

From his own cellar Evans had taken magnums of '48 Malartic Lagravière, '70 Ducru Beaucaillou, '70 Montrose and '70 Lynch Bages, single bottles of '61 Lagrange, '61 Pontet Canet and '57 Pichon Longueville Baron and the judges had arranged a host of other wines including a great collection of old Australian wines of which eight were older than 1955.

"I can't believe this, Mr Evans," said James. "What can I do for you? Clean your car, your shoes, or something?"

Not long after, James was judging at the Hunter Valley Wine Show, for which Evans found to his horror that no one had arranged any entertainment for the judges. So Evans invited them over to "Loggerheads" for dinner. "We had a good time with nice wines and simple food," he says. Towards the end of the evening he strolled outside, hearing a commotion and poorly suppressed laughter. "Tim James had got up from the bloody table and cleaned my Pajero!" he laughs. "Right there in the carport there was this gleaming bloody Pajero!" Inspecting his car again in the more revealing light of morning, Evans found that James had only cleaned the half that was showing and that the car's other side remained filthy dirty!

As a chairman, Evans was quick to devote his energies to recommending judges and encouraging the show committees to bring in more and more associates, firmly convinced of the importance of developing and training them, for the show system's future.

He has always made it a practice to spend time with associates, developing their understanding of wines and of the show system. Although he has always put them under a degree of pressure to perform, he has been there for help whenever they needed it. His contributions did not pass unnoticed by his novices.

At a dinner before the first tasting session of the 1989 Sydney show, he addressed the assembled judges and associates: "Right. This is the year of reckoning for the associates. A lot of you have been around for a while. Hill-Smith, you are a professional associate. You have been around here longer than anyone. Merrill, Weaver, Bulleid, this is the year you have to earn your stripes. Either you show you can make it this year, or you don't come back."

By the show's conclusion, the associates in question were together, racking their brains for a gift to present to Evans. Nick Bulleid had the answer, drove to a saddlery in Randwick and found a large, long whip with a short braided end, the type used for a team of horses pulling a carriage. It was presented to Evans at the Bulletin Place dinner after the show, with the words "To help you keep associates in line in the future as well as you have done in the past".

History reveals that each of these associates has since progressed to the status of full judge. When, after many years, Nick Bulleid was finally given his guernsey at Sydney a year later, he sent Evans a letter. "I am delighted to accept my place as judge for the Sydney show," he wrote. "Who died?"

Evans enjoys stirring up Australian judges by placing overseas judges and experts into the judging panels in Australian wine shows, a practice he initiated at Canberra and now standard across the system. Once again, the impact has been to enormously broaden the horizons of Australian judges and winemakers. Its most obvious benefit is witnessed in the rapid improvement in the Australian wine industry made by that most fickle grape of all, pinot noir.

Evans believes those with the most to offer Australian wine are the internationals with true international palates, such as John Avery, Nick Clarke and Peter Sichel. Specialists from particular regions like Burgundy, Bordeaux or the Napa Valley are of lesser value, since they might be blinkered towards their own familiar styles and may not relate to the entire spectrum of wine made in this country. "Internationals who come here are very impressed with the Australian system," he says.

However much the international judges may have contributed, Evans believes that Australians encourage a greater interchange of ideas than others and have raised the broad technical understanding of wine to new levels. "Australian judges are more incisive," he says, "although that's not to say that we haven't a lot to learn." Whereas the English and French especially, have influenced style, Australians have highlighted faults and cleanness in wine.

Len Evans has judged wine in France, Germany, America, England and Hong Kong and was Chairman of a brilliantly-credentialled international judging panel at the Victorian International Exhibition of Wine in 1985 (VIEW 85) held in the Exhibition Buildings, Melbourne. On occasions he has found that different nationalities tend to interpret the same wine character in peculiarly different ways.

Michael Hill-Smith, wine writer, owner of an Adelaide wine bar and Australia's first Master of Wine, was judging as an associate and stumbled across a wine he was convinced had an unpalatable excess of hydrogen sulphide (H_2S), colloquially known as rotten egg gas. Glancing over the shoulder of James Halliday, who was judging on his panel, he observed that Halliday has written, "H_2S and mercaptan ruin otherwise good fruit flavours".

Then, peering over the shoulder of Michael Broadbent, who was also on the panel, he saw that the great English wine critic had described precisely the same wine as: "A farmyard festooned with a garland of flowers". His words could be interpreted as the identical thing to Halliday's, although in a typically European manner.

Amused by these vastly different impressions of the same phenomenon, Hill-Smith showed the wine to Evans, the chairman, who then took a glass of the wine over to the great German wine man, Helmut Becker, and asked for his verdict. Becker took one sniff and cried: "Ah – Devil's Farts!" – yet another perfect description and interpretation of reduced sulphur in wine!

Australian wines are now regular entrants in international wine shows, and their results are invariably encouraging for the local wine industry. "We have got to allay the myth that French wines are the best wines, just because they're there," says Evans. "Some of the best wines are indeed French, but that doesn't mean that we can't compete against them."

In recent years, international shows have benefitted from the Australian show system, although no one would seriously suggest that the Australian show system is perfect, Len Evans included. It still has its faults, some more serious than others. The show system is still evolving, although it is often hindered by the outdated attitudes of certain show committees as they valiantly protect their fiefdoms against any possible loss of influence or authority.

Evans has furthered the show system in other ways. He has pushed for the improvement of conditions for wine judges and initiated a rotation system of judging which prohibits the possibility of two judges ganging up against a third for the duration of a show and thereby distorting results. The senior member of that panel, as appointed by the chairman, remains fixed with that panel, while the other judges are shifted around, a system now adopted by every major wine show. It became the responsibility of the senior panel judge to manage his panel and to act as a spokesman between it and the chairman.

Most of the top Australian wine judges are senior winemakers for large companies. "It is true," says Evans, "that a senior winemaker cannot help but favour his own company's style. But there are two other judges standing beside him, and also a chairman to argue with him, just in case he wants to put his point of view too strongly. There's a very good system of control."

Evans is firmly convinced that only those with the best credentials should judge at shows, even if the same names tend to repeat themselves in judging panels. Those chosen to judge at Sydney, Adelaide and Canberra, known in the trade as the "Evans XI", reflect his view. There is no question that he regards the panels of certain other shows as decidedly inferior.

It is frequently argued in the wine trade that the Evans team has excessive influence and tends to judge wine in a particular and blinkered fashion. Although it could be said that while perhaps the key members of this team, namely James Halliday, Brian Croser, Philip John, John Duval, Tim Knappstein, Ian McKenzie, John Hanley and Jim Brayne share a common broad perspective of wine, Brian Croser is certain that at the end of the day, each has entirely different slants to his judging. "It is a false accusation," he says.

The wines made by Coldstream Hills, Petaluma, Lindemans, Penfolds, Knappstein, Seppelt and McWilliams lend weight to his view by showing quite clearly that the various winemaker/judges each measures his quality and fixes his styles in different ways.

That the Melbourne show does not admit winemakers whose companies exhibit there as judges is quite beyond Len Evans. "It is just ridiculous. The top judges are

The Chairman with his international judges at the National Wine Show, Canberra. From left: Nicholas Clarke, Evans, Peter Sichel (d'Arngludet-Palmer) and Darrel Corty.

highly experienced people who can work off each other, but also by judging together, control each other in the best sense of the word."

Many awards are presented to unfinished and unbottled wines in major shows. Of these, Melbourne's Jimmy Watson Trophy is clearly the best known. It is awarded to the best one-year-old red wine at the show, usually judged from unblended samples taken straight from barrels. Although it honours a justifiably famous man who contributed a great deal to the Victorian wine industry, it has become Australia's most celebrated wine trophy without any real justification from a technical point of view.

"It's over-rated; and it's totally abused by winemakers who make sophisticated wines to suit the judges for the purpose of winning the Jimmy Watson Trophy, rather than to make wines for the future," Evans argues. "The best red should be a great wine that can be kept in the bottle and tastings of Jimmy Watson winners show that very few cellar well.

"The trophy was nothing until Blass won it three times. He made it famous and now its public image is very well fostered by those who run the Melbourne show," he says.

Evans believes the Canberra system is best, where only finished and bottled wines are able to be shown. Test samples of wine are bought from the retail shelves to compare to the show samples entered. Once at Canberra, a major company which had done very well there was caught flat-footed and found out. It was immediately forced to withdraw all its entries. "If the industry knows this happens, they will not try and create special 'show' samples," says Evans, who firmly believes that since "the Adelaide, Canberra and Sydney shows are better run, their medals should be a lot more highly regarded than those of other wine shows".

Judges at Australian wine shows are regularly expected to taste around two hundred wines a day, a number considered by most international authorities to be wildly excessive. Some well-known international guest judges have literally walked out of Australian show judgings, having hit the wall after the first couple of hours.

Like most people, Michael Broadbent, not to be inferred as one of the walkers referred to, says he is exhausted after tasting thirty wines but, according to Evans, a "good hard-working Australian judge getting on with it, not carrying on, can taste between a hundred and eighty and two hundred wines in a day. There's no question of that, but it is bloody hard work tasting between 60-80 young cabernets, for example. It's a hell of a job. The ideal class consists of thirty to thirty-five wines. You start getting tired at that point and need to be very much on your guard to do the bigger classes."

The aspiring judge's first sight of a large hundred-plus class at an Australian wine show is a daunting one that usually stays in the memory for life. "When I started judging I would walk up and down, up and down the rows, then I'd smell them, taking smelling notes," says Evans. "Then I'd taste them and put them into categories. I'd play chess with them, and then I'd go through them, taste them and write more notes, and then I'd bring the top ten wines to judge and then taste them again. By the time I'd finished I was exhausted.

"I reckon I judged like that for ten years. More and more I felt what's the use of it? I've got two more judges to help me if I make a mistake – that's the whole point of having three judges – and my ego is not that big that I have to be perfect all the time. So I decided to get to number one, judge it and then move to number two."

Evans has never felt comfortable with the existing show system in which each of the major capital city shows assume equal status. Today, some regional shows are beginning to tread on the toes of the major ones by admitting wines from all over the country. In the mid 1970s, while Chairman of the Wine Show Committee of the Federal Council of the Australian Wine and Brandy Producers Association, Evans recommended the initiation of a national hierarchical show system.

Following his concept, regional shows would be encouraged and developed, all their medal winners would then be granted automatic admission to their own State shows, which would therefore judge only the produce of their own State. The Melbourne show, for example, would only judge the best Victorian wines, as determined by the various regional shows around the state of Victoria.

Medal-winners in each State would then go on to a National Wine Show, such as Canberra (although this suggestion was made before the present National Wine Show at Canberra was initiated), which would therefore make it the most important show of the year.

Evans still thinks that would be a better system, although he recognises it is hardly likely to happen. The only danger I perceive would be that some high quality wines might be missed out at the regional show stage, as indeed good wines are often missed in the existing system, and would therefore have no hope of gaining any award throughout the entire year. At least the present system offers them another chance, with different people and in different conditions.

While he also concedes difficulty with some aspects of the Evans system, Brian Croser is firmly convinced that if Evans had a better show structure to work with, he would have achieved more with the show system than he has. "And he has already done more than anyone else before him," he says. "Wine companies have vested interests not to move to a pyramid system. They would be reluctant to compromise the attention their awards and trophies collect in the media."

Successful show wines are often held back from release to the market, simply for the publicity that shows generate, often in obscure fortified and spirit classes, where their habitual collection of trophies contributes to the prestigious overall title of "Best Exhibitor in Show". Ultimately, the wines are of pathetically little value to the wine public, for whose enjoyment and consumption they were initially made.

In the mid 1980s, Evans approached the Wine and Brandy Corporation with the idea of forming an Association of Wine Judges, whose role would be to co-ordinate schedules, the development of young judges, the continual training of established judges, and to communicate to the wine industry and the public what wine shows are all about.

That the corporation refused Evans' request for $10 000 funding still disappoints him. "I think they would probably help today, but I offered to get the whole thing going for the industry, and it said to get stuffed. The wine industry still does not recognise what the show judges do for it."

In future, Evans would like to see wines judged in their price categories and more of an emphasis placed on wine style. "Technical judges sometimes miss stylistic interpretations and we have possibly gone too far in favour of the technician judge, although many faults in Australian wine have been largely eradicated because of this. Now it's time for pendulum to go back a bit."

I am amazed at how often Len Evans is criticised in discussions about wine shows and his role in them. Certain people would suggest that Evans has used the show system to identify and promote the wines he has been associated with, especially those from Rothbury and Petaluma.

To put it simply, Evans has actively discouraged Rothbury and Petaluma from entering wines in shows in which he is involved. The facts are that Petaluma never shows its wine and Rothbury only enters wine in his shows on very rare occasions. Those in the wine industry who suggest that Evans has the ability to identify Rothbury wines in show classes, and then promotes those particular wines to his judges, could hardly be more distant from the truth, however beyond reason they are flattering even his palate.

Others criticise Evans claiming that, by selecting judges who follow his ideals, Evans therefore promotes through the show system the style of wines that he enjoys. What a naive suggestion! Who could be better qualified than Evans to dictate style and quality and train his judges to appreciate them? Isn't there a chance that if Evans considers a wine to have quality, others might as well?

Secondly, there is a notion that Evans only points up the wines he personally likes. Evans is a complete wine professional whose personal likes and dislikes, which are not to be confused with his interpretation of style, never interfere with his evaluation of wine quality. Through his fostering of style, says James Halliday, and his ensuring that, with its appreciation, the direction of Australian winemaking doesn't lose its flexibility, Evans has made a major achievement. "It comes down to his broad perspective," says Halliday, "his understanding of overseas wines, and his generosity of spirit, all without any vested interest. He has never pushed a particular style, wine company or industry barrow."

Brian Croser affirms that Len Evans has never had a vested interest in a wine show. "He would have to be the most misunderstood person in the wine industry. Everyone has an opinion on him, but nearly all those with a negative opinion on Evans hardly know him."

Each year the Royal Agricultural Society of New South Wales presents the RAS Medal, awarded to a person who has made a large and tangible contribution to the Royal Sydney Easter Show, selected from across a diversity of industries and endeavours. In 1992 it was presented to Len Evans, who has done more than anyone else to ensure that the Australian wine show circuit justifies the high regard in which the public hold it.

For
Services Rendered

*I delight in people, and it seems to me that almost the best
thing about wine is sharing it with someone you like.*
L. P. E.

*L*en Evans' years of service to the wine industry and the community were
recognised when he was awarded an OBE in 1982. Despite that honour, the
wine industry has generally been slow to recognise Evans' work on its behalf
although, through McWilliams Wines Pty Ltd, Evans received a considerable
distinction in 1991, becoming only the second recipient of the Mount Pleasant
Maurice O'Shea Award for excellence in the wine industry. In its previous and
inaugural year it was awarded to the creator of Grange Hermitage, Max Schubert.

The award, a silver sculpture valued at $10 000 made by Sydney artist Ernst
Pfenninger, recognised Evans' "historically significant contribution" to Australian
wine. Although Evans never met O'Shea, who had died two years before he started
washing glasses at the Ship Inn, he was very familiar with many of his great wines,
especially, he acknowledges, through the cellar and the generosity of Max Lake, John
Collins, a manager of Hardys wines in NSW, the late Johnnie Walker and the NSW
Wine & Food Society.

Although he has never been a initiator of charities, Evans has generated millions
of dollars for dozens of them by being what he describes the "icing on the cake".
That's no exaggeration. Evans has a great ability to manipulate and dominate a room
full of people and is one of the most talented hosts, MCs or auctioneers ever seen.
He has always been a highly skilled and quick-witted natural writer and raconteur.
Max Lake rates him as one of the world's great writers. "He is so bloody good it's
unbelievable," he says. "And that's a function of how he can hold an audience now.
Evans owns every audience he's ever had."

At the *Wine Spectator*'s 10th Wine Experience in New York, one of the world's
major annual wine events, organiser Kevin Zraly announced from the podium that
Evans had been voted the most highly regarded and popular presenter in the nine
years of the event. He was even invited to San Francisco in 1992 to compere the entire
11th Wine Experience, about which he was naturally proud and delighted but
somewhat concerned at the response he might receive from certain Californian
would-be MCs in the crowd.

As a natural storyteller, Evans is the equal of anyone I have ever seen, and by all accounts, was quite brilliant on television in the *Would You Believe* show. To Colin Richardson, another speaker and MC of considerable class, Evans has a "wonderful ability, part bombast, part arrogance, plus a very good sense of humour".

"He will stand up and deliver this terrific, nonchalent and spontaneous speech at five minutes warning, which has probably taken a week of preparation. He would know exactly whom he was addressing, how long he's got to speak, the key points he's to make and the whereabouts of any prominent individuals in the audience. He'd bounce topical jokes off them and use them to keep the audience involved with his marvellous sense of humour. First he wins an audience, then at the appropriate time, comes in and makes his point."

Evans began his public-speaking career on behalf of the wine industry. "Then, as I evolved," he says, "I was asked to make speeches more frequently. I got more and more bored by delivering the Rotary kind of speech, but said I would gladly do them for charity."

Evans in money-raising mood at Mount Isa, 1986.

Raising funds for charities now occupies about one month of Evans' every year. Although some of the time this year (1992) had been taken up with the Sydney wine show, he told me that although he had been working flat out for the first seven weeks of the year, none of his efforts had actually made him any money.

From relatively humble beginnings raising just a few thousand dollars a hit, and as his ability to project himself in public became more practised – this man had never had any problem expressing himself – Evans' fund-raising ability enlargened. For several years he has helped advise people how to raise money for their charities and then shown up at the critical moment to provide his unique combination of noise, colour and movement.

In fact, once he discovered that some so-called charities at which he performed raised such a pathetic amount of money, Evans decided to stipulate the base amount of money he expected a charity to raise before he would agree to perform. Below this amount he said he was quite happy to be hired for his not insubstantial but entirely realistic appearance fee as a celebrity speaker – another potential and brilliant career he has not milked as hard as he might have done – although for some time he performed as a speechmaker at three functions a month, year after year.

This typical Evans straightforwardness is again prone to interpretation by those quick to criticise as outright egocentricity, but it does reveal quite forthrightly that not only does he put a value on his own time and efforts, but he draws a line where a night on the skids comes to an end and genuine fund-raising begins.

One day, speaking professionally before the Poultry Growers Association of Australia, his fee was to be made as a presentation painting. His brief was to speak on the subject of chickens at the association's annual dinner.

"Apparently I gave one of the best speeches on chickens that has ever been heard – or so I was told by them," he says. "But when I finished with an impassioned plea to the poultry growers to put more flavour back into chickens, I sat down to one-handed applause. Until that moment the speech had been very funny, and even then, I felt that the point was there to be made." The painting, when it arrived much, much later, was largely dominated by a toilet-block.

Evans has since moved away from speech-making because the challenge was waning. "I got bored with talking about my life and times with wine. I am happier when given a brief, and feel best doing charity work."

Len Evans doesn't see any problem in constantly switching hats from being wine expert to funny man. "It all depends on the brief. There are no laughs at the Australian Wine Foundation (a wine industry body established to deal with the question of alcohol education in society) or at Rothbury Board meetings. These are different facets of me doing different facets of my work. Wine judging, although we used to have laughs at night, wasn't a barrel of laughs. If you want a serious speech from me about the future of chardonnay in Australia, I will happily give you that speech.

"At the Johnnie Walker Memorial Lecture for The Wine and Food Society, I spoke about the future of the wine industry as requested. Some people came up to me afterwards and said they were disappointed it wasn't very jovial. I wasn't told to be jovial, nor was I expected to be jovial.

"Playing the fool Evans' can go over very big in certain areas. It's an entertaining thing which I am happy to entertain with – provided it's the requirement. If it is not the requirement, then I don't, and I am perfectly happy not to."

In a life with so many compartments, Evans has an internal cast of thousands to call on. Tired of hearing his own voice, he revels meeting a challenging brief.

"A year or so ago I got a brief I couldn't fulfil only because I was unable to attend. It was from a conference organiser, who wanted to pay me a very good fee to address the international organisation of onion growers, who were coming to Tasmania, to Australia, for the first time. 'We'd love you to give a speech on onions' they said. But I just couldn't do it. I wasn't able to do it, but would have loved to."

Popular Sydney social writer Diana 'Bubbles' Fisher is positive she knows why both she and Evans are so regularly asked to conduct fund-raising raffles or auctions. "We are two of the noisiest people in Australia!" she exclaims. "He was a great one for saying 'Come on you old bugger, fork out another few dollars!'"

"We help with charity for all sorts of reasons," says Evans. "I have never been fooled into thinking I was doing it simply for other people; I enjoyed doing it. I enjoyed feeling good about it, feeling it was worthwhile and being effective at it. I believe strongly in that, in being able to help others one also helps oneself. It would be dishonest to say otherwise."

Similarly, it would be wrong to create the impression that Evans is not crucially aware of the need to help those less fortunate than himself. It is simply typical of his attitude that if he is going to get involved in anything, charity included, two things will happen. He will do it to the best of his ability, and wherever possible will have some fun while at it.

The first AAP sponsors luncheon in 1987 involved seventeen people. At the third dinner (1989, Bulletin Place) Evans is seen attempting to take control of an audience which featured Ronnie Corbett (to his left) and Clement Freud (opposite Corbett). David Jensen of AAP reveals a healthy scalp.

"There is an obligation to anyone who has made good in Australia to put something back into the country. It is a great cliché, but I strongly believe in it. You can't continually take from any society."

Evans is presently spending a deal of time considering ways to help elderly people. "I am very interested in old people. I think a lot of old people get a pretty shabby go in Australia. I would certainly like to do more for them, especially in the way of establishing self-help schemes, so they could become better organised for themselves. There is an awful lot of talent and wasted person power among old people and, if given an organisation, they could do a lot of good for each other."

Six years ago Evans became involved with a charity scheme developed through AAP and the financial markets, which is today Evans' major annual charity activity. Evans was involved from the beginning and in each of the first couple of years they raised around $130 000. Evans then said to Len Casey, MD of AAP and to David Jensen, AAP General Manager, Marketing, that after two years they were on to something. The following year they included an auction and raised $360 000, the next year, $540 000. In 1991, when they raised a total of $720 000, the auction alone collected nearly $400 000.

"We have since refined our ten lot auction concept," says Evans, "selling things you couldn't buy for money. Each year different charities are nominated, so the AAP and I sit down and sort out those to benefit," he says. The target in 1992 was a million dollars, from which ten charities would then receive $100 000 each. Evans and AAP raised $1 019 500!

Prior to each auction, Evans is aware of precisely the minimum amount he expects each of the ten lots to raise. Since he is notorious for calling up favours to compile lots for the auction from his international network of wine connections, some of the lots for sale are spectacular in the extreme.

The 1992 year got off to a flying start, with the various heavily-sponsored preliminary events including a celebrity golf day and sponsors' luncheon raising $580 000. Therefore the auction target was $420 000. Working hard, Evans found himself flagging half-way through, although the start had been encouraging. It took all the energy he could muster to sell an Arctic adventure for $25 000, although he anticipated fetching nearer $35 000 for it.

Just prior to the auction, Wynns Coonawarra had donated ten imperials (bottles the equivalent in volume of eight of normal size) of John Riddoch Cabernet Sauvignon. Thinking they might spark some interest in proceedings, Evans decided now was their time. Before he could sell them singly, as was his original idea, someone bid $30 000 for the entire lot and the auction was back into full swing. A New Zealand adventure went for $30 000, a Bordeaux adventure for $50 000, a Remy Martin gastronomic tour of France for $40 000 and Evans easily found the $40 000 he anticipated for a tour to the US Masters Golf. The ten charities, which included The Smith Family, The Heart Foundation, Leukemia Research and Odyssey House all received their $100 000.

In case you think the prices bid rather unrealistic, it's worth considering that the tour to Bordeaux included twelve days hospitality visiting all of the great houses to spend time with their owners, and the tour of France featured visits to all the properties associated with Remy Martin in Champagne, Burgundy, Bordeaux, the Rhône Valley and Cognac.

In previous years, Evans has auctioned a ten-day educational trip to Champagne, staying over each night with a different Champagne House and, in 1991, he sequestered ten imperials of Grange Hermitage from Penfolds for auction.

"By the end of the 1992 auction I was very stuffed and very emotional," he says. "I don't often get choked up like that." Afterwards, Evans was thanked for his efforts and presented with an object he is certain to treasure, a silver-plated and personally inscribed Mashie-Niblick golf club.

Another charity auction in which Evans participates is that held annually by the Primary Club, an English-based cricket charity which assists blind children, of which Evans has been a Vice-President. Lots are compiled together by requesting that the club members who attend bring along wines as lots for other members to bid for. One member might bring an old Grange and in return purchase a set of Coonawarras. Some members, unable to cut the emotional ties with their own, even buy back their stock. Evans remembers Graham Mapp once bidding furiously for three bottles of '67 Penfolds St Henri he had donated himself!

One particular bottle of Valpantena Valpollicella has raised well over $1 000 because various members, initial donor included, keep on buying it and then resubmitting it for sale the following year!

There are times when Evans winds up on the paying end of auctions as well. Bidding at the 1967 Barossa Valley Festival auction for a lot of old Frontignac, he raised the call to $1.25. His opponent then bid $1.50, before Evans realised it was Bob Raymond, the director of a Channel Nine television series and actually a member of his own syndicate.

"Hey," shouted Evans, and the auctioneer, Ian Bruce, called "$1.75 on my right".

"What?" called Raymond.

"$2.00 on my left," said the auctioneer.

"You idiot!" cried Evans.

"I'll take that as a bid," said Ian Bruce, as he knocked it down for $2.25!

The public component of the Evans persona is considerably larger than life. He has been the chairman of the wine industry's three most important national wine shows, National Director of the Australian Wine Information Bureau, Chairman of the Australian Wine Foundation, critic, commentator, promoter, consultant, educator and wine's unofficial, and at times, official front man. He has been involved to a greater or lesser extent in many international and Australian food and wine societies, a fistful of charities and several highly publicised business ventures.

Yet he says he was always horrified to think that he would become the Australian guru of wine and food. "I worked hard not to," he says. "I could see it happening when I turned fifty – if I played my cards the right way, became the head of this, and the President of that, and contributed more to the Wine and Food Society, the Chaine de la Rôtissières, and to the restaurant associations and the small winemakers competitions and all those sort of things, I could have become a godfather of Australian food and wine. I didn't want to be the godfather, so I actively avoided becoming it."

I'm not so sure that isn't one of the few things Evans has failed to do. Capisci?

Reflections

It's been three decades since Len Evans, inspired by wine enthusiasts such as the highly respected Rudy Komon and others, helped him to take wine seriously. Since then, having tasted more great wine than any other Australian, his knowledge and appreciation of wine sets him apart from any other and has set him on the path to becoming one of the world's leading authorities on wine – every reason to respect his reflections and opinions of the future of Australia's wine.

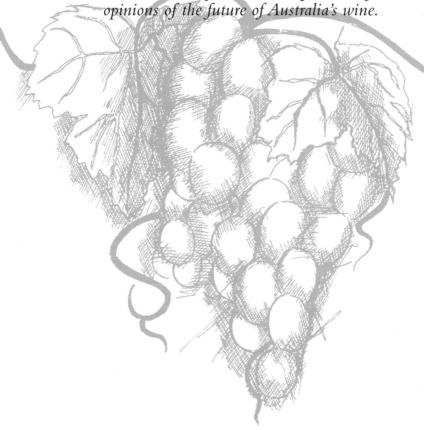

The
*A*pprentice's Sorcerer

Rudy Komon could be a terrible bastard and at times a real
old sod, both rude and common.
L. P. E.

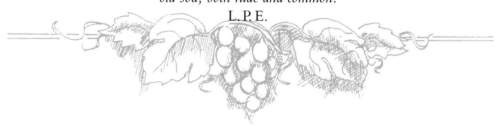

Rudy Komon, MBE, died in 1982. For many years he was the most important person in Len Evans' life in wine. Today Evans acknowledges him as his great mentor, father-figure and friend. I introduced him in the chapter *The Chevron Hilton: the Alternative University*, but such was his importance to Evans that he is worth dwelling on a moment longer.

Brian Croser best describes their relationship by comparing the relationship between Evans and himself. "As Len is to me, Rudy was to Len; very much a mentor and adviser on issues, not just those concerned with tasting wine. Rudy would discuss with Len the philosophies of life, how to conduct yourself, how to be an aesthete and how to appreciate the finer things. "Rudy admired the way Len could gather, perform and create, and was equally generous in letting Len share a little of his own rich, diverse life, and his art."

As Cellarmaster of the New South Wales Wine and Food Society and a regular wine judge at the wine shows of Adelaide, Canberra and Sydney, where he judged for many years until 1979, only three years before his death, Rudy Komon made an immense contribution to Australian wine.

That which Evans rates most highly was his strong promotion of regional wines at a time when very few Australians were aware that either regional or vintage variations even existed. Komon forced Sydney's developing wine community to drink Coonawarra and preached the qualities of Hunter Valley wines, red and white, long before they were recognised even in Sydney, its closest and most parochial market.

In his fine reference work, *Coonawarra,* James Halliday records that Rudy Komon watched as the first five places in the claret class at the 1951 Adelaide Show went to Redman. Standing straight up from his table, he drove directly over to Coonawarra, only to discover that no Redman wine was left unsold for either tasting or sale.

Passionately requesting that Bill and Owen Redman leave back several hogsheads (250-litre barrels) of wine from each vintage, he returned in 1952 to find the wine they left was untouched! But, as Evans acknowledges, Komon's enthusiasm for it put Coonawarra on the wine map in Sydney.

"Komon always said that had he not been an art dealer, he would have made a very good fist of being a wine merchant," says wine historian, David Dunstan, who puts the view that Komon's altruism led him to introduce Coonawarra wine to Sydney, suggesting in a way that he wanted to help Australia establish a sophisticated wine industry to meet his own personal needs. "It was all part of the lifestyle he wanted to create," says Dunstan.

Murray Tyrrell acknowledges a special debt to Komon and openly recognises him as one of the main reasons for his own success in the wine industry. Tyrrell was a cattle dealer when his uncle, Dan Tyrrell, slipped off a ladder after the 1956 vintage and was unable to perform in the winery cellar for a couple of years. Finding himself handed the reins of fully-operational winery, Tyrrell was uncertain what next to do, so Komon, along with Graham Gregory, Max Lake and Evans' admiral support, pressed him hard to continue at the winery business.

Anne Ellis, Tyrrell's daughter, remembers that Rudy Komon, Evans and others would arrive at the Tyrrell property laden with bottles of great wine for Murray to try, encouraging him that he was capable of matching those styles. "Rudy was incredibly generous," she says, "and would bring to us amazing foods from

Rudy Komon (left), Frank Margan (seated) and Evans tasting a range of Mildara red wines.

delicatessens in Sydney that at the time we had never even dreamed existed."

Some years later, Komon was one of those people, Evans included, who persuaded Murray Tyrrell to take the next step, and bottle his wine for sale under his own label.

As an art dealer, Rudy Komon gave a great start and encouragement to a number of now famous Australian artists, including John Molvig, Robert Dickerson, Leonard French, Clifton Pugh, John Olsen, John Perceval and Fred Williams. He would sign up his artists and put them on a regular salary.

Keith Dunstan, who has known most of the Komon stable, says they shared a common attitude towards their employer. "They all described Rudy as having done a tremendous amount for them, and said they couldn't have existed without him," he says. On the other hand, many said he would cheat his artists mercilessly. Loving and hating him at the same time, his artists all drew the conclusion that their relationship was symbiotic, neither party able to exist without the other.

All his life Rudy Komon was generous with his wine and his art. He would lend paintings to friends like Diana Fisher, to hang on the walls of their homes and offices. "You would get so accustomed and attached to them that you had to buy them," she confesses.

A dominant, forceful personality, Komon was never afraid to tread on toes and would voice his opinion whenever it suited him. Dining at Hobart's famous seafood restaurant, Mures, his host insisted he try a Tasmanian wine. Finding it contrary to his favour, he asked the restaurateur, George Mure, how much he charged for it. The price was $9 a bottle. "Then you should be in jail!" accused Komon. The restaurateur, patently a reasonable man, explained to Komon that he had paid $7 each for the wine. "Then you should be in the asylum!" Komon exclaimed.

Rudy Komon was present at a dinner at which Tom Seabrook introduced a bottle of the newly uncovered cache of 1872 Sunbury Hermitage from Craiglee. Taking forever to withdraw its cork, Seabrook served the wine with great ceremony before being requested from the floor to comment about it. When Seabrook began to extol the old and revered wine in the most glowing of terms, Rudy Komon, a guest of Keith Dunstan's, began to mortify his host by loudly crying out, in his heavy Czech accent: "He does not know what he is talking about! Any fool can see the wine is finished. It's gone!"

Rudy Komon was tough on most people and totally intolerant of fools. His bearing often made life difficult for those associate judges who served under him at wine shows. "Picture this," says Colin Richardson, "that you are a fairly young colt amongst the big heavies at the National Wine Show at Canberra. You are plodding your way along a class where there are no pearls, no wine in particular showing anything special. You'd go to Rudy, who was an important panel judge, and he'd look at you and say: 'But there is only one wine there!'"

"Hell! Which wine was it?" The young Richardson, in a state of high emotion and panic would then hastily return to re-evaluate the entire class.

"He was a total rascal and a great judge," says Evans. "He would let people know what he thought of wines, he would try and persuade the judges by suggestion, by inference and by hints." Very much an interventionist, Komon was famous for remarks like: "Have you tried number 58?" which, on occasions, would propel the wine from oblivion to trophy status.

After Evans succeeded George Fairbrother as Chairman of the Sydney Show, and had introduced his concept of the senior panel judge, he declined to promote Rudy Komon because, in his own words, "I don't think he could ever add up!"

"He was quite aberrative, and sometimes missed wines," says Evans, "but there is no doubt in my mind that he was one of the best judges of a final line-up of ten wines." Brian Croser remembers Komon as an excellent judge of single wines and of great wines, but supremely intolerant of anything ordinary.

It is inevitable that comparisons are made between Evans and Komon, although the apprentice ultimately revealed talents in wine which far surpassed those of the sorcerer. Keith Dunstan has been a friend to both. He says that "Komon was a much shrewder businessman than Evans. He was rude, ebullient, gregarious, very generous and fair to middling ruthless, I suppose."

Whatever his motives – selfish, devious, friendly or otherwise – Rudy Komon has rightly earned his place in Australian wine through his character and contribution. The wine industry remembers him today through the Rudy Komon Memorial Trophy, presented each year since 1984 at the Sydney Wine Show, fittingly enough for the best red burgundy style in the show.

Much of what Rudy Komon had given was given to Len Evans, who recognises that much of his own concept of wine quality and style can be traced directly back to Komon. It is appropriate, too, that Len Evans has named his best batch of Rothbury Estate Shiraz after Rudy Komon, beginning with a brilliant wine from 1989.

Len
*E*vans on Wine

Wine is only ever. and never anything more than a drink.
It's something you should enjoy.
L.P.E.

I have already established that Len Evans has earned his right to pass judgement on wine. Internationally he is regarded as Mr Australian Wine and, since 1967, has championed the cause of Australian wine wherever wine is enjoyed. He has an unsurpassed knowledge of the great wines of all wine countries. Although he says it's awful to admit, he's probably been exposed, shall we say, to most great vintages of most of the major wines of the world.

Since Evans' palate is in a class of its own, it is doubtful that more than the occasional flagon was ever wasted on him. He is equipped to draw more from the taste of a wine than anyone else I know. Secondly, Evans' intellect and memory for wine is so acute that he can draw at will from his accumulated wealth of experience to evaluate any wine, new or old, against a mental library of classic benchmarks.

Can one accumulate such an ability? In the early 1970s, a well-heeled friend and Bulletin Place customer told Evans he wanted to learn much more about fine wine. He was the sort that, once he got a fix on an idea, must immediately master it. "How do I get a palate like yours?" he asked.

"It will cost you at least $25 000," replied Evans," for not only will we have to buy all the great wines, but several years of them. I will teach you about the great Bordeaux châteaux, the great champagnes and the great burgundies, and we will talk about their years and all about their different styles."

The price, as it then was, was not an issue.

"But it will take you at least five years," continued the would-be teacher, "during which I will map out the programme for you, set the questions and plan the blind tastings. We will have a lot of fun."

The man was in a hurry: "I couldn't possibly take five years!"

"He didn't do it, but stayed a friend of mine," says Evans. "A couple of years ago we were chatting about it, and he asked how much would it cost to do today. I reckoned probably nearer $400 000, if you were to do it properly. A bottle of mature Romanèe-Conti can now cost around $800."

Evans was obviously a fast learner. At the Chevron in the early 1960s, he was an avid listener to wine merchants and the representatives of wine companies. Strangely, for today he can't quite figure out how he took to French wine like a duck to water. "I remember arguing at the first Thursday Club dinner at the Chevron about what constituted Burgundian and Bordeaux quality, although God knows where I got it from at that stage. I don't know when the great Bordeaux and Burgundies first came upon me and I don't know why. It's a mystery now, but I can remember back to the time of of my hotel career enjoying good Burgundy and good Bordeaux and knowing how good they were."

Most of all, Evans was intrigued by the great red wines of Australia, which he says were pretty simple to master in those days, there being so few. "They either came from Maurice O'Shea in the Hunter Valley, Colin Preece at Seppelt Great Western or Roger Warren, master blender at Thomas Hardy, who was a great friend of Eric Purbrick at Chateau Tahbilk." Roger Warren, also a close friend of Maurice O'Shea's, would visit the Hunter to buy red wines for the Hardy blend.

"We would open lots of great old O'Sheas at Wine and Food Society meetings, such as the famous '49 Price Henry and that sort of stuff. We also saw lots of great Preece wines from the '40s and '50s, not to mention the great series of Mildara Yellow Label wines which Ron Haselgrove put together in the '50s and '60s."

Evans describes Colin Preece as one of the greatest winemakers Australia has known. Several years ago, in the *Weekend Australian,* he wrote "there was no question that Preece made the greatest sparkling wine ever seen in this country". Thirty years on, his wines were still winning everything they entered.

Colin Preece was a magnificent host, full of wit and charm. Len and Trish Evans stayed with him at Great Western for a few days in 1961. On their arrival, unable to find a cold bottle of Great Western, Preece pulled out a cold bottle of Krug 1953 from the refrigerator. "It's not as good, but I suppose it will have to do," he muttered.

Of the Australian whites of the time, before and around the introduction of refrigeration to Australian winemaking, which greatly boosted their quality, Evans was most impressed with the early Gramps 1953s and 1954s, the first of the so-called cool ferment whites made with riesling. "And while I always drank copious quantities of the Leo Buring Rhine rieslings and the old Hunter semillons, the reds were really the stars, my early '60s memories," he says.

"The two best Australian wines that I have seen (winespeak for 'tasted') are the Penfolds Bin 60A 1962 and the 1959 Bin 1590 from Lindemans, the definitive Hunter red. The Bin 1590 left the two great 1965 Lindemans reds for dead; they were clumsy elephants compared to the finesse and style of the 1959. It was the classic wine." When it was re-released for $12.50 a bottle Evans and the rest thought it cost far too much, but the wine finished by fetching $285 per bottle. "A great, great wine," he says today.

It wasn't long before Evans was cocky enough to place a one-column, one-inch advertisement in the *Daily Telegraph* which simply read: "Len Evans Wines, Bulletin Place, regrets to announce that it has sold out of 1928 Pichon Longueville."

Since he would unquestionably have consumed more good wine at Bulletin Place than anyone else, it's fair to assume that Evans would have learned more about wine there than any other.

He is the first to agree that, without the strong Australian dollar of the '60s and '70s, it wouldn't have been first-and second-growth all the way. "Great wine was available at very reasonable prices," he agrees. "I wouldn't dream of drinking like that today." I'm not so sure he wouldn't. John Parkinson says he drank more good wine between 1970 and 1975 than for the rest of his life put together.

"Beeston and I would be having lunch together," Evans says, "and by this stage we've probably had half a bottle of champagne and a bottle of red, and then the sweets trolley would come along. We'd look at each other and decide if we wanted a pudding. And then we'd say 'Go and get a bottle of d'Yquem', just as casually as that."

Through Bulletin Place, Evans imported some 1975 Chateau d'Yquem to Australia in 1979 and sold it for $16 per bottle in a dozen lot, his retail margin $2.50. He says Halliday refused to buy it from him, saying it was far too much money and that he was nothing but a profiteer!

The bargains were extraordinary while the world was still waking up about quality wine. "The year 1959 was a great vintage, and some lovely wines were made in 1948, but you never heard much about them because the wonderful wines of 1945 stole the show. The '47s were very good, the '49s marvellous, and '48 was caught in the middle. Some lovely wines were made that year. I remember tasting the 1947 Cheval Blanc against '48 and enjoying the '48 more, although the '47 has the enormous reputation."

It's fascinating to examine some early Evans impressions on wine, made in 1967 while playing a bibulous brother of Phineas Fogg with Graham Kerr on their *Galloping Gourmets* world tour. I am certain that, having tried countless great wines since then he has reassessed some of his opinions and judgements, but they capture the energy and obsession behind Evans' unstinting and unquenchable lust for wines old and great.

At the Royal Orleans Hotel, New Orleans, staying as guests of Jim Nassikas, the hotel's General Manager and Vice President, and Marilyn Barnett, Evans and Kerr were served dinner in the Rib Room. They began with a 1964 Pouilly-Fumé and concluded with a 1959 Laurent Perrier Blanc de Blancs Grand Siècle with dessert. The reds are far more interesting. Having opened a 1934 Château Lascombes which, according to Evans was in very good condition itself, it was immediately rejected by their host in favour of a stunning 1929 Margaux which, according to Evans, had a "rich, full flavour preceded by almost the best bouquet I had ever experienced".

"Why discard the Lascombes?" he asked. Redefining all limits of hospitality, Jim Nassikas answered simply that he "just wanted to serve an outstanding wine".

At the Tours d'Argent restaurant, New York, owned by M. Claude Terrail, Evans was granted carte blanche of the cellar. He spoke to the sommelier, saying he "would like a great wine, one of such nose and flavour that it will live in my mouth for weeks and in my mind for years. A noble wine, an aristocrat wine."

Rather to Evans' initial disappointment, the sommelier returned with a comparatively young 1964 Corton-Charlemagne, which Evans later described in *The Galloping Gourmets* as "the best white wine I have ever tasted". Then arrived a 1955 Corton-Grancey from Louis Latour and, finally, a very old 1865 Chambertin. "It was old and tired, not really much more than a curio. But the flavour showed what the wine must have been and the nose was ethereal and of unbelievable finesse."

albert

Remember, Evans was tasting these wines and writing these words in 1968. Ten years earlier he was still to become a professional glass-washer!

Reluctantly, Evans declares: "When you drink so much wine, as I have, you forever say the great wines will stick in your mind. They don't." But they kept on coming and something appears to have stuck.

He does remember the 1825 Gruaud Larose, which cost him £320. It was put on the table for lunch the day after a 13 000-mile flight from England courtesy of Michael Broadbent who accompanied it to Australia. "It was glorious, great old claret," he says.

The oldest wine Evans has ever drunk was the 1646 Tokay he brought out from Christies, the London auctioneers. "We drank it at the the Single Bottle Club Dinner in 1980. I cried. It was in great condition – all spiritous and full, nutty and round." Evans arranged for special glasses to be blown for that occasion.

The year 1978 was the year of Evans' controversial Great Wine Dinner, at which he served only the greatest vintages of the great wines. The meal commenced with champagnes: 1947 Veuve Clicquot and Pol Roger. Then to Bordeaux: 1953 Lafite, 1949 Mouton, 1947 Cheval Blanc, 1945 Latour and 1929 Lafite, before the Burgundies: 1955 Chambertin, 1953 Hospices de Beaune (Cuvée Charlotte Dumay) and 1921 Clos de la Roche. Maintaining the standard 'til the last were the Trockenbeerenauslesen: 1976 Bernkasteler Doktor, 1971 and 1959 Wehlener Sonnenuhr. The humble ports were the 1908 Cockburn and 1927 Crofts.

The very concept of assembling wines of that impeccable quality and age together ranks with conducting an exhibition of the Crown Jewels, Tutankhamen's tomb, the treasures of the Louvre and the Vatican at a single place. And then Evans drank them.

The Great Wine Dinner was a magnet for criticism, typical of the sort of jealousy-inspired analysis Evans has attracted throughout his career.

An example of this criticism is found in *One Continuous Picnic*, Michael Symons' highly politicised account of the history of Australian cuisine and eating. While describing the interest generated by people like Len Evans inwards the newly emergent styles of Australian wine, Symons says, "it is not without significance, despite the new obsession with wine, that Len Evans' contender for Australia's 'greatest wine dinner' did not include one Australian wine".

Symons clearly shares the classic Australian inferiority complex, which mistakes tokenistic nationalism for representation based on realistic assessment and quality. He, and many others like him, misses Evans' point spectacularly. Which Australian wine ever made could sit comfortably in a list of wines like that?

In providing realistic and honest assessment of Australian wine throughout his career, Evans is chided for not promoting it enough, although no one has promoted it more.

Evans doesn't simply admire the best French wines because on the label it says they're French, but because he appreciates what it is about them that makes them great. His approach has always been to revere the best, to decipher what makes it the best, and then to encourage others to aspire to those levels. If in 1978 he and others who followed his lead had begun to rate Australian wine with the top fraction of the best made in France, Australian wine would today be but a fraction of its present quality.

Evans has a fondness for the world's greatest sweet wine, Château d'Yquem, to which his friends will instantly testify. He used to visit Keith Dunstan in Melbourne for dinner, where he would call for bottle after bottle of wine. "Come on, Dunstan! You can do better than that. You must have a better bottle than that we can drink!"

"This would really devastate your cellar after a while," Dunstan explains. "Once I told him I had a bottle of 1969 Château d'Yquem, but that I was saving it for a special birthday, and he couldn't bloody well have it."

Evans: "Yes I can!"

Dunstan: "You can't, Len, it's mine and you're not getting it."

Evans closed the issue by saying they would drink it now and he would replace it later. "And he did," says Dunstan, "with a '67."

"He is such a determined man. I have never in my experience known anyone with such a capacity not just for wine, but for the best wine that you've got," he says. The whole Evans' theory of capacity, introduced in the final chapter, centres around that premise.

"I can still see him sitting there yelling 'Not good enough, Dunstan, not good enough!' Other people you might invite to dinner are polite and self-effacing, and say 'Thank you very much, I like that'. Not Len," shrugs Keith Dunstan.

Evans has tasted both the 1899 and 1900 Yquems, which he loved, but prefers the 1921, "a great, great wine". In 1975, after a luncheon at the Pyramid restaurant in Vienne, he sent a postcard to Max Lake listing the wines that had washed down his meal, namely a 1934 Corton Charlemagne, 1934 Montrachet, 1945 Veuve Clicquot, 1945 Romanée-Conti, 1929 Château Latour, 1921 Clos du Tart and two 1921 Château d'Yquem. "I don't know why I'm telling you this," he scrawled, "but like the nun raped three times in the orchard, I just had to tell somebody."

Two years later, at lunch with Alan David and Peter Fox at the same restaurant, he contemplated buying the 1806 Château Lafite, on offer at the time for a piffling $350. After the sommelier insisted that he paid for the wine, regardless of whether it proved to be very tired or not, he dismissed the idea. Two years later, the same wine was sold at auction at Christies for £30 000, one of the highest prices ever seen for a bottle of wine. Rather understandably, that episode remains one of Evans' great regrets.

Evans has been a popular patron of the Pyramid. He was lunching there with Anders Ousback and Geoffrey Roberts, when well-known English wine writer and educator Steven Spurrier arrived.

"What have you been drinking?" asked Spurrier.

"'65 Latour."

"Really? What did it open like?"

"Marvellous."

"Oh, I still have a case of that."

Geoffrey Roberts offered to buy it gladly, provided Spurrier still had it.

Thinking quickly, Spurrier suggested he would taste a bottle first and then reconsider. "I've never thought the '65 Latour very good, you see."

The penny then dropped, as Evans and table looked up at him gleefully and in unison said: "1865".

I find it inconceivable that Evans could have drunk so much 1865, one of the greatest years of all time. He brought out famous French chef and restaurateur Jean

Troisgros to Australia for the Great Chefs Dinner at Rothbury in 1981 and, in return, received a bottle of 1865 Château Lafite. The bottle met its destiny, if not its maker at the Single Bottle Club dinner held by Malcolm Fraser at The Lodge, in Canberra, in 1982.

"It was wonderful," Evans enthuses. "Full of life, marvellous breed, marvellous character and flair, although old wines do age. Sometimes you have to extrapolate backwards and attempt to fathom what they might have been."

Later that week, Evans noticed that a bottle of the same wine fetched $10 000 at an auction. Sending a copy of the article to all Single Bottle Club Members, he queried which wine they were going to donate next year!

André Tchelistcheff is a Russian who has lived in California for many years, described by Evans as the doyen of Californian winemakers. He enjoys the story of Tchelistcheff and Michael Broadbent taking an interminable time to open and decant a jeroboam of 1890 Château Lafite before a crowd of devoted enthusiasts, barely able to contain their patience. Tchelistcheff finally tasted the wine and delivered his verdict. "This wine is like making love to an old woman. It is possible, it can even be pleasurable, but it will require a great deal of imagination."

"They do require imagination on occasions, for some bottles do open up badly," Evans explains. The oldest Australian red wine he ever tasted was an 1855 Hunter red. He has also sampled the famous 1872 Craiglee Claret from Sunbury, Victoria, which on the occasion, he says, opened up gloriously.

"I have tasted some glorious 1945s, 1928s and 1929s, but 1961 has been the most seductive and most consistent of all the great Bordeaux vintages I have seen," Evans declares. In 1980, he was present in Bordeaux and guest at a dinner for André Tchelistcheff, then seventy-eight years of age and still brimming with dash and wit.

Sixteen château owners were present, each bringing six bottles of their 1961 vintage to the dinner. The wines were opened in four groups of four. Evans recalls that in the last group were Mouton-Rothschild, Lafite, Latour and Palmer, which was served as the last wine, the inference being therefore that it was the best wine of the year. "Without a question of a doubt it was the greatest '61," Evans states firmly.

"I have a high regard for 1970 and have enjoyed many '53s. I did not think they were over the hill, as a lot of English critics claimed. I have even drunk many '53s with great enjoyment even until recently, but to me the most outstanding surprise vintage was 1962. It was never heralded because there was so much about, and you could buy the wine for nothing. In 1969 I bought 1962 Latour for a retail price of $9 per bottle! Unbelieveably cheap. That vintage followed the incredible one in 1961, so there wasn't such a demand for it."

Before discussing Australian wine in more detail with Evans, it's worth noting what he and his guests sniffed, slurped and gargled their way through on the occasion of his sixtieth birthday in 1990. The list begins with 1929 Krug (year of Evans' conception), six Domaine de la Romanée-Conti Le Montrachets, seventeen DRC Romaée-Conti vintages back to 1952, the vineyard's first wine after re-planting, six Château d'Yquems back to 1922 and three old Australian reds, including the venerable 1855 Hunter.

"That sort of thing, more than anything else, has been part of my great experience which enables me to talk stylistically about great wine. But I had a slight headache next morning," Evans admits, "the most expensive one I've ever had."

To Len Evans, there is no claimant that surpasses Penfolds Grange Hermitage as Australia's top red wine. "It is recognised overseas as the idiosyncratic Australian wine," he says. "Which is better than it? I have had a great pleasure from a lot of Granges. Mind you, I don't think Schubert's risk was all that great."

The creator of Grange Hermitage, Max Schubert, battled intense criticism in the wine trade and, indeed, within the Penfolds organisation to persevere with his new wine, first made in 1951. He even carried on without informing them so for two years after Penfolds thought the wine had been discontinued.

Neither denigrating Schubert or his wine in any way, Evans thinks the situation has been romanticised. "Don't forget he was only making a small quantity of wine," he says. "He had the great support of George Fairbrother, the wine industry figurehead. While other people criticised Grange, George never did."

Evans maintains unwavering respect for Max Schubert, and regards his contribution with the evolution of Grange as very significant. Sadly, he believes Schubert has been eulogised by his former company in recent years for commercial gain.

"You'd never meet a more humble, modest man than Max. All this 'Man of the Year' stuff – it must have been as big a shock to Max as anyone." Schubert was named 'Man of the Year' by the important English wine magazine *Decanter* in 1988. He was also awarded the inaugural Maurice O'Shea award in 1990.

The habit of collecting Grange has forced up its price and today there are even dealers in Grange. 'Grangeomania' was a word coined by Evans years ago. "The rare '58, which was always a very ordinary wine, sells these days for about $4 000 to $5 000 per bottle because there was always so little of it around. It's just a number to make up the set. I don't think that's healthy."

Today, Grange Hermitage relies heavily on Penfolds' excellent Barossa Valley vineyards at Kalimna. "Until 25 years ago the Barossa was principally a fortified wine area. Kalimna has pushed Penfolds to the forefront, and if Kalimna can do it, so can other parts of the Barossa," says Evans. "But they haven't yet, apart from possibly the Old Block at St Hallett."

The son of a Lutheran pastor, Peter Lehmann, is a perennial, enduring stalwart of the Barossa Valley. "He is as of the Barossa Valley as Murray Tyrrell is of the Hunter Valley," says Evans. It's worth noting that Len Evans doesn't think that Murray Tyrrell has ever received the credit due to him, especially for being the one who, essentially, introduced the varieties of pinot noir and chardonnay to modern Australian winemaking. "He would be first to admit that he has done things with which others wouldn't agree, but basically he has been an enormous power towards the development of quality wine in Australia."

Evans once described Peter Lehmann as "a cheerful light heavyweight with a face lined like a dry mudflat". The nickname of "Mudflat" stuck, although these days, Lehmann tends to be more revered, and better known as the "Baron of the Barossa".

Lehmann's wines set the benchmark for full, extractive, generous, jammy reds, so big, Evans once wrote, that you could spread them on bread. A former winemaker and manager at Saltram, today Lehmann is the inspiration of Peter Lehmann wines.

According to Evans, a Frenchman tasted a Saltram Dry Red years ago and declared: "Magnifique! A lovely wine! Is this in Australia what you call port?"

Evans also recalls a Saltram Bin 33 Claret made by Lehmann that was such a soft wine it wasn't really a claret at all. For that very reason it was pointed down for being out of style in a claret class at the Adelaide show. Lehmann wasn't too fussed about the upset in nomenclature and declared:"While the wine is making up its mind, we will call it a claret. Clarets sell better!"

Evans is concerned, however, at the Barossa's lack of image. He suggests that Yalumba has no regional identity other than Pewsey Vale and Heggies, its two vineyards in the Barossa Ranges, well above the valley floor, the company's main sphere of activity. Neither does he consider that Seppelt, despite its huge Barossa Valley tourist attracting of Seppeltsfield, has a real regional identity other than its true Great Western wine, grown and made in western Victoria."One doesn't go feverishly searching for Seppelt wines from Drumborg or Padthaway," he says. "Padthaway is a great region of production of mean quality, but it's not the star area that everyone falls around raving about."

Evans looks forward to the day when stronger connections develop between the various Australian wine regions and wines of unique quality and character."Eventually, we will become like Burgundy and Beaujolais and Champagne and concentrate on doing certain things best. It's not sufficient to be the Yarra Valley or the Margaret River and have everyone in those areas producing a cabernet, a pinot, a chardonnay, a riesling.

"If I lined up six of the best wine judges in Australia, they would have great difficulty distinguishing between chardonnays and cabernets from several regions. The future of the Australian regions is not to have this scattergun approach, but to have a true understanding of what they do best," he affirms.

"Most Australian wine regions have still to find their own niche. The only areas to have developed their idiosyncratic identity so far are the Hunter Valley with semillon and shiraz, north-east Victoria with muscat and tokay, Clare with Rhine riesling and Coonawarra with cabernet sauvignon.You really can't go much further than that."

"I have always been pleased by Lindemans Hunter reds and the Mount Pleasant semillon, for at the price it is, it's a hell of bargain, one of the great bargains of Australian wine. Like most people, I have a fantastic admiration for north-eastern Victorian muscat, especially those by Mick Morris; and a great fondness for the top Coonawarra reds, like the John Riddoch 1982 and 1987 – both terrific wines.The new Hollick wines made by Pat Tocaciou and the Orlando Jacaranda Ridge have been very good of late, as have some Lindemans, if they can stay away from that dreaded mulberry character.

"Generally though, the big companies have got it right.They make an awful lot of very good wine for sale at very good prices."

"Having said that, I have great respect for all districts of Australia, including Griffith and those on the Murray for what they do. If Oxford Landing can produce 'X' huge tonnes per acre and make an attractive wine which sells huge quantities at £4.99 per bottle in the UK, you cannot but respect the commercial success of it. It's fulfilling a need that would otherwise be fulfilled by Chile or France or Italy or whatever.

"Don't sneer at it. If you do that, someone else will get the business."

Evans has no time for sauvignon blanc, although over twenty years ago suggested it be used to extend the palates of the early refrigeration-enhanced Rhine rieslings.

"I suppose it has a place in the hierarchy of wines; I just don't happen to like it. I don't like ugni blanc, either, but nobody seems to care about that." If you really want to upset Len Evans, invite him to lunch and serve him young veal, goats cheese and sauvignon blanc, each of which he finds repulsively pungent and nasty!

Although Evans recognises that Western Australia is home to some very good wines, he believes the State is basically assumptive in its rating. "Just because it's called Margaret River, doesn't mean that all its wines are good wines. I also think the Yarra Valley has produced some excellent wines, cabernet and pinot particularly, yet it doesn't mean that it does that all the time." Evans especially admires the pinot noirs made by James Halliday at Coldstream Hills and some chardonnays by David Wollan at Tarra Warra.

On the street corner hawking Australian wine. Evans and Rothbury's General Manager,
Dennis Power, in San Francisco.

I think Evans derives much pleasure from provoking those to whom a cool viticultural climate means everything. "It's a hype engendered by winemakers from cool climates," he declares. Most of the wine judges espouse cool climate wines, so why does the Hunter Valley win more gold medals for chardonnay than any other area? Are they hot-weather judges? Clare, whose riesling is Australia's best, does not have a particularly cool climate. A lot of nonsense is talked about cool climates most of the time."

"Like the Yarra Valley and Margaret River, Tasmania owes a lot to hype and localised wine success. Much of the progress of these areas has been due to the demands of their parochial nearby public. I have never forgotten the irony of not being able to buy a Tasmanian wine in the Hobart Sheraton because the hotel couldn't afford to buy them. Tasmania has yet to prove itself, which doesn't mean it won't prove itself. If I was an investor I would look to make sparkling wine there.

"But don't expect too much too quickly from the regions at this early stage," warns Evans. "It's only been twenty-five years since some regions like the Yarra Valley were resuscitated and only thirty years ago Coonawarra was moribund. What's taken place is extraordinary. Don't expect too much from the wine industry too quickly."

Despite that, Evans still remains impatient for Australians to recognise and grasp their opportunities in markets other than their own. Presently Australia sells just over 1 per cent of all wine imported onto the world market.

Although Australians tend to sneer at the English expression of the "New World", Evans believes it has done our wine industry the power of good. The Americans first broke into the English wine market in the early 1980s while the pound was strong against the US dollar. Consequently, American wines were very cheap there and individuals like Paul Masson spent a fortune spreading the word.

"Then, as American wine became more of a fashion," Evans explains, "other people like Geoffrey Roberts, who presently distributes Rothbury and Petaluma in England, imported a diversity of small vineyard American wine, becoming known as the "New World Wholesaler" in the process. Suddenly, the New World was a wine entity in England, and moved consumers' minds away from their rigid French and Italian purchasing habits. In a sense Australia was fortunate to be part of that New World image, riding ironically on the back of American success. All at once we were called 'New World' instead of mere 'colonial' winemakers."

Since then, Australia has taken more control over its own destiny, although not to the extent that Evans is satisfied. Australian wine exports have rocketed from a mere 8 million litres in 1982 to 65 million litres in 1991, nearly a fifth of total production, valued at $A200 million. Seventeen million litres were shipped to the United Kingdom alone.

If exports follow their present trend it is conceivable that Australia could actually run out of wine in the near future! The Australian Wine Export Council, the industry's new statutory body responsible for wine export, is confident that the growth will continue, and has begun to deal with the unexpected problem that may be created – insufficient investment to meet the demand.

Why has Australian wine taken off so well? It has nothing to do with Paul Hogan, Greg Norman, the Wallabies or Alan Bond and the America's Cup, despite the contribution they and others have collectively made to our stronger international image. It has everything to do with the quality that Australian wine can provide at the price it asks, from the cheapest level to all but the most rare, exclusive and expensive of wines.

"There's no question in my mind," says Evans, that the best remark about Australian chardonnay was made by Auberon Waugh. He said that if anyone was a lover of white Burgundy and could not now afford to drink it every day because of its ridiculous prices, and had not used Australian chardonnay as a substitute, then they didn't understand what was happening in wine in the world today.

"Californian wine is no better than Australian. Some are as interesting, some less interesting, yet Australian wine is half the price. Californians have made two mistakes: they have over-priced their wines and then gone for those so-called 'lean', so-called 'food styles'. Why pay $25 for a bottle of Mondavi when you can get a perfectly good bottle of Australian wine for ten dollars?"

Evans says the Australian industry and government are at last beginning to understand that Australia could indeed become a significant wine exporter. "Its ultimate success will depend on the major players and the Australian Government. More investment is needed and vineyards need to be converted from poor to good varieties.

"It worries me that neither the industry nor the governments understand the great potential that Australia has internationally. If government only put back into supporting the industry a small amount of the tax they take away from us as sales tax, we could have a great industry. Don't think I'm preaching for it; for it's not likely to happen."

But Evans is serious about pressuring the government to grant some form of tax relief to assist those seriously involved in wine export. He says it costs Rothbury $A500 000 to finance every 10 000 cases it sends overseas for a retail price around $US10 a bottle, so the company requires $A2 million to fund its current exports of around 40 000 cases. Relief could be given to wineries, Evans suggests, in direct proportion to their export turnover.

Evans says the two critical aspects are Australia's overseas marketing and an ability to establish joint ventures with major players overseas. He's thinking big. "There is so much area in Australia, in South Australia and central New South Wales, in places like Mudgee, Cowra and Orange – not the Hunter Valley, and not the Yarra Valley – which could grow huge quantities of quality grapes expressly for export at a price you could not believe.

"If someone produced a million cases of high quality chardonnay a year for sale overseas by the other half of a joint venture, like an Australian 'Blue Nun' Chardonnay, you could completely fund and pay back the total cost of the operation within two years." Peter Sichel, Chairman of the company which owns Blue Nun, has confessed to Evans he could be keen on the idea. "Even at $A36 a dozen you could probably get your money back in six years.

"As we make better chardonnay, as I'm sure we will, and as we use more malolactic fermentation and fill out the back palate more, and as we get better and better at it, if the government is serious about addressing the balance of payments they talk about till they're blue in the face, they will think about doing something for wine, instead of all this talk about the so-called 'smart' industries. Why do they bother, when in front of them they have the industry, which if handled properly, could service the world?"

Evans' first involvement in wine export was on his overseas trip of 1967 with Graham Kerr, vividly recounted by both in *Galloping Gourmets*. Although he was no longer with the Wine Board, its council heard he was going overseas and offered him a small fee to "preach the gospel" in London.

"I have forgotten how little it was," says Evans, "but it was unbelievably small. I went to the Australian Wine Centre in Pitt Street, Soho, and lectured to the Circle of Wine Writers and gave other talks. I have never kept clippings, but I made the papers all over the place in England.

"The circle of wine writers was incredible. It included people like André Simon, Harry Waugh, Gabor Denes, Alec Waugh, (Evelyn Waugh's brother), and Vyvyan Holland, Oscar Wilde's son, who was eighty-four at the time. Can you imagine this — I actually lectured to Oscar Wilde's son!"

That day was a famous occasion, according to Evans, who said it wasn't much good him teaching them about what they regarded as colonial wines. To help him, he asked, would they mind tasting six wines? Their labels weren't obscured, all were under ten shillings and there were two Australians in the line, which came fourth and fifth in the summary of tasting. Everyone then sat down and Evans served another six bottles, masked this time, for lunch.

When he unwrapped the six wines, everyone could see they were the same six wines, but this time around the two Australians came second and third. Gabor Denes, secretary of Circle of Wine Writers sprang to his feet, saying "It's quite obvious we've been exposed by this young man, and the palates of the Circle of Wine Writers is now very much held to question. There is only one thing to do with a man like this. Make him a member!"

Evans didn't return to England until 1972, but has travelled there regularly ever since. He finds it odd that whenever Wolf Blass, Chris Hancock (Rosemount), or Brian McGuigan (formerly of the Wyndham group) go overseas, they are just seen to represent their own company, but whenever he goes, it is assumed to be in the role of general spokesman for the entire Australian wine industry.

"It's as if I'm paid for it. I've been doing it for a long time now, so I take care to balance my overseas presentations for Petaluma and Rothbury with some other wines, say from Rosemount or Lindemans.

"I've done a lot of talking, but always find that red-faced Englishman in the front row, with a cut-away collar and an old school tie, who says "But I say, do your wines travel?" I've always had to put up with that sort of thing in England.

It's no surprise, then, that one of Evans' favourite wine stories, of which there is an indescribable number, concerns the British winemaker entertaining the Frenchman in his English garden. Sitting down in the afternoon, the Englishman had just carefully poured his young white wine when he said: "Isn't it remarkable to think that this wine was grown and made only a hundred yards from where we are sitting?"

The Frenchman's reply was: "It's a pity it doesn't travel."

International wine people enjoy the down-to-earth qualities of Australians, says Evans, and love our irreverence. "James Halliday is popular overseas because he's so bright. Brian Croser is popular because not only is he bright, but he's very good with wine. "We have a place, a very important place, a personality place."

Evans was one of the earliest speakers at the 10th Wine Experience held by the *Wine Spectator* magazine in New York in 1991. His General Manager at Rothbury, Dennis Power, said that was a huge advantage, for everyone would recognise him for the rest of the event. "I would stop for a moment to pick my nose and be surrounded by people like a shot," says Evans, who was made compere of the event the year later.

One factor that may hinder the growth and reputation of Australia's wine industry around the world is the ongoing, unabashed and unscrupulous use of generic European wine names for Australian wine.

The winegrowers of Beaujolais have come out victorious in a legal battle to prevent Australian wines from imitating their name. Not before, however, at least twenty Australian wine companies adopted it in the first place.

Evans is exasperated. "When the hell is Australia going to grow up? How can you expect us to develop any form of reputation anywhere in the world, when you produce Australian 'Beaujolais'?" he sneers. "It's a great laugh to the world." Evans was thanked by the French Appellations d'Origine Contrôlées for his stand throughout the debate.

"It was quite outrageous and morally indefensible. The name didn't even have a history in Australia. Australians have no right to any wine appellation which is heavily Appellation controlled by its region. Look at Champagne – the soil, the pruning time, the pressing time, the amount of wine left in the press and so on and so on…

"We have no such system in Australia, nor should we have for years to come. We're just not ready. We're ready for our Label Integrity Programme (which guarantees the validity of claims made on Australian wine labels within certain limits), but it's not nearly as broad as an Appellation Control concept would be.

"We had nearly got rid of the Chablis name in Australia, but then Brian McGuigan (Wyndham Estate) started promoting it again. When I fronted him about it, he simply said that it sells more wine.

"Why are we insufficiently proud of what we're doing in Australia? What a dreadful indictment on Australian quality and marketing ability that we have to use French names!

"You can't have it both ways if you're going to be international. If we are to be international players, we must play by international rules. We can't just say this is the way we do things in Australia. Australian wine must be identified with Australian integrity and honesty, all the qualities we claim now, but which in some cases aren't there yet. We are what we are, by being what we do."

Where lies the future for Australian wine? Len Evans is convinced that for Australia to develop a major wine industry, it will not do it internally. "If it relies wholly on its domestic market, it will only be a small player in the international stakes in production and supply." And that's one way Evans does not know how to think – small.

The
Real Len Evans

Len Evans will never slow down of his own accord. From his home, "Loggerheads", overlooking Rothbury Estate and much of the Hunter Valley, he maintains the frenetic creative pace of the past sixty-one years. Some of his new concepts are local, some are based overseas, most are typically visionary.

Finally, after all these words and time, will the real Len Evans please stand up?

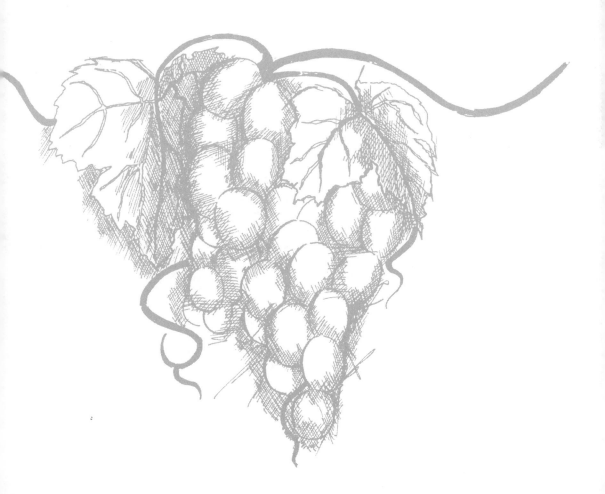

A
*F*uture at "Loggerheads"

I've always wanted to have a duel with Dan Murphy, with a
couple of muscats.
L. P. E.

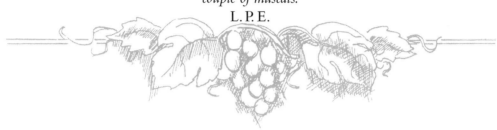

*A*s far as Len Evans is concerned, his most important plan yet is the next he is
about to implement. Somehow his energy keeps pace with his vision, and he
would be utterly desolate in retirement. Now beginning to appreciate the nature of
relaxation and leisure and the need for them, Evans is still able to get bored in fifteen
minutes unless things are buzzing and happening around him in triplicate.

Some of his best friends, like Peter Doyle and Bob Oxenbould are relieved to see
him slow down a bit, but Evans still finds watching the television news infinitely more
manageable if undertaken in conjunction with a cryptic crossword and a conversation.
"He's getting smarter now," says Doyle, "and spends more time fishing and skiing.
Those trips do him the world of good."

Since 1985, when he and Trish moved from Sydney to their Hunter Valley home
of "Loggerheads", Evans has also readjusted the geographical centre of his ambitions.
From his lofty residential perch, he is master of most of what he surveys and it is
within this visible horizon that most Evans' future dreams will materialise.

At present, it appears unlikely that any of the Evans children will follow him into
the wine industry, although they share in this and other of his interests. Len and Trish
Evans have three children, two daughters and a son. Sally was born in 1963, "a good
year for port", Jodie in 1964, "great for Pomerol" and Toby in 1966, a "good all-
round year".

Evans has a remarkable gift of foresight and, if anything, his new expectations
concerning the land around the Rothbury Estate are even more forward-thinking
than was the story of "Loggerheads", itself worth dwelling on for a moment.

In 1972, Len Evans bought the remaining unplanted forty hectares from
Rothbury, paying, he says, twice the price they paid for it. The reason? It would make
a magnificent site for a house.

Frank Christie and Doug Crittenden both remember Evans gesturing up from
the winery site, saying, "See up there at that hill; that's where I am going to have my

house; by that pepper tree." Although the block sat vacant for years, Evans would ferry people there on horseback or by four-wheel drive to show off the view. He imagined the house and rose garden long before he had cleared the space, says Max Lake, and planted the orchard in the most perfect position, long before the house plan was even drawn up.

Whereas all his friends agree that Evans has no interest whatsoever in hoarding away money for its own sake, he remains a hoarder nevertheless. For years he has accumulated and collected strange and often obscure artefacts, fittings and furniture, most of them antique, on the understanding that, at some future time he would put them to use. By combining them with others in his own way he has given them a new life, perhaps in roles totally foreign to their initial purpose but entirely appropriate, all the same.

"Loggerheads" is decorated with several Evans-made collages – large, surprising, busy and eye-catching compositions of his themes and ideas. "He has a great love of things and objects," Anders Ousback explains. "He loves the concept of creating and doing. 'Isn't that a gorgeous object', he might say. He possesses almost a metaphysical adoration of creation."

One drought year, only a few years ago, Anders Ousback remembers stumbling off to bed late at night at "Loggerheads", feeling very much the worse for wear after a huge dinner, topped off with half a bottle of muscat. Deeply perturbed, Evans had been discussing the ongoing drought: "Christ, we need rain! If this drought continues, I am really stuffed."

Beware of the resident. Evans and his newly-completed sculpture
along the driveway at "Loggerheads".

building Loggerheads

Around four in the morning Anders was abruptly woken by boisterous cries of "Ousback! Ousback!" and then bodily dragged outside, naked and half asleep, by an Evans clad only in nightshirt. Rain was bucketing down. "He started to dance, prancing around in the rain like Zorba the Greek, and he began to laugh and laugh with joy. It was extraordinary," Ousback recounts. "He was thanking the gods, thanking the earth, getting himself totally wet and playing in the mud."

Looking beneath the surface, the consistent theme of creation and the love of the thought process, its implementation and rewards, are a constant factor throughout Evans' personal and business lives. The legacy he has created, which few have the opportunity to really understand, will carry far beyond his material accomplishments in the wine industry.

But wait, I have almost fallen into the trap of talking about this stripling sixty-one-year-old in the past tense, which is grossly unfair. Hermann Schneider and I both agree that, if blessed with another twenty or thirty years of life, there is no telling what Evans might do.

Although his love of creation is most publicly expressed through his feeling for the finest of wine, it extends through Evans' many other avenues of interest – pottery, huge mosaics and ceramics, and his new-found interest in sculpture among them. His collages reflect a deep feeling for objects that interest him and have stories to tell, which pay respect to the skill, thought and creativity their conception first required.

People many times more qualified than I have observed that his collages reveal a genuine talent. Others have offered to buy them, which Evans refuses even to consider. He would no more sell one of these smaller works than he would part with his largest collage of all – "Loggerheads" itself.

Evans calls "Loggerheads" a "salvage" house. He would put aside things found in demolition sites, antique shops and yards. He knew exactly what he would use, from French windows to medieval Spanish doors, although he didn't know precisely how he would incorporate them. He acquired the ironbark beams of the Bennelong Point Wharf, which had made way for the Sydney Opera House, before knowing exactly what his house would look like. He bought the huge marble columns, sadly superannuated from the old Bank of New South Wales building in Macquarie Place, to construct a magnificent marble rotunda in the "Loggerheads" garden.

Doug Crittenden was habitually seconded into escorting Evans to discover some new antique shop in Melbourne. "He has a fantastic eye for antiquities," says Crittenden. "It wouldn't matter if it was tucked away behind somewhere, he would find something you wished you had seen for yourself. He has an eye like a hawk, a great eye for genuine antique furniture and interesting pieces he can do things with."

Evans' concepts for "Loggerheads" became architectural reality, although he originally intended the house to be built with mud bricks. Local council, however, had different ideas. Mud was out of the question until it had examined the condition of another new mud building in its shire, a verdict it would be unable to deliver until about twenty or thirty years time!

Then, since the guest bedrooms had no connecting corridor, the building was automatically classified as a motel. Towing the line, Evans applied for permission to build a motel, without any intention of ever using it as such. Permission was granted on the grounds he could assure that there was sufficient off-street parking.

Exasperated, he said: "Well, I've got about enough for 14 000 cars! But why are you all so against anything being done?"

He was told "You must remember that this is a strong Labor town, and we're all very conservative."

In typical form, Evans took to the building of "Loggerheads" with all-consuming energy. According to some close friends it became his major source of emotional release from the enormous pressures of refinancing his businesses, necessary after the death of his friend and financier, Peter Fox, in 1982.

Visiting it shortly after completion in 1984, Frank Christie said it was exactly the house he thought Evans would build – "Instant age".

On a now-famous occasion in its early days, a truckie arrived to deliver a load of tiles for one of the courtyards or walls. Unloading was a long process. Engaging Evans in a conversation, the truckie's wife said "Mr Evans, you're a marvel. No one else would do what you're doing."Everyone else would have simply let it fall down!"

Anders Ousback enjoys "Loggerheads" and thinks it works wonderfully well. "He puts things together because he likes them, not caring at all whether it is conventional or not. Totally unorthodox, "Loggerheads" is an extraordinary place and will be a lasting monument."

Now complete, a Dutch-style office has been added to "Loggerheads" and the Evanses are thriving there. Hospitality, Bulletin Place-style, has now found a new home, for entertainment continues there in familiar vein. Gerard and Francoise Rotel, part-owners of Château Pousse d'Or in Burgundy, once arrived at "Loggerheads" expecting a simple luncheon. It went enjoyably; tasting and drinking many fine Australian wines, before Evans showed them down to Rothbury in the afternoon to taste chardonnay and pinot noir, then washed down with two or three bottles of bubbly.

When they returned to the house for farewells, another visitor had arrived carrying an enormous fish. A unanimous decision was made to cook it immediately and to carry on. After many fine old wines had taken their curtain-call, guessing games were won and lost and singing commenced. "Someone sang all the arias from an opera," remembers Evans, "doing all four major parts and most of the duets and quartets, although I suspect something was lost in the translation."

Lunch finished around midnight. The following morning it was found that the ten people present had consumed thirty-seven bottles, and none, according to Evans, "were ever drunk, if perhaps a little happy and intoxicated".

In 1976, Evans began to plant vines on either side of the house site. He now has 4 hectares of chardonnay, 2.5 hectares of pinot noir and a small patch of gamay, making from them authentic estate-grown wine, processed at Rothbury and sold under the "Evans Family Wines" label. It's a very low-yielding vineyard and Evans' total annual production rarely exceeds 2 000 cases a year. He sells three wines – chardonnay, pinot noir and pinot gamay. As one might anticipate, the chardonnay is rich, powerful and voluptuous, made with the entire traditional winemaking textbook thrown hard at it.

Depending on how well they manage their schedule, visitors to the Hunter Valley can call at the arresting, Mediterranean-influenced, colonnaded cellar-door complex of Evans Family Wines, now open for business between 10 a.m. and noon on weekends. Brand new, the building could nevertheless convince many it had been there prior to the First Fleet. Being a typically expressive Evans phenomenon, either you warm to it instantly, or you do not.

According to one of Evans' very good friends, however well you think you know him, he always manages to surprise you. "Driving to 'Loggerheads', I was going up Palmers Lane and all of a sudden saw this atrocious building – all white and Spanish-looking. Good Lord, I thought, what would Len have to say about that? Who put this shocking building here? I drove on and then found I had to turn around. I couldn't believe it when I came back and saw the sign on the entrance – 'Len Evans Wines Cellar Door'."

The building includes a house for Evans' manager, a tasting room and a reception and dining area that James Halliday finds reminiscent of one of the floors of Bulletin Place. Dominated by a single long refectory table and high chairs, and tastefully cluttered with wine memorabilia, it is very atmospheric and directly challenges the visitor – "Walk out of here unaided, if you can!".

Again bypassing the retail trade, Evans Family Wines sells most of its produce through a mail-order system, offering discounts for larger purchases to its subscription members, who are also entitled to book into the glorious entertaining space at Evans Family Wines for tastings and lunches.

Evans merrily rules as king of his castle at Rothbury. "I would like to see this area as the centre of the web of my activities," he says. "I don't want to have to travel around the world to do things, I want to do them here."

Striking the first shots at the new Cypress Lakes Golf Course, Hunter Valley.

However, Evans still entertains the possibility of going back overseas. "I would like an Italian estate producing 5 000 to 10 000 cases of wine and, perhaps, a little piece of Portugal producing 2 000 cases of port. I would also adore a small vineyard in Champagne, to produce a single-vineyard wine of maybe 3 000 cases of champagne."

But as far as Australia is concerned, it's time for Evans to focus himself on "Loggerheads", where he plans to breed Clydesdales and conduct his other affairs. He wants people to bring their ideas and propositions to him, even if he happens to be going to Sydney. If people aren't prepared to do that, they can't be serious. "We don't have the time," they might tell him. "Exactly," he replies.

Evans admits it's harder these days to "charge around all over the shop and get the things done". He would rather have people working off him than find himself working off different people. He considers himself a focal point, not through selfishness, but because, pragmatically, it's the best way to get things done.

"If that sounds egocentric, which I am sure it does, then it's the time for egocentricity. It's practical. If I became richer and ever made any money, I would hire a personal secretary. I would be quite happy to have a continual party going on up here, with the people that I was to see coming and going, talking to me at the appointed hours. I could write books and plays, do television series and run businesses, with people milling around and working off each other."

Evans looks down the hill towards Rothbury. He has 140 hectares of land there, right in the heart of the Hunter Valley, all waiting to be used. Predictably, he has a vision for it. "I want to build a village down there."

Not a bad idea, adjacent to a colony of three excellent and up-market tourist, wine and hospitality ventures directly opposite Rothbury, encompassing Murray Robson's new winery, the newly relocated Old Convent guest house and Moulins Restaurant. Together Evans expects they will revitalise the area.

"I would love to have an accommodation village there, with a design that I am part of. The rooms would be much more spacious than visitors currently get, totally soundproof and totally alone," he says. In typical style, each room would have its own individual identity, there being no pattern or repetition of furniture between them. They would have old furniture, thick walls and their own little breakfast facilities.

"There would be a central breakfast room. Then an industrial tourist village. Rothbury wants a cask shop, we'd love a little brewery, a little distillery. I would love a ceramics shop, an antique centre. Somebody may want to make chairs, blow glass or make big terra cotta pots. If someone else wanted to make herb ointment we would provide an acre to grow herbs for a peppercorn rental, provided people could walk through the herb garden.

"Between those entities might be a little quayside on the dam, with little shops and restaurants, all linked by piazzas and walkthroughs and statue gardens which students could make.

"I hope that over the next ten years I can get on with this idea and start it. It may not be fulfilled in my lifetime, but it could certainly be started."

Now, who would bet against that?

Rough-cut Diamond

*I was always horrified to think that I would become the guru
of wine and food in Australia.*
L. P. E.

If you spoke to fifty people they would all have either a different version, either slightly or significantly, of who Len Evans is. To find out which person is, in fact, the real Len Evans is a challenge in itself, and quite possibly a futile one at that. He could very likely be all those people at once.

Len Evans, says Anders Ousback, is the most "egocentric, narcissistic, Napoleonically complexed, mentally retarded and emotionally handicapped" person he knows. "You can chronicle them all and I've heard them all over the years. I agree with all of them," he says. "Fortunately it doesn't change the fact that he is one of the most interesting, stimulating, kind, generous, warm-hearted most wonderful people I've ever met."

As many of us do, Len Evans has selectively incorporated into his own very complex and capable persona the qualities and characteristics of those he has admired: the passion for life of Rudy Komon, the quintessential style of Eric Purbrick, the dramatic impact made by Max Lake on Australian wine and the ability of George Fairbrother to judge wine; and yet ultimately, by doing it his own way, Evans has outshone them all.

What he has achieved with wine in Australia is all the more worthy since he is a migrant to this country, without any prior background in wine, family or otherwise. Wine is but one of the passions in Len Evans' life, although it is that which consumes him the most. In turn, to be fair, he consumes his share of it as well. He once estimated he tasted 13 000 wines a year.

Like him or hate him, you can't ignore him. Without even trying, he invariably provokes a reaction from any person, regardless of age, sex or background. There is a warmth and an aura about him which could possibly be charisma. Something would draw your attention to Evans if he just caught your eye in a crowd.

Evans is gregarious and generous, tenacious and bull-headed, irreverent and irrepressible. As Keith Dunstan observes in *Ratbags,* he is always likely to burst into song on festive occasions. His energy is limitless and he is physically incapable of wasting time. He can be anything from the most difficult to the most charming of people, yet I have not the slightest doubt that he is one of the most worthwhile.

Strangely, for although he is unquestionably one of the great communicators, he certainly remains one of the most misunderstood people I have known. Those familiar only with his public persona might be surprised at the depth and feeling that lies thereunder, and by his strict adherence to his own particular code of ethics. Evans is a born iconoclast and would be horrified at the number of people in whose mind he embodies the establishment.

Forever reluctant to turn his hand to things of little or no interest to him, Evans is determined to follow his own path. He is not infrequently accused of being over-ambitious, but claims he was virtually pushed into the three biggest things he's ever done. Rothbury Estate came about when Murray Tyrrell began breaking up his land in the Hunter; he was drawn into Petaluma when Brian Croser saw the possibilities of The Evans Wine Company's vineyards in Coonawarra and Clare; and Richard de Salis nagged him into setting up Bulletin Place. "So much for my vaulted ambition," he shrugs.

Try substituting "ambition" for "vision", for his vision is truly remarkable. Able not only to conceive how a project might begin, Evans will visualise it twenty years hence, even if his impatience might then have got the better of him. It's easy to forget how many of his innovations were far ahead of their time, because they have become part of the furniture so quickly.

Evans has a tangible sense of history and time, to which he feels compelled to contribute. Rothbury, Petaluma and "Loggerheads" are some of the more tangible elements of his legacy. To Evans the most worthwhile things are those with durability.

Wealth or power for its own sake has never remotely interested Len Evans, motivated, as he is, more by the entire experience of life. "He's wealthy to the extent

Len Evans

that he now is, only because he's bought or created things that he's loved," says James Halliday. "He's never set about creating a bigger pile to sit on." A bigger cellar, perhaps. Evans once wrote, "I love champagne and think champagne, French of course. I can understand what wealth is all about when I yearn to have buckets of it, appropriately chilled, for my friends."

Evans' ambitions, however as he may deny them, have never been individual, but altruistic. His generosity is overwhelming, for he delights in the sharing of everything he owns. One can imagine him thinking: "If we can build this winery, then we can have better dinners, for we will all be able to drink better wine at lower prices." Projects are conceived, initiated and nurtured for their own sake, and although naturally they must pay their way, which Rothbury, for one, has only started to, they are never driven purely for financial reward.

Despite having a mind like a trap, Evans' track record would suggest he hasn't been the world's best businessman. Given what fires him, that would hardly be possible. As Anders Ousback suggests, he'd much prefer to buy a better stainless steel fermenter to make a better wine, rather than squirrel away a few acorns for the future. "He always chose the hardest road," says Halliday. "He always has the grand vision and loves a challenge. He never lets normal practical impediments get in his way."

If life is a game, it has never been played better. After four days fishing, high in the Tasmanian mountains, Evans and Peter Doyle descended on the Hobart casino, dog-eared and slightly the worse for wear. They met downstairs at the bar a couple of hours later after a bath and a clean up. There at the bar, they met the manager who asked if they were going to have a drink. "Of course we are," cried Evans. "Then I am going to play the tables."

The manager asked what they would prefer. Evans said champagne. A bottle of Great Western was presented. "I said champagne, my dear. French Champagne."

"Oh. That's thirty dollars a bottle."

"Good Heavens, seeing it's that cheap we'll have two," Evans declared. "And charge them to the Manager, please."

A fanatical gambler, Evans won a lot of money that night. Late in the evening Doyle, who never gambles at all, removed about $5 000 from him as a safeguard, leaving a small bank. "Around 2 a.m. we were both down in the Hobart boat harbour trying to buy a yacht to sail around the world, in a very expanded state of intoxication," he says. "Later, I remember getting into bed after planting the money."

Their flight next morning was an early one, around 6 a.m.

"At 5.30 Evans was knocking down my door, demanding 'Where is the money?'," says Doyle. "I couldn't remember where I'd put it. We stripped the room, searched under the bed, in the toilet bowl, everywhere. He was going on a treat about the money while I was sitting at the end of the bed, trying to put on my shoe. Luckily the money was wedged in there.

"Once he got it, no matter how intoxicated he was the night before, he knew to the zac how much he'd won. We had to sit down and count the lot. God knows, if it was $10 short what we were going to do."

Evans' spirit is indefatigable. His is a full-frontal approach which doesn't know how to do things by halves. He attacks a venture oozing gusto, exuberance and devotion. A typical Evans project is characterised by its size and imagination, speed of conception and implementation, impact and quality. His life is too short for

Which one of these two would you welcome into your casino? Evans and Peter Doyle.

second attempts. Some suggest, without either implying he is spiritually naive or doubting his intellectual ability, that since any form of life after death is intangible to him, he has simply no time to waste.

"If there is a key to me it is my energy," he says. "Never ambition, always energy. I can't stop myself from getting involved in things," says Evans. "Although I have a better understanding of my limitations as I get older, I'm still unable to waste time."

I doubt there's been a person who has ever lived more for the moment. Combine a stamina that would do a marathon runner proud with an ability to surround himself with the things he loves and adores to do, and you have the Evans production line, which generally refuses to shut down. His secret, he says, is the diversity of things he enjoys. "If I get bored or exhausted by one," he says, "I'll pick up another. I might not go back to what I was leaving for another six months."

Resolutely guarding Evans' driveway are two huge blocks of stone, one now finished as a sculptured head, Easter Island fashion, another all but complete. He made them. In his store-room lay piles of strange antiquities and artefacts, useless to most people, but patiently awaiting their next incarnation as part of an Evans collage. Around his house numerous tiles, ceramics and mosaics demand construction or repair. Plays and stories need putting to paper, cryptic crosswords quickly dispensed with. Because every waking moment counts, Evans barely sleeps.

In 1976, Deeta Colvin went to visit his bedside at St Vincent's Hospital, only moments after he had come round from the anaesthetic. There was no question of his not participating in her champagne, although his angina had been just two days previously. He might have been drowsy, even groggy, but there was a moment to be seized.

His heart problem, according to Evans, was the result of genetic cholesterol. One of his arteries was diseased, so ultimately he underwent a single bypass operation on 30 November 1988. Although possibly a shade heavier now than he and his doctors would prefer, Evans is presently as strong as a bull, resolved not to let excessive moderation interfere with the those things he loves to do, i.e. eat and drink. Every minute counts.

One of his close friends, Bob Raymond, overcame his horror of hospitals to front at the Evans bedside. Fearing the worst, he arrived to find the convalescent dressed in silk gown and cravat, betting wildly on the television races and playing poker, while alternately gulping caviar and champagne in the company of two attractive women.

Another of his hospital guests after the bypass was Nick Bulleid, who sings with the Sydney Philharmonium Choir. He was accompanied there by a soprano, an alto and a tenor, who together with Bulleid sang Evans carols in five part harmony, the fifth part provided by a bottle of '75 Dom Ruinard. Evans later admitted there were tears in his eyes.

"You're not in a hurry are you?" he asked them. In the next ward, Evans told Bulleid, lay one of the founders of Rothbury Estate in the last stages of terminal illness. "He is on oxygen assistance," he explained, "but if you went in and sung a carol for him he would love it. Don't sing more than one; he can't concentrate for long."

His 24-carat generosity and thought for others is never far from the surface, even when recovering from major surgery. And, remembers Bulleid, he had a fairly generous share of that bottle too.

Evans' generosity is legendary and has always been the hallmark of the man, says James Halliday, who remembers finding it since the earliest days of his friendship with Evans strange, novel and appealing. At a dinner party at his home in 1970, Evans first introduced Halliday to the red wines of the Domaine de la Romanée-Conti, with a 1962 La Tâche.

"He has never hesitated to produce and open the very best bottle he could lay his hands on," says Halliday. "His reaction was always 'Christ, let's open and drink it and enjoy it', rather than to stick it in a rack and ponder how much it might be worth and how much its value might be appreciating." Peter Doyle thinks Evans has probably given away more quality wine in his life than anyone else in the world.

Keith Dunstan describes Evans' enormous spirit of giving to other people, "a rare capacity almost beyond that of anyone I've ever met. He is a tremendously warm, loving man in all respects. You could not set foot in Bulletin Place without Evans taking you into his room and opening a bottle of champagne."

In 1976, Evans sadly proclaimed he was getting older, and that since he might only drink another 8 000 bottles, they had all better be good ones. "Under the law of capability there may only be 2 500 succulent steaks left to me," he intoned and, with sinking voice, "I might make love only another 5 000 times."

Hence the Len Evans Theory of Capacity, which this and any story of the man could not possibly omit.

- THERE is an awful lot of wine in the world, but there is also a lot of awful wine.

- NO sensible person drinks to excess, therefore any one person can only drink a certain amount in a lifetime.

- THERE are countless flavours, nuances, shades of wine; endless varieties, regions, styles. You have neither the time nor the capacity to try them all.

- TO make the most of the time left to you, you must start by calculating your total future capacity. One bottle a day is 365 bottles a year. If your life expectancy is another 30 years, there are only 10 000-odd bottles ahead of you.

- PEOPLE who say: "You can't drink the good stuff all the time" are talking rubbish. You must drink good stuff all the time. Every time you drink a bottle of inferior wine, it's like smashing a superior bottle against the wall. The pleasure is lost forever – you can't get that bottle back.

- THERE are people who don't want to drink good wine, and are happy with the cheapies. I forgive them. There are others who are content with beer and spirits; I can't worry about everybody.

- WINE is not meant to be enjoyed for its own sake; it is the key to love and laughter with friends, to the enjoyment of food, beauty and humour and art and music. Its rewards are far beyond its cost.

- WHAT part is wine of your life? Ten percentum: Ergo, 10 per cent of your income should be spent on wine.

- THE principle should be applied to other phases of life. A disciple kissed a beautiful young lady and she demurred. He was aghast, and said: "Don't get the wrong idea. I've worked out that I can only make love another 1 343 times. I'm bloody sure I'm not wasting one on you!"

I doubt he will waste too many of the bottles in his rather expansive cellar.

One of the reasons he accomplishes so much at once is that Evans' mind operates concurrently on several levels. Deeta Colvin once ventured into his office to find him simultaneously discussing an article on the telephone to his editor at the *Bulletin*, Trevor Kennedy, writing a menu and conducting three separate discussions with people assembled there to see him.

Bob Oxenbould remembers times when they might be watching golf or else fishing together when Evans would blurt out "By gee, that would be a very good exercise, that one!" Initially taken aback, Oxenbould soon realised that Evans had been quietly talking an idea over to himself, and naturally assumed that he knew everything about it!

Len Evans is a highly competitive man. If he chooses to tackle something, he usually wants to be the best at it. Much of the time he has a fighting chance. It must have hurt him the day he had organised a cricket match at which he was clean bowled first ball and then to his chagrin, caught out the second. According to his own rules, a batsman could not be given out until he had scored a run. The umpire, Frank Hoffman, said: "Len, you are the first single batsman I have ever seen on a hat-trick." It is safe to bet the reply was unprintable.

Foremost in his natural talents were writing, golf, organisation and imagination. "He's a highly intelligent man," says Dan Murphy, "a master of organisation and design, getting the thing right. He has one of the greatest minds in every way."

As I have said, Evans gradually gave away golf and then writing, for wine. There wasn't a particular morning when he woke up, resolved to make wine his career, however much he might have enjoyed it. Some who have watched him over the years remain perplexed by the route he has chosen and even suggest that the worst thing to happen to Len Evans was to substitute his golf and writing for wine.

Although he disagrees, Evans was indeed potentially a successful golfer who won a professional golf tournament and despite the attention he has given to wine, he is genuinely a top writer. He is naturally blessed at both, but as some suggest, perhaps he never put a premium on these natural talents. History shows he preferred instead to pursue his wine interest, at the possible expense of a larger stage and sphere as a writer or golfer. "But I'm not very good at golf," he argues. "If I had been, I would have said so."

"I have lots of small talents. I have small talents in speaking, writing, drawing, organising, administrating and leading. I have wondered if I would prefer to have a single great talent or lots of lesser, different talents, but I prefer the latter, for this way I have a diversity of interests."

His personality and ability to choose words incisively stamp Evans a brilliant writer, although he never regarded writing as any other than a commercial thing to do. "I'm not a great writer, perhaps a competent one. I can be quite amusing." He considers that his best writing was early on, in his "enthusiastic" days, furiously churning out material in many directions, for such as the *Bulletin*, the *Observer* and the satirical *Mavis Bramston Show.*

Evans matches his love of words with an infectious sense of madness and fun. Five minutes after walking into a room of a thousand hostile or bored people, he can have them jumping with enthusiasm. He is a born storyteller with a great love for a good gag or a good story, a master of ceremonies without peer.

Oddly, Evans was drawn inches closer to wine with every step of his early career, never quite certain where it would lead him. Initially it offered financial security to foster his writing and to wed his bride, yet ultimately his choice makes perfect sense. Evans is part artist, part builder, part aesthete, part gourmand and a natural host, so wine is a logical extension for him. The pleasure, excitement and satisfaction it brings are both the means and the end.

At the end of the day, Len Evans has succeeded in what he wanted to do. He found his own direction, rather than feeling an obligation to commercialise other natural talents. "What I'm really best at is my profession. Not in terms of any particular role – a wine merchant, restaurateur or vigneron, but in terms of my understanding of wine. It's my chief talent," he says.

Frank Christie has no doubt of that, and remembers long ago Evans telling him that one day he would have his own vineyard and make his own wine. "That was always his driving force," says Christie.

One of the reasons Evans is so appealing is his infectious ability to inspire, motivate and exhaust those around him. He sees himself as an "agent provocateur", a catalyst whose ceaseless and spontaneous flow of ideas and energy will arrive at a concept, then find the people, the means and the materials to put it together.

This is easiest to visualise in his blending of wines, and he says nothing in his profession gives him quite the same thrill. "It's anticipation, fear, commerce and conjecture all mixed up. It's a thrill to discard each part of the make that you think is unsuitable, and to mature and cherish the rest."

Wine has provided Evans with his professional stature and has always contributed vastly to his social life. "I love being part of the international brotherhood of winespeople", he says. "Wine and food professionals are basically a gregarious lot and they like sharing." They are so bound together they call themselves the "Rafia", he once told Welsh goon and entertainer, Sir Harry Secombe. "You bloody traitor," answered Secombe. "I thought you were part of the Taffya."

Although he constantly reminds his protégés that wine is only, and only ever a drink, Evans reveres a great wine like the great work of art it is. The first time he met Joe and Marlene Bugner was while floating on Sydney harbour with Peter Doyle, Dave Allen, Lyn Redgrave and a few others. Evans had taken along some magnificent

Former boxer Joe Bugner, Lyn Redgrave, Peter Doyle, comedian Dave Allen and Evans striking land after a hot day on Sydney Harbour.

wines, including one extraordinary and very valuable bottle of French red he had secreted away and opened to breathe.

It was with alarm and horror that he discovered that Bugner, the former world heavyweight title contender and many times Evans' size, had stumbled by and had almost drained the entire bottle of his great wine, swilling it down by the midi glass. He was about to gulp the last of it down when Evans cornered him. "Joe Bugner, if you drink that, no matter who you are, or how big you are, you will have a fight on your hands," he bristled, in all likelihood meaning every word. After the heat of the moment, he and Bugner remained good friends.

Heaven knows, we are all biologically variable; some of us are shorter than others. Evans' height often enters conversation between those who know him best. He has the classic short, nuggety build of the Welsh miner, or pit pony. The brilliant Welsh golfer, Ian Woosnam is cast from a similar chunky mould. Evans once admitted in *Cleo* magazine that he would like to be a lot taller, although he says candidly that size has never worried him.

Napoleonically complexed or not, Evans does need to dominate. But since he is neither dictatorial nor incapable of admitting his mistakes, for his blunt honest style is disarming at the very least, those who would account for the Evans phenomenon by simple reference to the diminunitive Corsican are only partially correct. Like Napoleon, Len Evans will certainly be remembered for his achievements.

"I have never considered myself the dictator some people claim," he says. "I've done a lot of good-natured chivvying for a one-manned committee, but in the twenty-three years I've been around board tables we've never held a vote. Every decision has always been based on consensus. I don't like to throw any autocratic weight around, except when I own something myself."

But he will invariably take over in most situations. "There was no such thing as Len Evans coming over to dinner and not dominating the whole table," says Dan Murphy. "He is a bombastic know-all-bastard, but the point is that he knows his wine," says another friend. "You can be one if you are an expert, and clearly he is. But when he has been wrong in identifying wines like everyone else, he is always the first to admit it."

Sometimes Evans' climbing down may more resemble a justification than an admission, usually couched brilliantly into a story or a joke, only those who know him well enough tend to see it for what it is.

Until you get to know Len Evans, it is easy to be intimidated by his image and even awed by its projection. He is effortlessly, obviously, incredibly knowledgeable and entertaining, self-confident and forthright. Some suggest that elements of intimidation remain however well you get to know him.

Evans' garrulous and humourous approach has caused offence where none was intended. Sometimes, incorrectly assuming that others share his high-frequency wavelength, his fast throw-away lines that were not meant to be taken seriously are mistakenly interpreted by others.

His employer at the Chevron, Frank Christie, has enjoyed Evans, admired him, and at times, been frustrated and angered by him. "You either like him and enjoy him, or you can't. It's black or white, there's no grey. I know him well enough to be able to enjoy him and I'm quite at ease with his ego and his success."

There's no denying that Evans takes care to maintain his larger-than-life image. Without constant presentation to the public and its continual acknowledgement, he could feel somewhat, although incorrectly, a lesser person than he is.

Evans conducts himself with complete frankness and candour. He is the most honest man Peter Doyle thinks he has ever met and Doyle cannot once remember him telling a lie. He will not praise or promote a wine unless its quality is worth it and his criticism is invariably constructive. John Beeston says that even in Rothbury's own internal tastings against its Hunter competitors he would sometimes extol a wine made by Gerry Sissingh at Lindemans, saying it made his own look ugly.

Not infrequently, Evans has been accused of using his position to push his own barrow, either Rothbury, the Hunter Valley or Petaluma, by distorting and manipulating the facts. There is barely a wine figurehead or spokesman in Australia against whom that charge could not be levelled. It is nearly twenty-five years since Evans was last paid to promote the full spectrum of Australian wine. Put bias and jealousy aside, and his credibility is not found wanting.

Misunderstandings have undeniably occurred. Sometimes those being criticised by Evans have found themselves unable to handle his forthright, uncompromising delivery. In the same way, Evans has taken excessively to heart the attacks made against him by those prepared to defend their own positions.

In the mid 1960s while a popular and well-known figure in Sydney, Evans was almost entirely unknown in Melbourne, although words of his flamboyant and self-confident style had travelled south. However, he was regarded by the Melbourne wine establishment with much scepticism and suspicion.

As guest of a well-known Melbourne journalist at the Melbourne Club's Annual Wine and Food Night, he was seated between his host and Eric Purbrick. The club's new wine purchases, as chosen for the cellar by the club's wine committee were paraded out and tasted, then compared to older but similar vintages bought ten years previously.

After several speakers had complemented the wines, new and old, Evans was asked to comment, which, he at first, declined to do. His refusal, he says, was not accepted, and he was ultimately and reluctantly pressured into speaking. Although he had enjoyed the evening, he considered the food and wine served to be plainly awful. So, as I am reliably told, he let them have it.

The food was ordinary, the young wines had little future and the older vintages barely justified their keeping, he said, pointing out to minute degree what was individually wrong with each of the wines. Many of those present at the dinner were specialists in their own professions, he acknowledged, but similarly the buying of wine is a matter for wine specialists.

Dan Murphy agreed wholeheartedly with Evans, but says he would never have had the nerve to speak his mind like that in that particular environment. As much as I have heard about this speech, I sincerely doubt it was intended as a vitriolic attack on the club, however unfortunate its typically blunt delivery. But it stung.

A prominent member immediately rose to the club's defence, under the clear impression that the honour and integrity of the committee had been wrongly placed in doubt. Although he paled next to Evans as an authority on wine, his attack was as enduring as it was vitriolic, beginning with: "What right has this ignoramus got to talk about our wines like this?" The rest is predictable, however incorrect.

The effect on Evans was devastating, mortifying. His host was horrified, and taking Evans with him, stormed across Collins Street to finish their coffees at the Athenaeum Club.

Several years later, Evans bumped into one of the doctors who had been present at the dinner and who, as chance would have it, was the incoming President of the club. Thanking Evans profusely, he said his well-chosen words had helped him get rid of the cellar of "old mens' wine".

Years later, Evans was persuaded to return to the Melbourne Club for lunch. Remembering the entire affair, the porter recognised him immediately and smiled, his countenance brightening substantially. "Good day Mr Evans. Go in there and give them hell!"

So linear is his thought process that, when criticising a wine, Evans considers neither who may have brought it, who made it or whose feelings he might be treading on. He does not associate those people with the bottle, and looks only at the wine itself.

While employed at Bulletin Place Anders Ousback once proudly took in to a tasting what he then considered to be a special old wine from his fledgling cellar. It was a Penfolds White Hermitage from the Hunter. "What a piss-awful wine that is," Evans exclaimed.

"But I brought it," said an injured Ousback.

Evans just said: "I know."

To Ousback it was an important and very relevant lesson.

Despite the contrary opinions of many, Evans is not immune to criticism, justified or not, as the Melbourne Club experience illustrates, able to be as hurt and injured as the rest of us. It is true to an extent, however, that he is considerably less concerned with what others think of his efforts and accomplishments. For those with less than his spread of talents, this view could easily be interpreted as a bigoted one. A true perfectionist, everything must be done properly, the chief yardstick being whether or not it pleases him.

Wine is justly fortunate to have received the lion's share of Evans' attention. But while he considers it his main strength, how good is he really at it?

"I was often accused of having a great memory for wine, rather than having a decent palate," Evans despairs. "But how can you have a wine memory without a palate as well? You must have something to remember. It's like saying someone is a great historian just because he has a memory!"

Brian Croser rates Evans' palate, his ability to taste, smell and analyse, the best he has seen by far. "He really understands wine, its structure and its breeding better than anyone else; whether a wine really has great qualities or whether it's just a good wine."

Anders Ousback found his appreciation of Evans really grew when he went to work in the London wine trade. "I went to sit at the feet of the great experts of wine and was staggered by how little they knew", he says. "I then realised what a real palate Len actually has. With complete objectivity, his is the greatest palate I have ever encountered. Some regional specialists may know more of certain areas, but in terms of overall wine knowledge or, more fundamentally, what ultimately constitutes quality, he's it."

The real wine experts of Europe, those like Michael Broadbent, John Avery and Hugh Johnson were quick to recognise Evans' abilities. In the early 1980s, John Avery, one of the United Kingdom's leading wine merchants and palates, put up a tasting of three Bordeaux wines in front of Evans and some Bristol merchants, including John Harvey. "I think they're very good," he said. "They're from the same vintage, but that's the only thing I'm going to tell you."

"I picked up the three wines," Evans remembers, "and had no idea what the first was. I knew the second wine instantly. I had tasted it before, a typical Pauillac, a beautiful Mouton-cedar, and that lovely rich fruit character, violets and rose petals. I knew it was Mouton and I knew it was '49.

"That gave me a clue about the other two. The more, I looked at them, the more I realised they weren't Haut-Médoc wines. Having established that, I thought they were probably a Saint-Émilion and a Pomerol. If the first was in fact '49 Mouton, they were bound to be Cheval Blanc and Petrus – which in fact they were."

Evans had taken only a matter of minutes to pronounce his judgement, greeted by the gathering with gasps of surprise. He rose meteorically in their estimation but balance was restored, Evans concedes, when he pronounced the 1851 port served afterwards as a 1927. "I went the full spectrum from glory to culpability in one fell swoop!" he laughs.

John Parkinson expects that many of Evans' peers were intimidated by the strength of his palate. Some were resentful of his confidence and certainty in his own ability. "It never would dawn on Len," he says, "that some people are deliberately vague about wine, taking cover behind grey comments and taking every care to avoid committing themselves to an opinion."

"I always found the certainty of his palate decisions the most remarkable," continues Parkinson. "He could articulate about a wine particularly well." Neither does a wine have to be great for Evans to show it respect. "He has his finger on the pulse of what people want to drink at any level, from casks to first-growths," says Parkinson. "He has a great ability to say good, bad and why."

Long before his association with the Wine Information Bureau, Evans was a teacher of wine. He hasn't stopped teaching wine, either. Bob Oxenbould remembers he was always keen that those around him should discover more about how food and wine went together, "and making sure they had a bloody good time drinking the stuff".

Through Bulletin Place, Len Evans was able to bring up an entire generation of wine professionals. Some of the knowledge and feeling he imparted to his legion of protégés had as much to do with his philosophy of wine and how to understand it as it had to do with an appreciation of quality.

Anders Ousback was wine steward at a winter wine dinner held in the Beef Room. Evans and his friends, Tony Albert, John Beeston and James Halliday were in attendance, plus a host of others who paid a large sum to complete a glamorous and very grand wine occasion. Ousback was approached by a man who asked him "What's the best bottle of red you've got?" Ousback replied that it was the 1962 La Tâche, which then sold for around $65 a bottle, today equivalent to between $300 and $400.

"Give me a bottle," he demanded, slapping down the money.

The then young and very impassioned Ousback was distraught that this person, who clearly knew next to nothing about wine, was to drink the very best in his cellar. Finding the bottle, he promptly extracted the cork with the large lever de-corker attached to the bar, before thumping down a couple of glasses.

Evans had been watching him quietly, aware that Anders was furious. "Why didn't you decant the wine?" he asked him, who replied that the customer wouldn't even know the difference.

"He just looked at me," says Ousback," and said 'But you did the wrong thing by the wine'."

"I just shrank," he says. "The person is irrelevant, the wine is important. I was just nineteen at the time and that lesson told me a lot about fundamental integrity and honesty."

Another time, Ousback was watching Evans taste an old Lindemans 1949 sticky. "What a gorgeous, bloody wonderful wine this is," waxed Evans, "with lusciousness, depth of flavour and complexity," before he spat it out.

"If it was so good," questioned the game Ousback, "why are you spitting it out?"

"I don't like sweet wines."

Of course Evans does like sweet wine, but that wasn't the point, which was that opinion is independent of quality. "Don't ever confuse what is good and what you like, Ousback. They are two different things. It's nice if they are one and the same, but it's not a problem if they're not." That simple philosophy crosses most disciplines, into all areas of subjective appreciation.

For restaurateur Hermann Schneider to say that Len Evans has an incredible knowledge of food is rather a significant statement. Schneider says Evans knows exactly what needs to be cooked with what and for how long. "He understands great food and is very critical of food that is not good."

Evans used to make Schneider's Two Faces Restaurant his headquarters in Melbourne and, after most people had left in the evening, would suggest to Schneider, "Well, Hermann, now go and get a decent bottle."

In 1985, Len and Trish Evans visited Doug and Judy Crittenden at Mount Martha on Victoria's Mornington Peninsula. Evans had been promised a day or two fishing on Port Phillip Bay. Having been locked in by two or three days of heavy weather, Evans' patience was wearing thin. "It's no good, Len," Crittenden said. "With the breeze this stiff and the seas so heavy you will never be able to drift for flathead."

"Nonsense, it's not too rough. If you want to see some rough sea, come up to New South Wales! We're going fishing today."

Out they went. Even with his heaviest sinkers, Doug Crittenden couldn't get them to hit the bottom, in just 30 feet of water. Somehow Evans did, and he was the only one to pull in any flathead, enough anyway for a decent feed.

"We found some other seafood, and what he created as a bouillabaisse from scallops, mussels and flathead was quite amazing," says Crittenden. "He is an incredible chef. He just throws things in and always it finishes very well. And he is always looking for that extra ingredient."

Peter Doyle doesn't rate Evans a bad fisherman and one day lent him one of his old boats. "Impressing overseas people with his knowledge of the harbour, he ran the boat up high and dry on a shelf of rocks on Rose Bay, claiming they were an uncharted reef! By that time Sydney had been going for 190 years!"

Fishing for schnapper with Doyle off Shark Bay in Western Australia, Evans once hooked a very large hook into the palm of his hand, into the bone and out of his thumb. "It was a nasty one," says Doyle. "The old fisherman with him said he would have to cut the line and then pull the hook through, but Evans suggested he just cut the hook. But the fisherman said he didn't want to ruin the hook. So Evans endured this incredible pain for a few hours. We eventually got him to hospital, but there was no doctor, just a nurse.

"Evans had pre-cooked tea and we had invited a few skippers from other boats over for dinner, none of whom had ever heard of Len Evans, who must have been in agonising pain. The skipper asked Evans who cooked the meal, and he said that he had. 'Not bad,' said the skipper. 'If you want a job working on our boats, I'll give you one.' Evans asked about the pay, which turned out to be around $150 per week plus a percentage of the catch, which he would have to help with.

"Evans said that would be interesting. Then the skipper, who was quite serious about it, said, 'But you can't start until your hand gets better.'"

Doug Crittenden says, "The longer I have known Len the more I've liked him, although I'm sure almost every friend of his has experienced a love-hate relationship at times. We all understand that's Len, and although he doesn't really mean it, he's a cocky upstart Welsh bastard, as I call him. But he keeps a fantastic collection of friends in all walks of life."

"I'm a wine consumer, certainly not a wine buff," booms Bob Oxenbould, a banker turned actor who has never done a day's paid work remotely related to wine. "I like good wine, but I like lots of it. Evans is endeared to me because he knows that as long as I am alive, the wine industry will flourish. I didn't get this size by eating fruitcake, I can tell you! He's a great friend, and we've never had an argument at all. Not about wine, anyway, except maybe the volume!"

Evans' visits to Melbourne were tightly scheduled to fit in everything he wanted to do. He might ring Hermann Schneider: "I am coming for dinner tomorrow, but don't give me this crap that you're busy. I want to talk to you. See if you could arrange lunch at Vlado's. I'd like to see Doug Crittenden. See if Keith Dunstan is coming too. I haven't much time, but I want to go and see John Dunn, the antique dealer, then we will have dinner at Two Faces. Is Faye going to be there, because I will have so and so with me…"

Schneider laughs. "He is always organising his own things. He would give you a list of instructions of what he wanted. In a way it's a relief that he is in Sydney and I am in Melbourne!"

"I admire Len and recognise his good attributes," says Schneider. "He is a very true friend. He would stand by you through anything. He is often criticised by people in Melbourne, and I've often had to stand up for him there. 'Do you really know him?' I ask these people."

It was a pity that, after Peter Fox's death when Evans was caught so extremely tightly that some of the people who owed him so much were not there to support him, as he would most likely have supported them. Although Evans didn't raise this issue while discussing this book, there were, according to Anders Ousback, plenty of people who then owed him money who could have helped him financially. The entire experience separated his true friends from the hangers-on, he believes.

"Len has always demanded absolute loyalty from his friends and in return he gives absolute loyalty to you," says Keith Dunstan. "If he comes to Melbourne or wherever you happen to be, and you're not standing on the doorstep to welcome him, he gets very upset. And he'll also get upset if he gives an invitation that you don't accept."

In 1979, Marie and Keith Dunstan took the Southern Aurora, the overnight train to Sydney. On their arrival, they were astonished to see Evans, complete with his Bentleigh Continental, waiting at the station to drive them to their hotel. Dunstan said it was extraordinary that Evans should have interrupted his time for them like that. Evans said loyalty is the thing. "You have got to look after your friends." Bob Oxenbould says his close friends are the only people with the ability to hurt Evans.

"He is a bloody communist," insists Peter Doyle. "What's yours is his and what's his is his own." On one occasion, they both arrived in London from Heathrow, stopping at the Capel Hotel in Basil Street. Evans asked Doyle if he had any English money. Doyle had £10. "Give it to me," demanded Evans."

Doyle handed it over and, as the taxi pulled up, the doorman, who recognised him, said "Mr Evans, delighted to see you sir." With that, Evans put the £10 in his hand, at which the doorman asked "Which are your bags, Mr Evans?" He pointed them out and, of course, the doorman took his bags, leaving Peter Doyle to drag up his own.

Exactly the same thing happened the time when Peter Doyle ran into Evans in Melbourne. Evans was staying at the Hilton with Frank Christie, while Doyle had booked a small, cheap room at the Hotel Australia. The currency working in his favour, this time it cost Doyle only $10. "I could never win with him," he laughs.

Always keeping up the ties with his friends, Evans was a master of networking long before the word became part of the language. He takes trouble to maintain his relationships with people, especially his protégés from Bulletin Place and elsewhere, although it wasn't always easy when they first moved away and into their own territories.

Several had become almost like surrogate children to Evans, even adopting his mannerisms and modes of thinking. Anders Ousback now understands why Evans took his sudden departure from Bulletin Place for The Summit restaurant quite badly. Like the many other Evans' trainees, he has since established a new friendship with Evans on a more mature basis. John Parkinson remembers that Evans exploded in mock fury when he announced, in 1975, that he wanted to leave the Bulletin Wine Club. "You mean to say that I've wasted five years of my time training you?! Piss off then!"

Showing what Parkinson calls a healthy disrespect for youth, Evans has always given his pupils the impression that he considers them ungrateful for their training. "We, mind you," says Parkinson, "who are considered for life as his protégés, always returned it with mutual disrespect. But of course, none of us would ever hear anything said against Len."

Although he can be noisy and bordering on uncouth when he feels that circumstances demand it, much of Evans' humour is quirky and whimsical, often at the expense of others. He doesn't easily handle pomposity and wine. Finding himself at a particularly snobbish gathering, in full view of everyone, Evans dipped his fingers into a glass of wine. Someone asked him what he was doing. "You can tell much from a wine's feel," he explained. "Obviously this is a Hunter, it's quite different from a Barossa. Notice what a rubbery texture it has." Soon the entire room was dipping in their fingers, evaluating the feel! It's typical Evans humour for the joke to be his alone.

While staying at "Loggerheads" in 1991, I asked Evans to examine my golf swing. Beginning with my grip, its many and various flaws were detected and graphically conveyed. Having hit some forty golf balls between us from his lawn onto the paddock which doubles as driving range and short golf course, he suggested I take out the bucket and retrieve the balls.

It was late afternoon and the champagne was beckoning, so despite his frown I accompanied him inside for a couple of glasses. "Didn't you see that large crow?" he asked. "I didn't like the look of it and I reckon it had an eye on some of those balls."

By this stage, I was comfortably ensconced with my feet up, while the sun was about to go down, so I said I had played golf on many courses teeming with crows and had never been bothered by one yet. The balls could wait. But since Evans was fidgeting so much, I consented and, with bucket in hand, climbed over the style and into the paddock.

Apart from six or so golf balls, it was obvious the paddock was empty. My insides rehearsed a difficult, tumbling dive, with pike. Although they were old, some of them cut, it is still impolite for guests to lose thirty-four of their host's golf balls, whatever their condition. Suddenly it clicked. Evans had every opportunity to ring his staff and instruct them to collect most of the balls, leaving just a few scattered around for effect. That was it, I decided, so I would play along.

Try as I did, saying of course I'd found the lot, under Evans' intense, doubting glare I wilted. "You bastard, you know exactly where they are!" I accused, describing what I had deduced he had done. I was then hauled straight into his Pajero and spent the next ninety minutes driving around all 40 hectares of the Evans block and considerably more of those surrounding it, peering into the half-light for traces of enormous crows and their nests, or for the tell-tale droppings of golf balls.

It was useless. Either Evans or nature had won and, because I don't know which way, and doubt I ever will, I am still very much in the dark, just like the whereabouts of the thirty-four golf balls. Evans denies foul play but Brian Croser is convinced I have been set up. More and more I think he's right, but then I did see a very large black bird…

Anders Ousback regularly feeds Evans' collection of books with obscure titles. Some are really quite special: *A Tour by Horse and Sled to Outcast Siberian Lepers, Stone Quarrying Made Easy* and *The Irish Bee-Keeping Manual*. Evans keeps the books in a guest suite, together in their own shelf. "The most wonderful thing," Evans told Ousback, "is that I don't know how many people have stayed in that room, but not one person has commented!"

Once Evans and Keith Dunstan found themselves comparing their relative frequencies of book-writing. Dunstan gave Evans a copy of his latest, which had a retail price of $2.05. A week later Evans sent Dunstan his, with a $1 note cellotaped into the front, since it was $1 cheaper! There was a note inside: "You capitalistic poof!"

Some find Evans' style and persona too much to handle. Much to his chagrin, he was once prevented from attending a party because he was too noisy! The occasion was the seventieth birthday of Walter James, the brilliant old Australian writer on wine. Dan Murphy clearly enjoys the memory. "That sort of thing never happened to Len!" he cries, through tears of laughter. "He was absolutely crestfallen."

On occasions Evans has been fairly criticised for not tolerating fools but, in public, he is usually more generous and less patronising than most of us could ever be. Anders Ousback recalls many scenes when an elderly person might confront him with, "Mr Evans, I like a bit of sherry, now and then." "That's wonderful, darling", he would reply. "I enjoy a little sherry myself, you know."

Snobbery is an entirely different issue. A guest at the Chevron once ordered the most expensive wine on the list, a 1947 Château Latour, which he then promptly sent back, claiming it had been chilled and stored upright! In a position to know both these claims were perfidiously invalid, Evans tasted the wine and found it perfectly sound. "The only excuse I could offer for his appalling manners was his obvious desire to impress," he says.

In 1980, Nick Bulleid decided to take out to dinner at Le Café, where Oasis Seros is now, those who had helped him find a career in wine. He found some fabulous old Australian wines for his guests, who included James Halliday, John Parkinson and Len Evans.

Half-way through the meal, Le Café's chef, Patrick Chouillet, burst in on Bulleid's table, close to tears. "Nick, what do you think of this wine?" he asked. It was a lovely Bordeaux, a '73 Pomerol, La Pointe, and drinking beautifully. A table had sent it back, claiming it was ordinary. Bulleid handed the wine to Evans, who tried it and said: "Take this wine back to the table with my compliments and say that the Chairman of the Sydney Wine Show has been delighted to taste your delicious wine."

It is fair to say that Len Evans maintained an excellent relationship with the Australian wine industry until the mid '70s, when some companies began to distance themselves from him. After he had left the Wine Information Bureau, most had felt that if the time had now arrived for Evans to make some money out of the wine industry, to which he had contributed so much, then that was a fair thing. The majority of the industry both liked and supported him.

Australians are happy to allow their own to succeed to a certain, domestic extent, but if they do better than that and even dare to create an international profile, we turn on them, often quite viciously. Evans' profile rose too steeply for many. He was a tall, flamboyant, boisterous and successful poppy; most of the wine industry was staid, conservative and inward-looking.

As the Evans Wine Company's grand vision for an international wine concern took shape, as Rothbury raised its profile, as Bulletin Place cemented itself as Len Evans' own personal centre of Australian wine activity, and as his media profile reached new heights for one involved in wine and food, resentment and jealousy began to accumulate in the minds and around the boardrooms of the people and companies too small to cope with Evans and his success.

Although he had made some very good and close friends in the wine industry, several of the old wine companies became unwilling either to support him, recognise his endeavours or let him get too close to them. All the while aware of how much good he had done for them, Evans didn't fit the conservative, low-profile mould they demanded. Many companies were openly critical of him, although they still welcomed with open arms any of Evans' promotion of Australian wine wherever he went; they were all delighted to reap the benefits.

"I didn't talk to Penfolds for nearly ten years, for example," he says. "I don't know why, but they ignored me from the late '70s to the mid '80s. He now gets on particularly well with the Penfolds management and believes the company has a very healthy attitude towards the wine industry. "But before, they only had an attitude for Penfolds."

"I'm not at all bitter," he states. "I'm not saying that the industry hasn't been good to me. The biggest shame is the number of missed chances, the Association of

Wine Judges, for a good example. I used to be on several wine industry councils in the mid '70s including the Management Committee of the Federal Council. I was voted off it for insisting that we had no right to use the word 'Champagne' on Australian wine labels. It didn't worry me, but it really was a shame. Once I was off, I had no wish to go back or become a wine politician."

The bitterness directed towards Evans, which had effectively polarised the wine industry into two camps, pro and anti Evans, found an outlet in 1981, when his profile was at its zenith and Peter Fox was killed, and Evans' world began quickly to fall apart. Not only was he about to lose his entire grand vision, but Rothbury had entered all sorts of trouble.

"The knives came out," says John Parkinson. There was ammunition aplenty. Rothbury's early attitude to wine retailers had isolated him from many. His global plan, which he had so loudly and publicly proclaimed since the early 1970s, before he even met Peter Fox, lay in ruins. The bandwagon of knockers, another less than laudable facet of the Australian national psyche, rolled into gear.

I expect that this only fuelled Evans' resolve to save Rothbury Estate and look further ahead.

Today, of all things, he's close again. The wine industry is now better organised than it's ever been, but the only visible change in Evans is that his hair has become whiter. The newly constituted Winemaker's Federation of Australia headed by Ian Sutton, and the Australian Wine and Brandy Corporation under George Paciullo, provide the wine industry with a positive and well-managed bureaucracy. Evans sits comfortably and ever so naturally alongside, assuming the mantle of statesman, albeit in his own iconoclastic fashion, as the President of the Australian Wine Foundation, the industry's instrument of wine and alcohol education.

The wine industry has caught up with the times, yet the basic Evans attitudes have remained constant. "He's still anti-puffery," says John Parkinson, "and hates the Colonel Blimp mentality of petty bureaucracies. He still respects order and respects the system, but can't handle it being obstructive without good reason."

His style is very straightforward, quickfire and logical: "Cut the crap, get to the point and make an executive decision." It's not difficult to imagine that so many Evans proposals for promotions and training submitted in past years extended far beyond the vision and imagination of those on the committees ultimately responsible for their funding.

Evans recognises the industry still has its fundamental problems. "Small people are in it for the lifestyle, within the financial constraints the industry brings. The big people view the industry as theirs and still see no reason why they should support the poorer smaller people. They increase levies and take too much for granted: the wine judges, the writers and the industry figures who work on their behalf. And if that's a love-hate relationship with the wine industry, you're dead right."

Although he has never asked for it, and at the risk of sounding incongruous to those who do not know him, it would be stretching a point to suggest that Len Evans has been adequately recognised by the wine industry for what he has given it. A decade ago he received his OBE of which, as one might expect, he is extremely proud, but the following ten years were among his most philanthropical.

Evans has certainly not received the accolades he should have, for being what James Halliday described as the single most important contributor to Australian wine in the second half of this century, although McWilliams did redress the balance somewhat by presenting him with the Maurice O'Shea Award in 1991. That he hasn't been acknowledge is probably as much a result of his brusque, frank and utterly direct personality as anything else.

"He should have been given a knighthood," says Peter Doyle. "He has done more for the wine industry than anyone else in Australia but they shrugged him off."

Our greats are ultimately judged by their contributions to society and not for what they have taken from it. Few will be able to match that which Len Evans ultimately leaves behind. But it is undoubtedly premature, bordering on rude, to discuss Evans' legacy in ponderous detail. If he was Chinese, his contemporaries would be thinking, "Well, you've had your ups and downs, now you are almost wise enough to really achieve something for yourself and for others." Perhaps there's a dash of Chinese in his bloodline somewhere, for I expect Evans agrees completely.

There's still a project born every minute, Evans' vision has not faded and his contributions will continue as long as his health and lifestyle permit. But I don't imagine there's much green tea in the Evans diet.

"He's one of the great characters," says John Beeston. "He's growing old gracefully, but he's much the same now as he always was, ebullient, bull-headed, sparkling, living life to the full, and larger than life. He's always ready to be the spokesman, always ready for a comment and always very responsible. If there's a wine cause and it hasn't got Evans on its side, it's not much of a cause. He's very necessary, although you have to be prepared to concede him the chairmanship of the committee!"

While we are now coming to understand fully just what a wasteland of lies, staggering debt and lost opportunity the so-called great entrepreneurs of the 1980s left behind them, Len Evans has created genuine richness, little of which has to do with money.

On one level are the companies which should endure and prosper, Rothbury Estate and Petaluma, now both established and secure. On another level are the people to whom he has contributed vastly, a diverse collection thrown together by their love for wine and drawn to Evans for his presence, his generosity and his teaching.

The list is an extraordinary field of influential people now operating throughout all levels of the wine industry. But to name only a fraction – Anders Ousback, Brian Croser, John Parkinson, Nick Bulleid, Michael McMahon, Peter Morse, Michael Bright, Anne Ellis, Chris Shannon, Chris Hayes, John Hennesey and, if we look back to his early days, James Halliday and John Beeston.

Several of his "pupils" or "protégés" have since climbed to great heights after the start Evans propagated, but each retains much of the essential feeling towards wine engendered in them by Evans. Through these names and through others, including the many leading wine show judges trained by Evans, his understanding, attitude and love for wine will continue to snowball throughout the industry.

The third level of the Evans' contribution is almost impossible to measure. Through his teaching, writing, promoting and bludgeoning, Len Evans can witness to a vastly more mature Australian wine industry and wine public than he first encountered. Keith Dunstan believes that through sheer exuberance of personality, Evans has been the greatest person the wine industry has produced. "He has done more about getting Australians aware of and interested in wine than any one else," he says.

"He's a great motivator and he's responsible for a positive change in the Australian attitude towards wine and food," says John Parkinson. "He got us all going." His contribution stands alone. Ever since the early 1960s, through the Wine Information Bureau, Bulletin Place and Rothbury Estate, Evans has been telling Australians to raise their sights and enjoy the view.

Australia is no longer a quirky, old-fashioned producer of idiosyncratic regional wines, but an internationally recognised and respected maker of wines of individual quality that conform to the rest of the world's expectations of style. Evans has been a driving force behind this emerging adulthood of Australian wine, without which, it would have no guarantee of a long-term future.

To infer he's an angel, however, would be grossly inaccurate. Evans can be impossibly aggressive, egocentric and dominating. Some say he is excellent company as long as he is in control. He's too easily threatened and has been quick to walk away from embarrassment, unable to handle it properly. He doesn't like being upstaged, and he wrongly believes he loses face by not being the centre of attention. He's played life hard and, along the way, has given many people what they feel is just cause to resent him.

No conclusion concerning Len Evans can hold water unless the case against is considered. The point of the matter, however, is that when all arguments for and against are compared, Len Evans finishes so far ahead. The closer you look, the greater the margin.

Len Evans used to discuss with Keith Dunstan what they would like written on their tombstones. "Evans is such a restless, nervous soul," says Dunstan. He's always wanting to know what's around the corner. "His favourite saying was 'What's next?' That should be his epitaph."

Timeline

1930	Len Evans born at Felixstowe, England.
1948	Refused Cambridge scholarship to study architecture, in favour of professional golf.
1950	Demobbed from the air force.
1951	Appointed assistant professional at Potters Bar Golf Club.
1953	Emigrated to New Zealand.
1955	Arrived in Sydney.
1956	Won The Selectar Cup, a golf tournament in Singapore, before moving to Mount Isa, Australia.
1958	Worked at the Ship Inn, Sydney, also contributing scripts to television and radio and humour articles to the *Observer*.
1959	Married Patricia Hayton on 18 July. Evans first meets Rudy Komon.
1960	Joins the Chevron Hilton as a Beverage Systems Controller, shortly afterwards becoming its Assistant Beverage Manager.
1962	Frank Christie promotes Evans to the position of Chevron's Food and Beverage Manager. Evans begins to write as "Cellarmaster" in the *Bulletin*.
1963	Evans appointed the Chevron's Executive Assistant Manager.
1965	Len Evans joins the Australian Wine Board on 1 January, as its first National Promotions Executive.
1966	Evans publishes the *Cellarmaster's Guide to Australian Wines*.
1967	Evans leaves the Wine Information Bureau. Evans highly publicised overseas trip with Graham Kerr, recorded in their book *The Galloping Gourmets*.
1968	Evans publishes *Cellarmaster Says*. The birth of Rothbury Estate.
1969	Len and Trish Evans open the Bulletin Place cellars with Graham and Treena Kerr on 20 July, the same day man first stood on the moon. The beginning of the Monday Table, Bulletin Place.
1970	Evans launches the Bulletin Wine Club with John Parkinson.
1971	Rothbury Estate's first vintage.
1972	Evans buys the remaining unplanted 40 hectares of Rothbury as a site for his home.
1973	Evans publishes the first edition of the *Australia and New Zealand Complete Book on Wine*. Establishment of the Rothbury Estate Society and the Rothbury Ribbon Dinners.
1974	Amalgamation of the four Rothbury syndicates.
1976	At a Queen's Birthday fireworks party at Brokenwood, Evans experiences an angina attack. Peter Fox subsequently helps rescue Bulletin Place. Evans begins to plant the vineyard around the site of "Loggerheads" for Evans Family Wines.
1977	The inaugural Single Bottle Club Dinner, in honour of Michael Broadbent, on 4 February. Rothbury shares reorganised, with Len Evans, David Chen and Peter Fox taking control of the company. The Evans Wine Company buys its vineyard in Coonawarra.
1978	Evans appointed Chairman of Judges, Royal Sydney Show. "Indulgence" appears for the first time in the *Weekend Australian*. The Evans Wine Company buys its vineyards in Clare and the Hunter Valley. The Evans Wine Company buys Château Rahoul and Château Padouen in Bordeaux. The Evans Wine Company buys the Weaver Ranch in the Napa Valley.
1979	The grand diet.
1980	Evans turns fifty with a private three-day wine festival.

1981	Evans leaves the *Weekend Australian* and begins to write for the *Women's Weekly*. Rothbury's first vintage of Cowra Chardonnay. Peter Fox dies in December, aged forty-three.
1982	Rothbury Estate's shareholdings reorganised yet again. The Evans Wine Company forced to sell its assets in France and California. Len Evans awarded an OBE for services to wine and to the community. Rudy Komon dies. Rothbury Estate buys its vineyard at Cowra.
1984	Publication of the fourth editions of Evans "big book", as *Len Evans' Complete Book of Australian Wine*. "Loggerheads", the "House on the Hill" in the Hunter Valley is finally completed.
1985	Evans moves with his family to his "salvage home" of "Loggerheads".
1986	Evans returns to the *Weekend Australian* to continue "Indulgence" and then to commence the "Hunter Diary" column, which lasted until 1990. Awarded a medal by the French Ambassador for the 'Personalité de l'Année, becoming the first Australian to be honoured in this fashion. ("Congratulations," said James Halliday. "And what year was it for?")
1988	Evans undergoes a single heart bypass operation on 30 November at St Vincent's Private Hospital, Sydney.
1989	Evans appointed President of the Australian Wine Foundation.
1990	Evans closes Bulletin Place. Publication of the fifth and last edition of *Len Evans' Complete Book of Australian Wine*.
1991	Evans becomes the second recipient of the Mount Pleasant Maurice O'Shea Award for Excellence in The Wine Industry.
1992	Evans is presented with the RAS Medal by the Royal Agricultural Society of New South Wales for his contributions to the Royal Sydney Easter Show.

*B*ibliography

Dunstan, K. *Ratbags*. Golden Press, 1979.

Evans, L.P. *Cellarmaster Says*. The *Bulletin*, 1968.

Evans, L.P. *Cellarmaster's Guide to Australian Wines*. The *Bulletin*, 1966.

Evans, L.P. *Complete Book of Australian Wine*. Paul Hamlyn, 1978.

Evans, L.P. *Good Evans*. Methuen, 1981.

Evans, L.P. *Indulgences*. Methuen, 1980.

Evans, L.P. *Len Evans' Complete Book of Australian Wine*. Lansdowne, 1984.

Evans, L.P. *Len Evans' Cookbook*. Golden Press, 1985.

Féret, E. *Bordeaux and Its Wines*. Éditions Féret et Fils, 1986.

Halliday, J. *The Australian Wine Compendium*. Angus & Robertson, 1985.

Halliday, J. *Clare Valley: the History, the Vignerons and the Wines*. Vin Publications, 1985.

Halliday, J. *Coonawarra: the History, the Vignerons and the Wines*. Yenisey, 1983.

Halliday, J. *Vintage Halliday*. Magazine Promotions Australia, 1982.

Halliday, J. and Jarratt, R. *The Wines and History of The Hunter Valley*. McGraw-Hill, 1979.

Halliday, J. *Wine Atlas of Australia and New Zealand*. Angus & Robertson, 1991.

Kerr, G. and Evans, L.P. *The Galloping Gourmets*. A.H. & A.W. Reed, 1967.

Ousback, A. *Words on Wine*. Hill of Content, 1977.

Symons, M. *One Continuous Picnic*. Duck Press, 1982.

Glossary of Wine People

Addison, John. Former New South Wales head of Hamiltons Wines, member of the Australian Wine Board's Promotions Committee and a friend of Len Evans.

Albert, Tony. A solicitor and now head of his family's Albert Investments company, which amongst other interests, prints much of the sheet music available in Australia. Tony Albert was one of the regular members of the 'Bulletin Place Front Row' and the Monday Table.

Avery, John. Master of Wine, friend of Len Evans and internationally respected palate who manages his family's English firm of wine merchants.

Baker, Neville. Friend of Evans and regular patron of Bulletin Place who, at Evans' instigation, became the *Australian*'s first wine and food columnist.

Beeston, John. One of the regular members of the 'Bulletin Place Front Row' and the Monday Table, John Beeston is a former solicitor now turned full-time wine writer, judge, consultant and author. He is one of the founding partners in Brokenwood, the Hunter Valley wine company.

Bohdan, Tony. Simultaneously appointed the Chevron's Catering Manager when Evans was made Food and Beverage Manager. Straight-talking American who, after early difficulties, became a good friend of Evans and with him formed a highly successful team at the Chevron. Evans recognises Bohdan as the individual who taught him most about food.

Broadbent, Michael. One of the world's great palates and wine writers, Michael Broadbent, Master of Wine, runs the wine division of Christies auction house in London. He is a long-standing friend of Evans and was guest of honour at the first dinner of the Single Bottle Club.

Bulleid, Nick. Sydney-based wine writer, educator judge and consultant, also partner in Brokenwood, presently a brand manager with the Penfolds group. Previous to his current appointment, he worked with John Parkinson at Cellarmasters, the direct-mail wine operation. Nick Bulleid is a more recent Evans protégé, who met him through the Rothbury Estate Society and was welcomed as a regular at the Bulletin Place tasting panel.

Chen, Daniel. Major financier and shareholder of Rothbury Estate since 1977. Before Rothbury's float in 1992 he controlled 24 per cent of the company.

Christie, Frank. General Manager at the Chevron Hilton in Sydney and Evans' employer from 1960 - 1964. He left the Chevron in 1966 to go to the Hotel Australia, Sydney. He is also remembered for running the Melbourne Hilton from its construction in 1973 until his retirement in 1987.

Cleaver, Sally. Took over from Bobby Patterson (now McNee) as restaurant manager at Bulletin Place in 1980.

Cole, Nat King. Popular black American singer whose one-week season at the Chevron was the biggest sensation ever seen there. He once explained to Evans that: 'He is a star when no one clears a plate during his show.'

Crittenden, Doug. Popular and well-known Melbourne wine retailer and merchant, once jokingly described by Evans as having "the best grocer's palate in Australia". Crittenden remains a close friend of Evans since first meeting him in the early days of the Australian Wine Information Bureau in the mid 1960s.

Croser, Brian. Close friend of Evans since 1973. Arguably Australia's finest contemporary winemaker and a protégé of Evans, Brian Croser is presently the managing partner and chief winemaker of Petaluma and the Chairman of the Winemakers' Federation of Australia. For a young man, he has been Australia's most active wine politician and will undoubtedly be a guiding force in its future. Croser was the winemaking consultant to the Evans Wine Company in its French and American exploits. Today he owns a significant winemaking operation in Oregon, the Dundee Wine Company, which sells wine under the Argyle label.

Doherty, Frank. Hired by Len Evans as the Wine Information Bureau's Victorian writer and educator, later to become a popular freelance wine journalist.

Doyle, Peter. Sydney's best known seafood restaurateur, Peter Doyle is a close friend and fishing partner of Len Evans, introduced to him by Rudy Komon.

Dunstan, Keith. Very popular and whimsical Melbourne journalist at the very top of his profession, Keith Dunstan has been a friend and supporter of Len Evans since first meeting him through the Wine Information Bureau. Dunstan was encouraged by Evans to write about wine in the 1960s and today owns a small vineyard and winery growing pinot noir on Victoria's Mornington Peninsula.

Ellis, Annie (*nee* Tyrrell). Murray Tyrrell's daughter, now married to Hanging Rock winemaker, John Ellis. She was the first manager of the wine cellar at Bulletin Place.

Fairbrother, George. Famous Australian winemaker, personality and show judge, rated by Evans as his show-judging mentor. Fairbrother appointed Evans to his first judging post at the Sydney Show and then handed over the reins to him as Chairman of that Show.

Fox, Peter. Evans' great friend, financier and patron, who was tragically killed in December 1981 aged only forty-three. A classic and very creative entrepreneur, he had made a large amount of money in the tax minimisation industry and lived lavishly, taking great pleasure from his association with Len Evans.

Franks, Joe. President of the Australian Catering Institute in the early 1960s and a member of the Chevron's Friday Table.

Fraser, Malcolm. Well-known wine enthusiast and Prime Minister of Australia from 1975 to 1983, Malcolm Fraser is a member of The Single Bottle Club and once hosted a club dinner at The Lodge, the prime ministerial residence in Canberra.

Gough, Sarah. 'Châtelaine' at Rahoul for eight months from March 1980, a former wine writer who is presently with the Victorian wine company of Brown Brothers.

Greatorix, Blue. The wine industry's PR man before Len Evans, whose role was to keep any unsavoury reference to wine out of the newspapers.

Gregory, Graham. Officer in the New South Wales Department of Agriculture, friend of Evans since the Chevron days in the early 1960s, wine judge and respected palate.

Halliday, James. Australia's most important contemporary wine writer, wine judge and winemaker at his company's Coldstream Hills winery in Victoria's Yarra Valley. He has known Evans since attending one of his wine courses in the days of the Wine Information Bureau and became one of the regulars at Bulletin Place, one of the tasting members of the 'Bulletin Place Front Row'. He was one of the founding partners in Brokenwood, but no longer retains his shareholding.

Hardy, Sir James. Internationally known yachtsman and winemaker of the Hardy wine company, of which he is the present Chairman. He has known Evans since early wine-buying trips to the Hunter Valley and was a guest at the Chevron's Friday Table.

Haselgrove, Ron. Former chief winemaker of Mildara and member of the Australian Wine Board. As a winemaker, he pioneered the blending of different varieties and wines from different wine regions, especially between Reynella, the Hunter Valley and Coonawarra. He was awarded an OBE for his services to wine.

Hastings, Peter. The Editor of the *Bulletin* magazine who admitted Evans to it as Australia's first-ever regular wine columnist and, without letting on to Evans, invented the 'Cellarmaster' byline.

Healey, Dr Ray. Sydney wine enthusiast and wine judge who loaned money to Evans to assist him set up Bulletin Place and who, with Rudy and Evans, helped to persuade Murray Tyrrell to persevere with his family winery in the late 1950s.

Heath, Dick. Former Chief Winemaker of Thomas Hardy and, later, a member of the Australian Wine Board, Heath was a close friend of Evans from the Chevron days, when he and others from Hardys would trek to the Hunter to buy local wine long before the Valley's boom years.

Hill-Smith, Mark and Margie. Part of the family which owns the Yalumba wine company, and great friends of Evans since 1957.

Hill-Smith, Michael. Son of Mark and Margie Hill-Smith, wine writer, merchant, judge, Australia's first Master of Wine and owner of an Adelaide wine bar.

Horgan, Dennis. Well-known Western Australian entrepreneur and owner of Leeuwin Estate in the Margaret River area, who helped finance Petaluma after Peter Fox's death in 1981. He subsequently sold his shareholding to Brian Croser.

James, Walter. Fabulously talented but very private man who stood alone as Australia's foremost writer on wine for many years until the emergence of Max Lake and then Len Evans. His books included *Barrel and Book: A Winemaker's Diary* (1949), *Nuts on Wine* (1950) and *Wine in Australia* (1952). Greatly admired by Evans, who sat with him once when Dan Murphy awarded Graham Kerr a bottle of 1934 Château Margaux. "Why is that?" asked Walter James. Evans replied that 1934 was his birth year. "Hmmffphha," said Walter James. "If they want to give me a bottle tell them I was born in either 1945 or 1947."

Joyce, Peter. Victorious President of the Wine and Food Society of Victoria whose team defeated the Bulletin Place Front Row in circumstances bordering on the acrimonious in 1975. The title was later taken from him by Evans in Adelaide.

Kendrick, Ken. The Chevron Hilton's Catering Manager during Len Evans' time there until replaced by Tony Bohdan.

Kerr, Graham. Described by Evans as 'a tall, self-confident English Scot from New Zealand', Kerr met Evans in 1962 while Kerr was a guest at the Chevron. In 1967 he and Evans made a highly publicised *Galloping Gourmets* tour around the world's leading eating establishments. A polished expert and presenter of information on food, Kerr then launched a highly successful career in the media.

Komon, Rudy. Sydney-based but Czech-born art dealer, bon vivant, wine judge, and President of the New South Wales Wine and Food Society. Recognised as one of Australia's leading authorities on wine from the 1950s through to the 1970s. A member of the Friday Table and very much a mentor and father-figure to Len Evans. He was one of the founding partners of Rothbury Estate.

Lake, Max. Surgeon, winemaker and now aromatologist, Max Lake was Australia's leading wine writer in the early 1960s, with occasional contributions to magazines and several published books, including *Hunter Wine*, *Hunter Winemakers* and *Classic Wines of Australia*. His enthusiasm and energy were the driving force behind the explosion of interest in the Hunter Valley. A wine visionary, he planted cabernet sauvignon grapes at what became Australia's first 'boutique' vineyard in 1963, when considered utterly unconventional, there then being no cabernet sauvignon planted in the Hunter Valley whatsoever. A member of the Friday Table at the Chevron, he has been a very good friend of Len Evans, although they are not as close today.

McDiarmid, Mary. Evan's first manager at Bulletin Place, joining him there for its opening in 1969.

McKeever, Fred. One of Evan's promotional team with the Wine Information Bureau.

McNee, Bobby (*nee* Patterson). Evans' most celebrated manager of Bulletin Place, who married Ian McNee, whom she met there. Evans is godfather to their son.

Mann, Jack. Famous old Houghtons winemaker and father of its benchmark 'White Burgundy'. Fanatical about wine, cricket and Western Australia, Mann was a genuine friend of Len Evans. His son, Dorham, continued his family's winemaking tradition.

Manuel, David. Member of the Chevron's Friday Table who had to drop out because of an ulcer.

Margan, Frank. Hired by Len Evans as the Wine Information Bureau's New South Wales writer and educator. He became a well-known wine writer in Sydney.

Moore, Arthur. One of Evan's promotional team with the Wine Information Bureau.

Murphy, Dan. Respected Melbourne wine retailer and merchant and Victoria's first regular wine columnist, with a weekly contribution to the Melbourne *Age* beginning in 1967. Regarded in the 1960s and 1970s as the best palate in Victoria, he was frequently pitted against Evans in tasting duels. He has been at the forefront of Australian wine retailing and gave the author of this book his first job in the wine industry.

Nassikas, Jim. Evans' friend and former General Manager and Vice President of the Royal Orleans Hotel, New Orleans, he met Evans while on the *Galloping Gourmets* tour of 1967, when Evans stayed with Nassikas and Marilyn Barnett.

Newton, Wayne. American singer of the 1960s whose booking by Frank Christie at the Chevron's Silver Spade restaurant Evans cancelled. Christie countered the cancellation and Newton became the Chevron's second biggest hit after the Nat King Cole season.

O'Shea, Maurice. Legendary French-trained Australian winemaker for Mount Pleasant Wines, purchased by McWilliams, in the Hunter Valley.

Ousback, Anders. A well-known Sydney-based wine writer, commentator, caterer and Evans protégé, Anders Ousback joined the staff of Bulletin Place immediately after leaving school. He is currently devoting much of his attention to pottery.

Oxenbould, Bob and Jan. 'The Dreaded' Bob Oxenbould and his wife, Jan, are best of friends with Len and Trish Evans, although Oxenbould confesses his interest in wine is quantitative rather than qualitative. A very theatrical couple, they were an essential ingredient in the successful Evans Christmas parties. A fanatical fisherman, Oxenbould is a regular fishing partner of Len Evans.

Parkinson, John. Another Evans protégé, John Parkinson was employed to set up and manage the Bulletin Wine Club and was then recommended by Evans as the first Editor of the *Wine and Spirit Buying Guide*, Australia's first national wine magazine. At Bulletin Place he was a prolific researcher for Evans and contributed greatly towards the various editions of Evans' *Complete Book of Australian Wine*. He presently heads the Australian office of Cellarmasters, the country's largest direct-mail wine selling operation.

Pascall, Geraldine. Sydney-based food critic who took over Evans' 'Indulgence' column in the *Weekend Australian* once he left for the *Women's Weekly*, saying she would be tougher than he.

Preece, Colin. Another great Australian winemaker for Seppelts at Great Western in western Victoria. Preece was another good friend of Evans and is famous for his sparkling wines and shiraz.

Purbrick, Eric. Very cultivated and stylish former head of the famous wine family which owns Victoria's Château Tahbilk, and a great friend of Len Evans. A lawyer, he arrived back in Australia at the suggestion of his mother in 1932 at the age of twenty-eight to take over Château Tahbilk, knowing nothing about winemaking, which he had to learn, very successfully at that, from books.

Reid, Ken. Former New South Wales head of McWilliams Wines member of the Australian Wine Board's Promotions Committee, and friend of Len Evans who persuaded him to take the appointment with the Wine Board.

Richardson, Colin. Popular Victorian wine media personality, wine educator and judge, presently with Rémy Australie.

Rodriguez, Lawrence. King's Cross doctor, member of the New South Wales Wine and Food Society and of the Chevron's Friday Table.

Schneider, Hermann. Highly acclaimed Melbourne-based restaurateur and former wine distributor, Hermann Schneider was chef-manager of what Evans long regarded as Australia's finest restaurant, Two Faces. He is currently manager of Delgany's private hotel at Sorrento, Victoria, where Two Faces has been relocated to all its old standards.

Seabrook, Doug. Prominent Melbourne-based wine merchant, judge and show chairman.

Sissingh, Gerry. Well-known Hunter Valley winemaker, currently with Hungerford Hill (part of the Penfolds group). During his working life, Sissingh had several spells with Lindemans and was the first winemaker at Rothbury Estate.

Stanford, John. One of Evans' promotional team with the Wine Information Bureau, where he became a State Manager. Later, Stanford became a popular wine writer, consultant and judge with a well-known leaning towards spirits.

Stevens, Kit. A Master of Wine, Kit Stevens is a long-time friend of Evans who discovered that Château Suduiraut in Sauternes was possibly for sale, which ultimately led to the Evans Wine Company buying two châteaux in Bordeaux.

Tarrant, Ron. Celebrated journalist, editor of *Pix* magazine in the early 1960s and a member of the Chevron's Friday Table.

Tyrrell, Murray. Now outspoken and well-known winemaker of Tyrrells Wines in the Hunter Valley. Known today as the 'Mouth of the Hunter', Tyrrell was the first to introduce the Burgundian varieties of pinot noir and chardonnay on a large scale to modern Australian winemaking, for which Evans does not believe he has been suitably recognised. Then a cattle dealer, he took over Tyrrells in the late 1950s when his uncle Dan Tyrrell, winemaker for seventy-six consecutive vintages, was injured and unable to continue. Murray Tyrrell credits Rudy Komon for persuading him to continue with the family wine business. In 1962, Evans and Komon persuaded him to bottle his wine for the first time. Tyrrell was a founding partner and initial Vineyard Manager of the Rothbury Estate.

Vinding-Diers, Peter. The Danish-born winemaker who worked for Evans at Château Rahoul. He has since been recognised as a leading light in the dramatic improvement of white wine in Bordeaux, but it is worth remembering that he was taught the techniques Evans wanted him to use there by Brian Croser.

Warren, Roger. Great Hardys winemaker and blender of the 1940s and 1950s.